ROGER STEVENSON
AUGUST, 1995

REAGAN
and the
ECONOMY

REAGAN
and the
ECONOMY

The Successes, Failures, and Unfinished Agenda

Michael J. Boskin
Foreword by Herbert Stein

ICS PRESS

ICS

Institute for Contemporary Studies
San Francisco, California

Inquiries, book orders, and catalogue requests should be addressed to ICS Press, Institute for Contemporary Studies, 243 Kearny Street, San Francisco, California, 94108. (415) 981-5353.

Distributed to the trade by Kampmann & Co., New York.

Book design and production by Marian Hartsough

Library of Congress Cataloging-in-Publication Data

Boskin, Michael J.
    Reagan and the economy.

    Bibliography: p. 287
    Includes index.
    1. United States—Economic policy—1981–
2. United States—Economic conditions—1981–
3. Supply-side economics—United States.   4. Reagan, Ronald.   I. Title.
HC106.8.B656   1987   338.973   87-22544
ISBN 0-0917616-80-4

Contents

Preface

Seven years ago, on the eve of the Reagan Presidency, the Institute published a broad study on the U.S. economy, edited by Michael J. Boskin. The study, *The Economy in the 1980s: A Program for Growth and Stability*, was undertaken at a time of great economic difficulty, perhaps the worst decade since the Great Depression. Inflation was high and rising, the average American family had seen no gain in its standard of living in six years, and taxpayers were growing restless with the rapid growth of government spending. The study presented a broad program for reforming economic policy, and it helped change the terms of debate on economic policy and led to the wholesale reforms that occurred in the past six years.

The central thesis of the 1980 study was that much of America's economic malaise was the result of policies that perpetuated disincentives to produce income and wealth and allocate resources efficiently. To reverse this, the study proposed a combination of traditional and revolutionary policies that included slower and more predictable monetary growth, reduced nondefense spending, budget balance, fundamental tax reform, and deregulation.

Seven years later, the long-run effects of the Reagan economic program are beginning to be known, but evaluating the connection between the program and its effects is a complicated endeavor, requiring a balanced perspective and careful judgment. For this task, we approached Professor Boskin to evaluate the program in relation to the current state of economic knowledge and set forth elements of the unfinished agenda.

As Boskin notes herein, making this evaluation is difficult for several reasons. One problem lies in the popular tendency to correlate contemporaneous policies and performance, ignoring the significant lags that separate them. Furthermore, economic policy is inherently political, and clear perpectives on long-term economic growth and stability can be distorted by looking only to the next election. This was certainly true of the extravagant forecasts made by certain supply-side proponents in the early 1980s. Partisan critics are now judging the Reagan economic program against these claims; this could obscure the Reagan Administration's many achievements.

The economy will, as always, be an issue in the 1988 presidential election; and it is thus important that a balanced judgment be made of the successes and failures of the Reagan program. This volume represents an important, comprehensive attempt to provide such a judgment. Policymakers and the public would do well to study Professor Boskin's conclusions as part of an ongoing effort to understand our changing economy and improve economic policy and performance.

Robert B. Hawkins, Jr.
President, Institute for
Contemporary Studies

San Francisco, California
August 1987

Acknowledgments

The period of Ronald Reagan's presidency will be recorded as one of the most interesting in recent economic history. For economists, historians, and citizens in general, it is in many ways the most important in the United States since the New Deal days of Franklin Roosevelt. Shifting budget priorities from social spending to defense, de facto engineering of a new federalism, cutting and reforming taxes, generating unprecedented budget deficits, disinflating the economy, continuing deregulation, adding ten million jobs while structural changes in the labor market continued: all this and more occurred during the Reagan era. Some of the outcomes were the result of President Reagan's policies; some occurred independent of, or in spite of, them.

Changes in the economy, economic policy, and analyses of the relation between them moved at a breathtaking pace, stirred by the powerful message and sense of redirection and values the President enunciated. New economic theories were combined in interesting proportions in a sort of recipe economics in order to market certain parts of the President's program. Each of these theories contained elements of truth, but none of them was sufficient to describe the actual performance of the economy or to prescribe economic policy in all its important dimensions.

These policies are fundamental to an understanding of our economy, the role of government in it, and the future opportunities to improve economic performance while maintaining personal freedoms. Because of this, I decided under the urging of A. Lawrence Chickering of the Institute for Contemporary Studies to try to write a non-technical, accessible volume placing Reaganomics in perspective. My intent throughout this volume is to assist the reader in understanding the economic and intellectual background to Reaganomics, to recall the vast array of policies — including some policy reversals — that were proposed, enacted, or rejected, and to describe the economy's performance, with some emphasis on assessing what role economic policies had in achieving that performance.

I have attempted to remain as detached as possible for someone who feels strongly about the various issues involved, has conducted much research on them, and has been an adviser and consultant to many involved with them, including the President, the Treasury, the Senate Majority leader, and members of both parties on key committees in both houses of Congress (such as the House Ways and Means Committee, Senate Committee on Finance, Budget Committees, and the Joint Economic Committee). I have deliberately avoided elaborating on the roles of specific individuals in all but the few instances in which it was necessary to do so. I believe that what is important is the policies proposed and adopted, the alternatives that were available, and the outcome. Many persons far more important than I devoted countless hours to the making of the economic policy. Regardless of which side of the issue the person was on, or whether they were in the executive or legislative branch of the government, I do not doubt their sincerity in doing what they viewed was best for the country, at least as they saw it.

I owe a great intellectual debt to the numerous scholars whose work is mentioned in this volume, as well as to countless others whose research has influenced my thinking. To those with whom I disagree, I can only say that I have attempted to incorporate your theories and findings to the best of my ability.

It is inevitable that in a society as complex and diverse as ours, with an economy whose performance must be measured in many dimensions, points of view will differ despite attempts to examine common evidence. I have attempted to convey a bit of the flavor of those disputes throughout this volume, although that is not my primary purpose. I mention where one might find an alternative point of view and summarize it briefly, and refer those who would like to pursue the subject to original sources. This is not meant to be an academic treatise. The material presented is not technical, and requires little more than the ability to read a chart or table and bear with a small amount of the economics jargon used in the popular financial press in order to follow the arguments and to make up one's own mind.

I firmly believe that understanding this era in our history — this set of attempts to restructure the role of government in our economy and the major economic disruptions and achievements of the times—is vital if we are to pursue sensible policies in the future. That will not guarantee an economy free of future problems. We have not seen the last recession in the United States or in the world economy. Reigniting inflation will always be a temptation for politicians. Sluggish productivity growth and declining international competitiveness are not exclusively a phenomenon of the period of the over-valued dollar. Maintaining the dynamism, flexibility, and decentralization of decision-making in our economy will require more than an ideological predilection toward such features. It will require a careful understanding and evaluation of the achievements such approaches have to offer our citizens. It is in this spirit that this volume was produced. For sharing that concern and vision, and providing invaluable guidance and editorial assistance, I would like to thank the staff of the Institute for Contemporary Studies, in particular its Executive Director, Mr. A. Lawrence Chickering. I would also like to thank Mr. William Gale and Mr. Jong-goo Yi for invaluable research assistance and Ms. Rossannah Reeves for technical and editorial assistance in the preparation of the manuscript.

Michael J. Boskin
Stanford, California

Foreword

The perceptions of the economic policies and performances of Presidents Hoover, Roosevelt, and Kennedy remained alive and politically influencial for years after those presidents left office. Hoover was a symbol of failure and Roosevelt was a symbol of success: Democrats waved those banners for a long time. Kennedy was also a symbol of success: twenty years after his death even Republicans were seeking to identify their economic ideas with his. Reasons for these perceptions seem obvious. We did have a depression during Hoover's term, we did have a recovery during Roosevelt's term, and we did have a short period of unusually rapid economic growth beginning in Kennedy's term. Whether the presidents were responsible for these economic developments, and by what policies, are questions even today. But these questions did not weaken the popular perceptions and their political force.

The economic policies and performance of the Eisenhower Administration did not become political symbols. Even subsequent Republican politicians did not associate themselves with Eisenhower economics. This is despite the fact that the economic record of the Eisenhower period was probably superior to that of any other eight-year period in this century. But the economic performance of the Eisenhower years was commonly considered to be normal, or worse, because we didn't know what was to come. More important, President Eisenhower did not try to identify himself as the champion of any unique brand of economics, distinct from the ideas of the Democrats or other "wings" of the Republican Party. His pol-

icy was consensus, and that concealed anything especially Eisenhower-
like in economics.

Reagan economics is probably going to be a political issue for some
time to come. (I dislike the word "Reaganomics." It suggests that the policy is more simple and personal than it is. Moreover, the locution is only
good for those presidents whose name ends in "n." One can't imagine
"Bushomics" or "Hartomics.") Ronald Reagan has been an extremely
conspicuous president and his policy has been closely identified with
him personally. He and his supporters have made Reagan the issue and
have built up the idea that there is a brand of Reagan economics different
from that of any of his predecessors or even from other Republicans and
conservatives.

But what Reagan economics will stand for in the future is uncertain.
The Hoover depression, the Roosevelt recovery, and even the Kennedy
expansion were quite visible. But at this point, in 1987, the results of
Reagan economics that can be seen with the naked eye are quite limited.
The inflation rate has come down substantially and the national debt,
the budget deficit, and the trade deficit have gone up substantially. The
low point of the inflation rate was probably already seen in 1986; the
Reagan Administration may well leave office with inflation on an uptick.
As for the debt and deficits, while they are headline subjects, their effects
on the lives of the American people will not be seen until years after Mr.
Reagan leaves office. In other dimensions of economic performance —
the growth of output and productivity and the reduction of poverty, for
example — any break in trend associated with Reagan policy is hard to see.

The influence of the Reagan experience on politics of the next several years will be more influenced by the image than by the facts. That
is partly because image-making has become such an efficient and powerful instrument. It is also partly because, as I have just noted, the facts are
not self-evident, which leaves much more room for the image makers. But
to say that the effects of Reagan economic policy are not now visible to
the naked eye does not mean that there are no effects. It only means that
we have to look with a microscope, not with the naked eye. That is what
Michael Boskin does in this book. He applies to the Reagan experience
the microscope of economics — a cloudy microscope admittedly but the
best we have and better than the naked eye.

This effort is important. Even though the political resonance of Reagan economics will be mainly a matter of image undisciplined by facts,
nevertheless the facts will probably have some influence. Discovering the
facts would be helpful. Also, the analysis helps us to learn something about

economics, and also about political science. History is our laboratory—not a very good laboratory, but we have to use it. So we are interested in the relation between economics and Reagan's policy in two directions: what does economics have to tell us about Reagan's policy and what does experience with Reagan's policy have to tell us about economics?

It is important not to be distracted by the comparison of the 1980 campaign statements with the subsequent performance. In 1980 the Reagan campaign team was saying, or implying, that a large tax cut would raise the revenue, that inflation could be sharply reduced without a recession, and that tens of billions of dollars of expenditures could be cut out of the budget without injury to anyone except a few bureaucrats. None of these things turned out to be true or should have been expected to be true. The interesting questions raised by this experience are not for economists but are for students of politics and public opinion. Some of the 1980 campaign ideas had some relation—usually extreme—to trends in economic thinking, such as rational expectation, supply-side, and monetarist theory. One question is how far the campaign ideas were influenced by economics and how far the existing trend of economic thought was adopted and exploited because it helped to make the campaign plausible. How did these ideas escape effective challenge during the campaign? How did they affect policy once the Reagan team came into office?

For economists, the important questions concern the relations between the policy actually followed and the results. Here the Reagan experiment turns out to be less clear-cut than talk about the Reagan "revolution" would lead one to expect. We did not have a test of the consequences of a regime of stable and predictable monetary and fiscal policy because we did not have such a regime. We did not have much of a test of the consequences of deregulation because there was not much deregulation, especially if regulation of international trade is considered. We did not have much of a test of the effects of slowing down the growth of government expenditure because there wasn't much slowing down. Even the experiment of cutting marginal tax rates, the most obvious Reagan departure from previous practice, is clouded by the presence of the budget deficit.

Appraisal of the effects of Reagan economic policy is an exercise of prediction—whether we talk about past effects or about future effects. We are accustomed to laughing at Sam Goldwyn's remark that forecasting is difficult, especially for the future. But we are consistently engaged in forecasting the past, and that is difficult also. To estimate what the effects of Reagan's policies have been so far we must forecast how the behavior of the economy would have been different if the policies had been different. But in the Reagan case the need for forecasting is especially obvious. The most important Reagan policies are of a kind that are likely to show their effects only after a considerable period of time after the Reagan term is over. And by the time these effects may be expected to appear, there may be other policies to interfere with visibility.

If we turn to the other side of the equation and ask what can the Reagan experiment to tell us about economics, we encounter the fact that this experiment is only one episode in a long history of economic policy. We find, for example, that the relation between the money supply and the inflation rate was different in 1985 and 1986 than one would have expected from more than 100 years of historical experience. Should we now conclude that we are in a new era of monetary behavior or only that there will be temporary deviations from historical relationships?

I have been emphasizing the difficulties in doing what Mr. Boskin has undertaken to do. I also want to emphasize the importance of the effort, for future politics and for future economics. Boskin's work is a valuable contribution to the growing literature on Reagan economics, chiefly, in my mind, for two qualities.

First, he approaches the subject from a constructive point of view. He is sympathetic to Reagan economics but not idolatrous. He is hopeful that the policies will be productive but is not willing to suppress uncertainties in the evidence of results so far. This attitude lends credibility to conclusions that in many cases can only be judgments rather than facts.

Second, he applies to analysis of Reagan economics a body of estimates, some by himself and some by other economists, of particular quantitative relations within the economic system. For example, how big is the response of saving to a change in after-tax interest, how much does an increase in the budget deficit diminish domestic private business investment, what are the relative magnitudes of factors influencing the growth of productivity? Moreover, Boskin acknowledges that economists differ on many of these estimates, and gives the reader an opportunity to make up his own mind. This approach tends to rescue the subject from the grip of ideology and move it into a realm where learning is possible.

The lessons of this book can not be put on bumper stickers to be used in the 1988 campaign. The book is an exercise in thinking about real problems, something that we sorely need.

HERBERT STEIN

Chapter 1

Introduction and Overview

When Ronald Reagan first ran for president in 1980, the United States was suffering economic problems relatively more severe than at any time since Franklin Delano Roosevelt's first presidential campaign in 1932. Like Roosevelt (post-election), Reagan promised a dramatic change in direction. Reagan's economic program was a central issue in his first race, and again when he ran for re-election in 1984. His program remains controversial today, for it claims that traditional Keynesian economic ideas are out of date, and re-introduces elements of an older economic tradition, sometimes repackaged.

To what extent is Reaganomics based on sound economic principles, and to what extent does it ignore them? Are the extreme claims made in its name merely energetic public relations for realistic goals, or are they an inconsistent set of conflicting, superficial ideas? Will the program have a lasting impact on economic thinking, or will it be only a temporary aberration?

President Reagan's program contained elements of monetarism, supply-side economics, and traditional conservative orthodoxy. It embraced several goals at once: lower inflation, rapid growth, a balanced budget, less government, and high employment. Administration officials at various times stressed one or another of these schools of thought and policy objectives, which often seemed to conflict. While economics is not capable of achieving the precision of the natural sciences, it does have certain basic principles that cannot be violated without casting serious doubt on a policy's consistency and efficacy. Did the Reagan program properly mix ideas, theories, and objectives? Or did it violate basic economic principles?

Consider the major policies of the Reagan program. Reagan strongly endorsed the Federal Reserve's disinflation policy, despite extreme pressure to abandon it during the 1981–82 recession. He called for, and received, a substantial defense buildup. He also proposed, and partially received, large cuts in nondefense spending. The President got most of the large tax cuts he called for, cuts that focused on marginal tax rates and (until the 1986 Tax Reform Act) other factors, such as depreciation schedules, which stimulate economic activity. He also proposed limiting government regulation, continuing work begun under President Carter, and establishing a new federalism to shift responsibilities from the federal to state and local government.

In short, the President was steering in a new direction based on decreased reliance on centralized federal government programs and increased reliance on private initiatives. His program used taxing power to raise revenue and avoided using taxes, as the President himself put it, "to regulate the economy or bring about social change. We've tried that," he remarked, "and . . . it doesn't work."[1] These policies gave each intellectual faction in the Administration part of what it wanted. Monetarists wanted tighter and more stable money and disinflation. Supply-siders wanted tax cuts focused on marginal tax rates and investment incentives. Free-market conservatives liked the emphasis on slowing the growth of domestic spending. Reaganomics was thus a complex combination of positions, sometimes harmoniously blended, sometimes not.

None of the "schools of thought," however, got exactly what they wanted. Monetarists, such as Milton Friedman, complained bitterly that the Fed's control of money growth was too erratic. Supply-siders like Paul Craig Roberts argued that we waited too long for a tax cut, and that much of it was offset by subsequent increases. Fiscal conservatives, such as Martin Feldstein, applauded cuts in domestic spending and the structure of the tax reforms but were concerned about the prospects of huge budget deficits for the indefinite future. At times, members of the Administration openly disputed the relative importance of various goals and methods for achieving them. For example, then Secretary of the Treasury Donald Regan said of the 1984 Report of the Council of Economic Advisers (which heavily reflected CEA Chairman Martin Feldstein's concern over large deficits), "As far as I'm concerned, you can throw it away."[2]

But there were unifying objectives. For Reagan and his advisors, freedom, including freedom from government interference, was enormously important, far beyond the superiority of free markets to controlled ones. Less government, including nondefense spending, regulation, and so on, was desirable per se. This must be remembered, both because it affects the interpretation of claims and counterclaims, and because it partly explains the willingness to use large budget deficits, despite their short and long-run deleterious consequences, to attempt to pressure Congress to reduce spending. Permanently reducing the role of government in the economy—or at least stemming its rapid growth—was considered by many to be worth the problems associated with large deficits, even if they persisted for several years.

The President claims his program is responsible for enormous economic gains since he took office, while his detractors argue that many of the putative gains are illusory and that, in any event, they were achieved in the short term only by sacrificing the longer term. The task of untangling the complex claims and counterclaims, many of them with obvious political motivations, is greatly complicated by claims about the Reagan program that are simply misleading and inaccurate. This includes both the Administration's claims of success and the Democrats' allegations of failure and impending doom. For example, it is generally unrecognized that:

1. Federal spending as a share of GNP has gone up, not down, under President Reagan;

2. The defense buildup is *not* the primary cause of this increase in spending;

3. The 1981–82 recession was quite severe by many usual measures, but these measures themselves have a relative meaning, and the recession was much *less* severe than what was predicted as needed to achieve the substantial reduction in inflation;

4. The recession was a by-product of wringing inflation out of the economy, a policy begun by the Federal Reserve at the end of the Carter Administration;

5. The President is partially to blame for the large deficits, due to the defense buildup and his original tax cut. But Congress, too, has played a part by refusing to cut many non-defense spending programs and by adding substantially to the President's original tax cut;

6. Deficits *sometimes* matter for *certain* economic outcomes, but they are not always a matter for concern, let alone alarm.

There is much to learn from the Reagan program, enacted against the backdrop of a rapidly changing world economy and startling economic events that caught economists by surprise: the tenfold increase in the flow of foreign capital into the United States, for example, or the 50 percent reduction in energy prices. But before the Reagan economic program can be evaluated, it first must be defined. This alone is complicated because it requires knowing what was proposed and why, what was enacted or rejected, and what price had to be paid for the objectives sought. What have been the program's successes and failures? What remains undone? What will be the program's legacy? And is it exportable to other countries in their attempt to improve economic performance?

The answers to these questions will fundamentally influence the course of policy, and thus our economic well-being: growth, inflation, unemployment, international competitiveness in trade, and our general role in the world economy. They may help us to avoid unnecessary boom and bust cycles, sluggish economic growth, high inflation, and growing government intrusion into our lives. In this book I will try to answer these questions and others. The answers will have an important influence on the well-being of every American.

Evaluating the Reagan Program

In judging the Reagan program, it is important to understand that the economy is complex and its performance may be evaluated in many ways—including the stability of employment and prices, the rate of improvement of standards of living, the efficiency with which resources are allocated, and the range and cost-effectiveness of programs to assist those in need. At the same time, since there are many policy instruments that can affect an economy's performance—including government spending, tax and deficit policies, regulation, and Federal Reserve policies that control the supply of money and credit—it is unlikely that success or failure can be measured in any *single* dimension or attributed to any *single* policy action.

Finally, many discussions of economic policy are dominated by the unfortunate tendency to correlate contemporaneous policies and performance. The truth is that policies often work with long lags and reflect earlier negative economic developments which may have spanned many years. Further, preoccupation with present performance, encouraged by media concern for the present and by politicians' time horizons defined by the next election, often produces policies that promote the present at the expense of the future. The impact on long-term performance can be devastating.

What, then, of Reaganomics? A fundamental dilemma facing every advanced economy is to reconcile relatively stable economic growth with provision of a humane social safety net. This balance frequently goes up and down like a seesaw. After a burst of economic growth, an awareness grows a) that some families have been left behind but b) that resources to assist them have become available. Such periods are thus often followed by substantial expansion of government assistance to the needy. The political process in turn tends to become a free-for-all attempt to redistribute income toward particular interest groups, both needy and not. This process begins an erosion of incentives to produce income and wealth, and this, in turn, slows the growth of productivity.

This pattern was evident over the last two decades. The 1960s was a time of relatively rapid economic growth; subsequently, there was an increased awareness of the plight of those left behind. Various programs begun in the Kennedy–Johnson years continued their expansion in the 1970s. The federal government's role in this period was transformed from provider of goods and services to redistributor of income, taxing some people to provide benefit payments to others. In the late 1960s, a substantial productivity slowdown began, and this continued through the 1970s. While its causes and remedies are complex, certainly a major reason for the slowdown was the erosion of incentives to produce income and wealth. This erosion was caused in turn by high and fluctuating inflation and high and rising marginal tax rates, especially on investment income. In 1980 President Reagan was elected by a public concerned that domestic spending was out of control. An increasing number of people concluded that we could no longer afford ever-growing social programs at the neglect of defense and private incentives to produce income and wealth. President Reagan's policies were designed to redress this imbalance and restore the economic growth of earlier periods.

In judging economic policy, there is an unfortunate temptation to set perfect economic performance as the goal. By this standard no economic policy has been or will ever be successful. The reason is that perfection — full employment, stable prices, rapid economic growth, efficient resource allocation, and humane but cost-effective provision for the poor — is impossible. No economy has ever achieved all of these goals simultaneously over any length of time, and no known economic policy — regardless of the political views or school of economic thought of its backers—can guarantee to deliver anything near that kind of performance. The reason is that economies are subject to continuous shocks, such as dramatic, unexpected increases in energy prices, generation of new technology, and swings in labor and product markets induced by demographic bulges such as the baby boom. These shocks, as well as such things as imperfect information, the uncertainty of the future, and the nature of political institutions, make it necessary to judge economic policy by realistic standards. Although one always wants perfection, insisting on it is a sure way to fall far shorter of the goal than would be true given more realistic expectations.

The seeds of today's economic outcomes often were sown months, years, even decades ago, and many of tomorrow's economic headlines will reflect decisions made today. Since there is nothing analogous to a capital market in the political process to value long-term outcomes, as opposed to short-term performance, we must do more than correlate current policies and outcomes when judging issues that profoundly affect all citizens. For example, President Reagan often argued that the 1981–82 recession was caused by the increase in government spending and the inflation of the 1970s, and that his commitment to disinflation and to increased reliance on private initiative was not only desirable, but inevitable. He was correct to blame the recession on past policies, which produced the inflation, but he could have stated the issue more more convincingly. Acknowledging that the 1981–82 recession was severe by any standard, he might have asked whether inflation could have been reduced *without* it. Made in this way, his point would have been extremely powerful because, looking back, a remarkable reduction in inflation was achieved at a much lower cost of lost output and (temporary) increased unemployment than many expected. Likewise, the more than $1 trillion of national debt accumulated during the Reagan presidency will leave large interest payments in the budgets of subsequent administrations, and may cause other problems as well.

These issues are especially important because a change in administration might well bring renewed attempts to return to previous policies in an effort to achieve certain social goals. Unless the successful and sensible parts of the Reagan policy achieve some recognition and support, based on historical experience *and* an evaluation of the economic principles upon which they are based, it is possible that a new president will return to increased regulation and social spending, or support excessive money growth, rekindling inflation. It is possible because bad policies, unfortunately, do not always die; they simply wait to be revived. As David

Stockman said, "Whenever there are great strains or changes in the economic system, it tends to generate crackpot theories which then find their way into legislative channels."[3] Similarly, sensible policies can get a bad name by historical accident. Avoiding past mistakes will require careful evaluation of opportunities, options, and outcomes.

Goals and Organization

This volume will analyze Reaganomics in terms of such opportunities, options, and outcomes. My purpose will be to clear the record, sort out achievements and failures, and assess likely long-run consequences. It places President Reagan's economic policies (as well as those policies followed by Congress and the Federal Reserve that were not proposed by the President) in the context of prior economic events, and compares likely alternative policies to those actually followed.[4]

To understand the Reagan economic program and alternative future policies, one first must understand the intellectual and economic history of the program and how it influenced the major indicators of performance. These include the results and prospects for inflation and recession, the budget, taxes and deficits, long-term growth, and fairness. This background will provide a basis for understanding how to extend the successful policies of the Reagan Administration, and ameliorate those that are undesirable. Such an assessment will reveal future policy options and reforms, and suggest the exportability of Reaganomics to other countries.

Chapters 2 and 3 trace the economic and intellectual history of the 1970s respectively. They recount reasons for the partial decline of Keynesian ideas, the rise of monetarism, and the development of rational expectations and supply-side economics. They document the great productivity slowdown, the enormous growth of government, and the booms and busts of inflation and recession. Most important, they document how the interaction of inflation and the U.S. system of taxation conspired to reduce incentives to produce income and wealth—incentives to work, save, invest, and innovate. In recalling the economic policies over the decade of the seventies, I conclude that the economic malaise of this period may be traced to a combination of reduced incentives and major structural changes in the economy, aggravated by unusually severe economic fluctuations resulting from rising energy prices.

In 1980, we faced a fundamental choice about the future course of economic policy: either to attempt to restore an economic climate that would encourage growth and rising standards of living, or to degenerate into continuous squabbles over the division of a stagnant output. Underlying that choice was the fundamental issue of the true source of economic vitality: was it to be found in decentralized private initiative, encouraged by an environment that minimized uncertainty, or in centralized government interventions, actively encouraging individuals to channel their efforts in directions chosen bureaucratically? By 1980, increasing numbers of economists had come to reject government manipulation of the economy, which increases uncertainty and stifles private initiative. Increasingly it became clear that rules rather than discretion are better for monetary and fiscal policies unless substantial long-term diversions of the economy from its potential output occur. It also had become clear that many government programs were losing their effectiveness while becoming more and more costly.

Out of this economic malaise, a reasonably clear consensus emerged:

1. Remove disincentives to produce wealth and income;
2. Disinflate the economy;
3. Restructure the tax system;
4. Resort to government intervention only in extreme situations;
5. Eliminate remaining controls on wages and prices; and
6. Enhance the potential supply of output (via points 1–3), as well as stabilize aggregate demand.

In 1980, disputes existed among economists about a number of issues, including the precise nature and magnitude of reduced government spending, disinflation, tax reform, decrease in regulation, and implementation of known and predictable rules of behavior by fiscal and monetary authorities. But there was a general agreement among economists on both the problems and the reforms necessary to correct them. How much could be accomplished, how quickly, and at what cost, remained to be answered. It was undeniable in 1980 that the economy was performing far below its potential, and that a continuation of past policies would only contribute to the decline.

The Reagan economic program was born out of this new consensus. The program drew its ideas and policies from various strands of economic thought: monetarism, supply-side economics, rational expectations, and traditional free-market conservatism.

Monetarism focused on slower money growth to disinflate, supply-side economics on the beneficial incentive effects of lower marginal tax rates, and traditional free-market conservatism on reducing the role of government in the economy. Each of these strands of thought contained elements of truths, but were over-simplified, and were sometimes unharmoniously blended. Compromises had to be made. Some unanticipated events caught virtually all economists by surprise. And the politics of selling painful but necessary choices produced overly optimistic forecasts of what could be achieved and at what cost.

Chapters 4 and 5 present an overview of the Reagan economic program: what was proposed and what was adopted. The chapters consider to what extent the Reagan Administration merely accelerated or expanded past administration policies or policies adopted by the Federal Reserve — for example, the Reagan Administration's crucial support of the Fed's policy of disinflation, which began before Reagan took office. Chapters 4 and 5 also document budget policy proposals and outcomes in relation to the deficit. Spending has gone up, not down, under President Reagan. Some naively attribute all of the increase to the 1981–84 defense buildup (Congress abruptly halted the defense buildup in 1985 and 1986). Actually, interest on the national debt and Social Security benefits account for a larger share of the increase than the defense buildup, despite years of virtually no *new* programs, but the effects of this will only become apparent in the next decade when there will not be a myriad of such programs to cut or eliminate.

New problems have been created by large deficits; and new structural procedures, such as the Gramm-Rudman-Hollings Balanced Budget Act, have been instituted to deal with them. Can our political process really deliver a balanced budget? In evaluating the Administration's tax policy (as amended and implemented by Congress, and revised periodically since) in the context of structural tax reform and the overall need for revenue, I consider the fairness issue as well as the impact on capital formation and growth — all in relation to the problem of incentives. I discuss the President's drive for tax reform and simplification, and the bold new tax reform that has emerged.

Besides issues of deregulation and international trade (almost all economists were stunned by the massive flows of capital into the United States), I also examine those policies that were explicitly *rejected*: industrial policy,[5] national economic planning, major protectionism, short-term monetary expansion to reduce unemployment temporarily, and massive public works and job programs to ease the pain of recession. In fact, one of the most important achievements of the Reagan program has been a very considerable influence on the range of economic policies that are considered respectable. A few years ago, many policies, such as wage and price controls and guaranteed public employment for the unemployed, were considered serious policy options. Today such policies and others are understood to be unwise in the general policy debate, not just by the Reagan Administration. Will this change endure? Will the economics upon which such policies were based remain discredited? If so, changing the terms of debate may well be President Reagan's greatest legacy.

Further chapters examine various economic results and prospects, policy lessons learned, and Reaganomics' unfinished agenda. They consider the failures as well as the successes of monetary and fiscal policies chosen to deal with inflation and recession, structural budget policy, tax policy, deficits, fairness, and long-term growth. Each of these chapters discusses the relevant economic issues and the views of most economists regarding them (or the main alternative viewpoints and reasons for them). It then compares the Reagan program to this consensus, with special emphasis on consistency and plausibility against the backdrop of a changing economy. The net outcome of the Reagan program is evaluated both for its effects on the economy and its effects on the field of economics. Finally, I discuss Reaganomics' exportability to other countries. Many advanced economies suffer from excessive government regulation, extremely high tax rates, and bloated budgets. The productivity slowdown that plagued the United States is a worldwide phenomenon. The Western European economies in particular have experienced massive unemployment and little growth in employment. What parts of Reaganomics are suitable to deal with these problems? Are there any lessons for the less-developed countries to learn from the Reagan program?

◆ *Chapter 2* ◆

An Economic History of the 1970s

By 1980, discontent with the policies of the previous two decades and the disappointing economic performance of the 1970s led a growing number of economists, businessmen, and politicians to support different economic policies than those in favor since 1960. These changing attitudes were not limited to a narrow ideological band, but were embraced by a broad group of people drawn from various political and economic persuasions. President Reagan's economic program, which represented a significant departure from previous policies, reflected this new outlook and differed only in degree and packaging from what was rapidly becoming a consensus among economists. Although Reaganomics was oversold ideologically and politically, it was simply something of an exaggerated expression of mainstream economic thinking at the time. It was not an aberration.

The changing views of economists may be understood by recalling economic events from the end of the 1960s up to 1980.

The Growth Slowdown

From the late 1960s to 1980, the country's primary economic goal shifted from increasing to redistributing income and wealth. The effects of this shift are striking. In the decade prior to President Reagan's election, the

FIGURE 2-1   **Annual Growth Rate in GNP per Employed Worker**

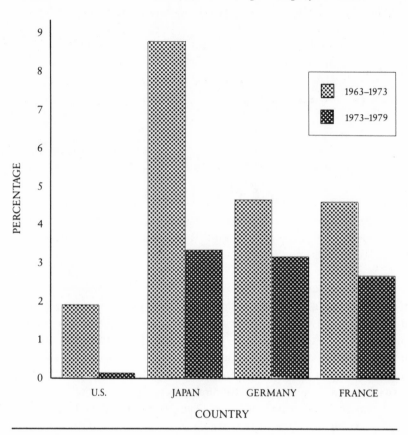

standard of living for most working, taxpaying Americans improved
hardly at all, as most of the gain in income came from increased employment, *not* productivity and real after-tax wage increases. This contrasts
strongly with the experience of most advanced economies, which experienced slower, but significant productivity growth. The past century saw
living standards (measured roughly by real GNP per capita) grow a little
under 2 percent per year in the United States, France, Germany, and many
other economies—with more spectacular growth episodes sometimes
occurring for less-developed economies. When living standards are
improving at a 2 percent annual rate, each generation becomes almost
twice as wealthy as the one before it. The general population becomes

better off, and opportunities for upward mobility are maximized for the poor. It is also politically easier to redistribute income than it is in a stagnant economy. All of this explains why long-term economic growth is perhaps the most important element holding together the social fabric.

Between 1973 and 1980 real growth per worker had declined to virtually zero, compared to about 2 percent per year in the previous decade (see Figure 1). The growth slowdown was a worldwide phenomenon, but as Figure 1 shows, other advanced economies went from rapid to modest growth. We went from sluggish to virtually zero growth. Although the causes of the slowdown are disputed, its consequences are not. One consequence, without doubt, was the tax revolt at the end of the decade. Among explanations advanced for the productivity slowdown are reduced average hours of work, a more rapid shift in the age/sex composition of the labor force, declining growth of capital per worker, changes in the legal environment, and a slowdown in gains from economies of scale. Other important factors have been the sharp increase in energy prices in the 1970s, and the continuing shift in the economy toward services.

Among all explanations advanced, the decline in incentives to produce wealth and income is perhaps the most important. The reasons for this decline include high and rising inflation, which increased uncertainty in returns to investment and saving; rising marginal tax rates, especially on the returns to saving and investment, aggravated by the interaction of inflation and the unindexed tax system; and the growth of government regulation, which increased costs and uncertainty in long-term investment planning.[1]

Inflation

Table 1 shows the substantial rise in inflation, beginning in the late 1960s and continuing through the end of the seventies. Substantial inflation has occurred in the United States primarily after removal of price controls at the end of wars, though it has never been anything like the hyperinflation which ravaged central Europe in the 1920s. By international standards, our inflation has been quite modest, but keeping it in perspective has been a problem: by 1983–84 inflation was regarded as "more or less" under control because it had declined from the high, double-digit rates of 1979–80 to about 3 or 4 percent, while President Nixon imposed wage and price controls in 1971 when inflation "soared" to 4 percent. The point is that inflation rose from its relatively low rates (averaging two or three percent per year) in the 1950s and 1960s to double-digit levels at the end

TABLE 2-1   Quinquennial Average of Inflation: 1954-1979

Period	Percentage
1954–1959	2.49
1960–1964	1.47
1965–1969	3.52
1970–1974	5.82
1975–1979	7.10

Inflation measured as percentage change in GNP deflator.
Note: Data are continually being revised and therefore numbers throughout the text
may vary slightly from updated figures.
Source: *Economic Report of the President,* 1986.

of the seventies; worse yet, the economy came out of each recession with
higher inflation than at the corresponding point of the previous recession and subsequent recovery. This sharp rise, along with rising unemployment, forced economists to reconsider basic macroeconomic theory
and policy.

While it was popular to blame inflation on the energy price increases
in the 1970s, they probably caused no more than three percentage points
of the 12 to 13 percent inflation of 1979–80.[2] Myths about energy prices
reflect the habit of explaining broadly accelerating inflation by recourse
to the problems of one specific quarter or year. At one time the culprit
might be energy; at another, food. Unfortunately, this is like saying that
the cause of alcoholism is that Fred drinks too much gin and Joe drinks
too much wine. *The primary cause of inflation in the 1970s was excessive monetary expansion.* Figure 2 shows the close connection between
inflation and money growth in this period. This connection was highlighted in the work of Milton Friedman and other "monetarists," and led
many to believe that reducing inflation could only be accomplished by
reducing monetary expansion. However, such a policy brings with it substantial *temporary* costs, to which I will return in a moment.

As inflation reached double-digits, the perception and mood of
Americans changed dramatically, and it soon became their preoccupy-
ing concern. This was true even during the 1976–79 recovery, when real
incomes were growing rapidly. In October 1979 the Federal Reserve Board
seemed to face inflation head-on when it chose to target money growth,
not interest rates, to bring about a deliberate, *gradual* deceleration of

FIGURE 2-2   **Inflation and Money Growth**

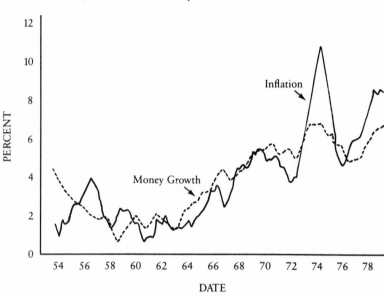

Inflation measured by the average rate of growth of the GNP deflator over the previous four quarters. Money growth is the average growth rate of M_1 over the previous three years.

money growth rates and reduce gradually the double-digit inflation rate by a percentage point or so a year.

Many economists understated the costs of high and fluctuating inflation, and oversold its benefits in reducing unemployment. Many politicians and economists argued that double-digit inflation could be made tolerable simply by indexing various features of contracts and the tax system. This view was not confined to a particular party or political persuasion. Such eminent economists as James Tobin of Yale argued inflation was not very costly, and my Stanford colleague Robert Hall argued we could index contracts against inflation and live with it. Numerous studies, however, have analyzed how inflation distorts incentives and increases uncertainty about the future.[3] Figure 3 presents data on inflation and unemployment in the United States for the past quarter century, illustrating the so-called "Phillips Curve." Clearly, if there ever was a reasonable short-run tradeoff between unemployment and inflation, it had worsened considerably. Each recovery from recession started with a higher infla-

FIGURE 2-3   The Phillips Curve

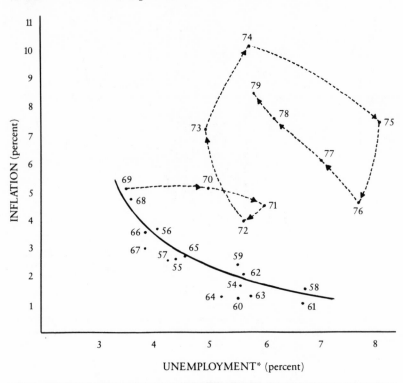

*Unemployment is the unemployment rate for all workers; annual average inflation is measured by the rate of change of the GNP deflator, fourth quarter, over fourth quarter of previous year.

tion rate than at the corresponding stage of the previous recovery, and inflation then accelerated. Why is this so? Is the Phillips Curve a statistical artifact? Would a disinflation from the 1979–80 inflation rates to, say, 3 percent, imply a huge increase in unemployment and low output for a long time? I will return to these questions in subsequent chapters.

Growth of Government Spending

Government spending increased substantially in the 1970s, but more significant than this increase was the change in its composition, both by level of government and type of expenditure. By the late 1970s the federal gov-

TABLE 2-2a   Government Outlays, Total by Level of Government, and by Function Selected Years

	Total Government ($ Billion)	Per Capita (1980 Dollars)	Percent of GNP
1929	10.3	384	10.0
1940	18.4	773	18.4
1960	61.0	1,300	21.3
1970	311.9	3,056	31.8
1980	869.0	3,900	33.1

TABLE 2-2b   Composition of Government Spending by Level of Government

	Total	Federal	Federal as Percent of Total
1929	10.3	2.6	25.2
1940	18.4	10.0	54.4
1950	61.0	40.8	66.9
1960	136.4	93.1	68.3
1970	311.9	204.2	65.5
1980	869.0	602.0	69.3

TABLE 2-2c   Composition of Federal Outlays by Function ($ billions)

	Purchases of Goods & Services	of which Defense[1]	Transfer Payments to Persons	Transfers as % of Transfers plus Purchases	Other[2]
1952	47.2	41.3	8.5	15.3	—
1960	52.9	43.8	20.6	28.0	16.1
1970	97.0	74.6	55.0	36.2	41.6
1980	190.2	125.9	234.7	55.2	148.7

Source: *Economic Report of the President* (1978, 1982).
[1] Defense outlays for the above fiscal years are derived from calendar year figures of defense spending as a percent of government purchases of goods and services. This percent is then multiplied by the figures given above for overall purchases of goods and services.
[2] Other includes grants-in-aid to State and local governments, net interest paid, and subsidies less current supplies of government enterprises.

ernment was spending more on transfer payments to individuals ($235 billion in 1980) than on purchases of goods and services ($190 billion). Table 2 shows that by dollar volume, the government's major role was to redistribute income, not provide goods and services. The result was a tremendous social achievement — a sharp reduction in poverty, from 22 percent of the population in the early 1960s to about 11.7 percent by 1979 (and perhaps only one-half or two-thirds this rate if the value of subsidized food, housing, and medical care is included in the income measure). Among other effects, the growth of government transfers and the large growth of Social Security benefits led to a substantial amelioration of poverty among the elderly, who were particularly prone to it. The increased spending for social programs was offset by a dramatic reduction in the share of GNP spent on national defense (see Table 2). In addition, investment-type expenditures, such as those on infrastructure, dropped. Since the federal budget does not have a separate capital account, the problems were disguised in the 1970s, delaying public awareness of their impact.

Taxes

The growth of government spending was accompanied by a large increase in taxes during the 1970s (see Figure 4). Increases were not as great in *average tax* burdens as in *marginal tax rates* — the tax an individual pays on incremental income — due to bracket-creep and various policies. The fact that these increases were in marginal tax rates rather than average rates is important because taxes affect incentives to work and save mainly at the margin — on the last dollar earned, rather than on the average dollars earned. If one's average tax is 25 percent, but the tax on the last dollar earned (the marginal tax rate) is 50 percent, the decision whether to work overtime will depend primarily on the marginal rate. The same is also true for saving and investment.

The increase in taxes is evident in various ways. To begin with, the percentage of taxpayers subject to high marginal tax rates quadrupled between 1966 and 1980, while average marginal tax rates increased from 25 to 37 percent (see Figure 4). No longer were high marginal tax rates imposed exclusively on the rich. *The middle class now saw that for every additional dollar they earned, between one-third and one-half of it disappeared in taxes.* At the same time, the effective marginal tax rate on capital income, especially on business investment in plants and equipment, rose dramatically. There are various estimates of these rates. One

FIGURE 2-4   **Growth in Taxes, 1960–1980**

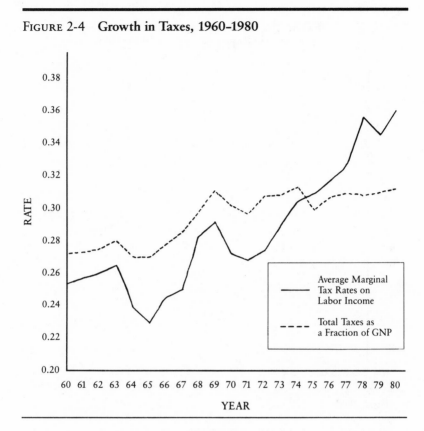

prominent set is shown in Figure 5. Finally, corporate-source income from business investment faced high and rising marginal tax rates throughout the 1970s, due to the failure to index for inflation, the use of historic rather than replacement-cost depreciation, the taxation of nominal rather than real interest, and the double taxation of dividends.

The growth of government regulation in the 1970s caused compliance costs to soar. One estimate by then soon-to-be chairman of the President's Council of Economic Advisers, Murray Weidenbaum, placed the cost to business of complying with federal government regulations at over $100 billion by 1979.[4] While cleaner air and water, greater health and safety, and other such nontraditional goods and services are certainly important, initial attempts to provide them created a series of regulations that often made no serious effort to relate benefits to costs. The regula-

FIGURE 2-5   Effective Tax Rates on Capital Income of the
              Nonfinancial Corporate Sector, 1964–1986

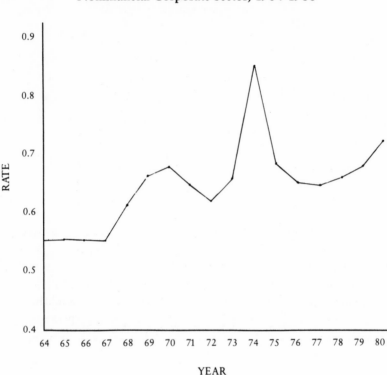

YEAR

tions also added to the time necessary to complete major investment
projects — years, in some instances — as well as adding enormous direct
costs and great uncertainty.

Saving and Investment

With the erosion of incentives, it is not surprising that the level of savings and investment declined in the 1970s, as shown in Table 3. In addition, there was a turn toward investment in shorter-lived assets such as equipment, as opposed to structures. Substantial relative growth in investment in residential housing (as opposed to business plant and equipment) was also encouraged by the combined effects of the preferential tax treat-

TABLE 2-3   U.S. Net Saving and Investment, 1951–80, Decade Averages

	1951–60	1961–70	1971–80
Total Net National Saving	6.9%	7.5%	6.1%
Net Private Saving	7.2	8.0	7.1
State-Local Govt. Surplus	-0.2	0.1	0.9
Federal Govt. Surplus	-0.2	-0.5	-1.9
Total Net Investment	7.0%	7.5%	6.3%

Notes: Data are averages of annual flows, as percentages of gross national product. Total net saving and total net investment differ by statistical discrepancy. Detail may not add to totals because of rounding. Source: U.S. Department of Commerce prior to revision of national income accounts (to provide the data as viewed from the 1970s).

ment for housing and the rising marginal tax rates for the general population.

The share of GNP devoted to net investment fell from the already dangerously low level of 7 percent in the 1950s and 1960s to only 2 or 3 percent in the *late* 1970s. It fell at precisely the time when it should have been rising to equip the additional (primarily young and inexperienced) 20 million workers with the capital and technology to make them productive. In short, we were mortgaging our future.

The Labor Market

I have already noted the demographic changes in the labor market, but Table 4 reveals some additional changes in the nature of employment and unemployment, as well as labor force participation in the 1970s. Despite several recessions, with substantial increases in unemployment, the absorption of an enormous influx of additional workers was a major economic achievement. Thus, what was traditionally considered the "full employment rate" was bound to change because there was a much higher percentage of workers with a more marginal commitment to the labor force and greater job mobility prior to settling into careers.

Among the important features of the labor market in the late 1970s was the unusually large growth of public-service and public-sector jobs. Despite the reduced demand for various types of state and local government services because of the "baby bust" of the 1970s—decreasing the

TABLE 2-4   Labor Force, Employment, and Unemployment Rates, Various Years

	Males and Females			Males			Females		
	L/P	E/P	U/L	L/P	E/P	U/L	L/P	E/P	U/L
1962	59.7	54.2	5.5	82.8	74.1	5.2	38.0	35.6	6.2
1967	60.6	55.8	3.8	81.5	73.8	3.1	41.2	39.0	5.2
1972	61.0	56.0	5.6	79.7	72.5	4.9	43.9	40.9	6.6
1977	62.8	57.1	7.0	78.3	70.9	6.2	48.5	44.4	8.2
1979	63.7	59.3	5.8	77.9	72.1	5.1	51.0	47.5	6.8

Note: L/P stands for Labor Force as percentage of the Population
E/P stands for Employment Rate as percentage of Population
U/L stands for Unemployment Rate as percentage of Labor force
These data describe individuals age 16 years and over.

demand for school teachers, for example — state and local government employment continued to rise. This was encouraged by federal programs that financed public-service jobs at the state and local levels. The original intent of programs such as the one established by the Comprehensive Employment and Training Act (CETA) was to encourage work and experience that would help train people for private-sector employment. Unfortunately, the success rate of these programs was very poor. Since they were not terribly productive and did not tend to lead to permanent private-sector employment, they were extremely costly ways of assisting the disadvantaged, far more expensive than other forms of public assistance.

International Trade and Other Changes

Other major structural changes occurred in the U.S. economy during the 1970s. Besides the demographic bulge caused by the baby boom and the increased labor-force participation of women, changes included the continuing shift in output from manufacturing to services, the growth of world trade (sparked in part by rounds of tariff reductions and the growth of income worldwide), the move from fixed to flexible exchange rates, and the energy price shocks. The U.S. economy became much more open to both trade and capital flows in the 1970s. While international trade was still only a small percentage of our economic activity on average, at the margin we bought and sold a growing number of goods on world markets. Further, fluctuations in the foreign exchange value of the dollar began to lead to swings in our trade balance, affecting domestic production and employment. The dollar plummeted to a low of 83.2 in 1979 (with an index of 100 for 1973), then rose rapidly.

This appreciation in the value of the dollar made our exports more expensive and imports cheaper. Largely ignored by most economists and policymakers, this dollar appreciation would soon place severe downward pressure on the domestic economy. Within a very short period, exchange rates and the trade deficit would move drastically and drive home to every American citizen how interdependent our economy had become with those of our trading partners. The quadrupling of energy prices, for example, not only caused short-term disruption but also changed the relative productivity of different sectors of the economy and types of capital. The automobile industry saw major changes in the demand for its products, due to increased oil prices. This "crisis" came at a time of increased foreign competition and growing pollution and safety regulations. Combined with higher wages and short-sighted management, it made the U.S. auto industry quite vulnerable to imports, which in turn led to industry and labor union demands for protectionist quotas and controls. Other industries such as steel followed a distressingly similar pattern.

Macroeconomic and Monetary Policy

Macroeconomic policy was also changing. The Kennedy-Johnson tax cut of 1964 was the first major attempt at aggregate demand management when the economy was not even in a recession. Because the growth rate was too low, it was argued, the tax cut might stimulate the economy. In the early 1960s, inflation in certain sectors was dealt with by federal jawboning and threats, such as the plan to dump excess supplies of government commodities on the market if prices rose too rapidly. The Federal Reserve Board through 1979 continued activist attempts at demand management through frequent changes in monetary policy.

Monetary policy prior to 1979 was quite accommodating. The Fed lectured the Congress on the evils of growing spending and deficits, but expanded money and credit sufficiently to sustain rising inflation. It simply refused to impose the severe monetary restraint necessary to curb inflation, focusing primarily on the nominal level of domestic interest rates. The combination of high inflation and our unindexed tax system made the after-tax and inflation cost of funds and return to savers negative for much of the late 1970s. The money supply grew rapidly, if erratically, and the Fed appeared to be unwilling to take the lead in the fight against inflation. It was no longer just academic monetarists who were critical of the the Fed.

Monetary policy changed abruptly in 1979 when the Fed announced it was altering its stance to target decelerating money growth rather than interest rates. Under the leadership of Chairman Paul Volker, the Fed committed itself to a policy of gradual disinflation. To place this change in perspective, recall that President Carter's October 1978 economic message and anti-inflation program included some early versions of the proposals made by him in the 1980 campaign. In that 1978 message — included in a half-hour television address — President Carter's only mention of monetary policy was his expression of hope that the Federal Reserve would keep interest rates down. Within two weeks the dollar plummeted on foreign exchange markets, and the Federal Reserve was forced to arrange a line of credit at foreign central banks to help prop up the value of the dollar relative to foreign currencies. It was an episode made more poignant by recent events.

The worst episode in macroeconomic policy was the wage and price control scheme imposed by President Nixon, closely followed by the incomes policies adopted in the mid- and late-1970s. These attempts to *suppress* inflation, rather than address underlying problems, probably *increased* inflation. For example, the enormous administrative bureaucracy of the Council on Wage and Price Stability, and its demands on business, highlighted the inflation issue politically but undoubtedly did little or nothing to combat it effectively.

The notion that wages, prices, and inflation can be controlled through a presidential appeal for cooperation between businessmen and unions is, at best, naive. Thousands of price decisions are made daily, and an attempt to keep a large number of them under government control would lead to a costly and absurd nightmare. Further, the economy is not so heavily unionized that keeping down the wage demands of the larger unions would do much for the inflation rate. Only 18 percent of the labor force is unionized, and not all members belong to powerful unions. The unions with power may cause their products to be priced out of the market, especially relative to foreign competition, but they are not the primary cause of inflation. A policy that explicitly or implicitly condones excessive monetary expansion while attempting to cajole firms and workers into slowing the rise of prices and wages is doomed to failure. Nevertheless, economists such as Walter Heller, President Kennedy's CEA Chairman, and Charles Schultze, President Carter's CEA Chairman, recommended such policies in the late 1970s, despite all the evidence indicating their ineffectiveness.

Regulation

The 1970s saw a new phenomenon in "social regulation," the attempt to correct market failures in areas such as pollution, safety, and health; simultaneously, it saw a major expansion of government economic regulation. Most notorious were the foolhardy energy regulatory policies developed in the 1970s, from which we still suffer. Fortunately, in the late 1970s the Carter administration began a general move toward deregulation of traditionally regulated industries, perhaps Carter's most important contribution to improved economic policy. Deregulation of the airlines was initiated during his administration, together with other forms of transportation and financial institutions. Deregulation has continued under the Reagan administration, and is likely to lead to better economic outcomes in the future.

Where Were We Headed?

Before evaluating the economy at the time of the 1980 election, it would be worthwhile to recall the economic policies that were considered reasonable during the mid-1970s. For example, many analysts were concerned about the low rates of saving and investment. To address this problem, President Carter, with prominent business and labor leaders, proposed the creation of a national reconstruction bank to help "revitalize"—as the shibboleth went—American industry. The idea was that an appointed group of business and labor leaders would decide where tens of billions of dollars of badly needed capital would be allocated. Some thought this would provide funds to rebuild American cities. Others, including most economists, saw it as a way to protect declining industries that were hurt by foreign competition and union wage pressure. Such nationalized agglomerations of capital almost certainly would have guaranteed a flow of capital to low- rather than high-productivity uses, starving those industries where investment *should* occur. Such a government body would probably have led us down a sinkhole, as indicated by recent attempts in the United Kingdom, Mexico, New Zealand, France,

and other countries to "revitalize" their economies by nationalizing industry and banks, reallocating capital, and attempting other, similar schemes.
A government reconstruction bank is not a prescription for productive
investment: while it might have brought increased saving and investment
rates, the returns on that investment would not have been great, and if
the experience of other countries is any guide, much of the investment
would have produced only negative returns.

The call for an industrial policy was a closely related phenomenon.
Proponents contended that government should target specific industries
as "sunrise" industries, providing them future opportunities at the expense
of obsolete "sunset" industries — a view most often associated in the popular press with the economist Lester Thurow. This policy of aiding new
industry with growing government subsidies, tax breaks, and other plums
was commonly misperceived to be the primary reason for rapid Japanese
economic growth. A *de facto* industrial policy in the United States could
be said to exist in some ways through the interaction of monetary, fiscal,
regulatory, tax, and trade policies, but this new call for industrial policy
would have elevated it to a national priority and raised the stakes enormously with the possibility of government misallocation of resources.
There simply is no reason to believe government generally can allocate
resources more efficiently than private markets.

By the end of the 1970s, the economy was threatened by sluggish
growth and high, rising, and wildly fluctuating inflation. We also faced
calls for growing government intrusion in the microeconomics of resource
allocation, especially capital markets. Attempts at active demand management led to disappointing outcomes, and calls for incomes policies
and controls seemed to increase as inflation accelerated. Had we continued
the policies of the time, and tried to supplement them with stricter incomes
policies and other attempts to steer economic activity, economic performance would have been far worse, with a continuation of high and rising inflation, further erosion of incentives to produce income and wealth,
and greater government intrusion in relatively efficient private markets.
Continuing these policies was hardly the best way to deal with our economic dilemma.

The Fundamental Problem

The conundrum was how to increase *long-run* growth, thereby improving living standards for the general population while providing resources
for both a humane social safety net and a necessary defense buildup. This

required action on a number of levels. Incentives to produce income and wealth had to be restored, which implied reducing inflation substantially, by means of reduced and more stable money growth. Increasing incentives would also mean reducing marginal tax rates, especially those on capital income. The relative size of government would have to be reduced, and private resources for investment, saving, and research and development increased. Other necessary measures were to remove tax distortions and reform regulation. This would lead to increased saving and investment, generation of new technology, and increased growth of productivity. This, however, is a *long-run* process. Nobody had a right to believe that higher productivity and growth would come immediately. Nor was it sensible to believe that the economy could be disinflated painlessly.

By 1980, economists were badly divided over what to do about inflation. On the one hand, there were those, such as James Tobin of Yale University and George Perry of the Brookings Institute, who thought we should learn to live with inflation because the costs of reducing it exceeded the benefits. Perry argued that there is great momentum to inflation — through such things as inertia in wage settlements — and thus there would likely be an enormous cost to disinflation, perhaps $200 billion (1980 dollars) in lost output per point of reduction in inflation.

On the other hand, there were those, such as Thomas Sargent of the University of Minnesota, who thought that the costs of inflation were high and the costs of disinflation, while substantial, not nearly so severe as most Keynesians predicted. Sargent argued that a changed *regime* by the Fed and fiscal authorities, if it was believed, could quickly disinflate at a much lower cost. The late William Fellner of the American Enterprise Institute also stressed the importance of credibility.

Views on these issues by individual economists were closely related to their theories on resource allocation and long-term growth. Many who thought it not worth reducing inflation also tended to ignore evidence that deteriorating incentives were at least partly responsible for declining growth. They thought the economy could do well enough with the existing tax structure and greater government spending; growth would take care of itself, or in any event, would not respond to changed incentives.

Conclusion

By any economic standard, the decade of the 1970s was the worst relative performance since the Great Depression. The economy was battered

by booms and busts, by recession and ever-rising inflation, while simultaneously suffering wrenching structural changes and a frightening long-
term productivity slowdown. After rapid gains in living standards during most of the 1960s, income per worker simply stopped growing for
an entire decade. All gains in GNP, adjusted for inflation, were products
of growth in the labor force, not increases in output per worker. For the
first time since the Depression, Americans experienced a long stagnation
of their standard of living.

Structural changes in the economy, however, concealed the real
dimensions of the slump. To begin with, the slowdown was not a smooth
transition to a lower growth path. The economy suffered several recessions, including the especially severe downturn of 1974–75; the recovery
from each recession left us with a higher rate of inflation than the corresponding stage of previous expansion. Somehow, the economy seemed
capable of simultaneously generating rising unemployment *and* inflation—a paradox known as stagflation.

The Keynesian economics of the 1950s and 1960s seemed to indicate that during a recession, straightforward government manipulation
of aggregate demand could raise output and employment more quickly
than the private market, while during times of inflation, a government
reduction of aggregate demand could dampen economic fluctuations.
Keynesians argued that demand management could transform the roller-
coaster economy into a moderately bumpy ride. Unfortunately, the Keynesians overestimated the accuracy of economic models, the reliability of
short-run forecasting, and the speed with which the political process could
implement policies. The promise of expunging the business cycle from
the list of society's problems was a noble (and hallowed) one, but the most
naive Keynesian theory overestimated the government's ability to achieve
this goal.

More than a decade of demand management—from tax cuts and
monetary fine-tuning to wage and price controls and incomes policies—
had produced discouraging results. Direct government intervention in the
economy—transfer payments to deal with poverty and regulation to deal
with cases of potential market failure—resulted in increasing marginal
costs and shrinking incremental gains. Alternative economic views
stemmed from two desires: first, to explain simultaneous inflation and
rising unemployment, and second, to provide macroeconomics with a
sound basis in individual maximizing behavior, stressing the importance
of incentives and expectations. Out of this ferment of economic malaise
and intellectual discontent came a better understanding of the economy

and of the shortcomings of traditional economic analyses. New data, measures of performance, concepts, and methods of analysis appeared — all of which, in turn, produced alternative policy prescriptions. Neither a change in the politics of economists, nor a change in the views of the broad population, was necessary to bring a clamor for something new.

The Reagan Administration used — some would say misused — strands of economic thought that had come to the fore in the 1970s. Understanding these policies, the problems of the economy which prompted them, and the intellectual turmoil in the economics profession is essential to understand the Reagan economic program and separate the extravagant claims and salesmanship from a careful analysis of policy. For a better understanding of Reaganomics, we must turn to a more complete discussion of the important developments that raised serious questions about traditional economic analysis and suggested new lines of argument and reasoning.

Chapter 3

Changing Views on the Changing Economy: The Alleged Crisis in Economics

Economic thought underwent significant changes in the 1970s as the prevailing Keynesian theories had difficulty accounting for emerging economic events. The Keynesians, who had dominated macroeconomics since the 1930s, placed great faith in government's ability to "fine tune" the economy by constant adjustments in taxation, government spending, and the money supply ("demand management"). They stressed the importance of the "multiplier effect" (whereby a government spending increase or tax cut would expand GNP by a multiple of the amount of the change in spending or taxes), and the short-run tradeoff between inflation and unemployment, otherwise known as the Phillips Curve. In the Keynesian perspective, policymakers could direct the economy simply by choosing the most desired combination of unemployment and inflation rates.

As the post-Keynesian models became more sophisticated and complicated, macroeconomists became increasingly confident of their ability to forecast, prescribe policy, and control economic fluctuations. Keynesian policy culminated in the 1964 Kennedy tax cuts. For the first time, economic policy was being forcefully applied to stimulate aggregate demand at a time when the economy was experiencing sluggish growth, but was not in a recession. The Kennedy tax cuts were generally thought to be a spectacular success, and the reason for the success was thought to be the stimulation of demand through the famous Keynesian multiplier effect.

Unfortunately, this interpretation was oversimplified. For although the economy did grow more rapidly after the Kennedy tax cuts, it was not due to a demand stimulus. Indeed, Edward Denison estimates there was no gap between potential and actual GNP by 1964. Further, in the late 1960s inflation also began to rise. Although the beginnings of the inflation may be explained (in classic Keynesian terms) by the deficit spending caused by trying to finance the wars on poverty and in Vietnam without a tax increase, the deficit problem does not explain what happened in the 1970s, for reasons I will explain below.

Monetarist Counterattack

Another school of thought, generally called monetarism and led by Milton Friedman, emphasized the role of fluctuations in the money supply in predicting short-term fluctuations in the economy. From the famous quantity theory of money, $MV = PQ$,* it can be seen that if velocity is relatively stable, changes in the money supply will be highly correlated with changes in nominal GNP (PQ). Add to this the idea that the economy has a natural tendency toward full employment, and it is evident that changes in the supply of money will generally affect the price level, rather than real output. Though highly simplified, this description highlights the monetarist's case that inflation tends to be primarily a monetary phenomenon. The contention that velocity is stable has been the subject of much dispute among economists, and the behavior of velocity in the 1980s will be discussed in Chapter 6.

For the moment, consider that if the economy falls into a recession, there is a natural self-correcting tendency to return to full employment. This may take time, but *eventually,* increases in the money supply will affect primarily the price level, i.e., inflation, not real output or employment. The simple quantity theory also suggests why monetarists tend to favor a simple, steady monetary growth rule: if velocity is relatively stable (at least grows predictably), appropriately stable money growth will lead to stable nominal GNP growth, which, given the economy's natural

---

*Nominal GNP, the product of the overall price level (P) and real output (Q) is by definition equal to the product of the supply of money (M) and its rate of turnover, called velocity (V).

tendency toward relatively full employment, can minimize fluctuations in output and provide price stability. Continued fine-tuning of the money supply will lead to fluctuations in nominal GNP growth, unless adjustments in money growth happen to counteract unexpected changes in velocity. Since this coincidence will rarely occur, fluctuation in money growth caused by fine-tuning will increase instability in nominal GNP, as well as real GNP and/or the price level.

Thus, monetarists tend to be skeptical about activist demand management, and they have advocated nondiscretionary rules to guide monetary, and often fiscal, policy rather than a discretionary policy of continuous "fine tuning" the economy. They espouse stable money growth as the best way to minimize unnecessary fluctuations in output. In both monetary and fiscal policy (or any other economic policy for that matter), the issue of certainty and the ability to predict future actions is very important. Those who promote "fine tuning" the economy may claim that a current discretionary action will occur only once, but how can one be sure that Congress or the Fed will not attempt other discretionary moves again in the future? With no guarantees, the private sector will be subject to great uncertainty. A monetary rule—or a tax or budget rule—would reduce this uncertainty, and, it was argued, greatly stabilize the economy.

This desire for rules rather than continuously applied discretion explains the various proposals advanced in the 1970s to establish constitutional amendments to limit discretionary behavior considerably. Most of these took the form of tax or spending limitation amendments, which eventually evolved into a movement for a balanced budget amendment. Among the foremost proponents of such constitutional amendments were economists Milton Friedman, James Buchanan, and William Niskanen. Although monetarists remained a minority during this period, their critique of the dominant Keynesian analysis did cause the Keynesians to expand their theories to place much more emphasis on monetary policy.

The Natural Rate Hypothesis

In the late 1960s Friedman and Edmund Phelps of Columbia caused a major change in macroeconomic thought by arguing that despite the traditional, short-run Phillips Curve tradeoff between inflation and unemployment, a "natural rate" of unemployment made impossible a *permanent* stable tradeoff between them. The natural rate of unemployment was the point at which inflation neither accelerated nor decelerated. When unemployment rose above the natural rate, inflation would fall, and when it fell below, inflation would rise. The "natural rate" theory had an important effect on the traditional notions of standards of economic performance. Throughout the 1950s and 1960s, Keynesians nurtured the hope that activist demand management could fine-tune the economy along a path that kept it at the top of its performance year after year. This goal was stated numerically as "4-4-1": 4 percent real GNP growth, 4 percent unemployment, and one percent inflation. When the economy strayed from this ideal standard, demand management was used. While in its best years in the 1950s and 1960s, such a goal was achieved, it had no sound theoretical basis. The natural rate hypothesis indeed argued that if the natural rate (established by various demographic, institutional, and economic forces in the labor market, including how well skills matched jobs) was above 4 percent unemployment, any attempt to bring unemployment back to 4 percent would accelerate inflation and would not succeed in keeping unemployment permanently below the natural rate. Therefore, more would be necessary to evaluate the economy's performance than merely selecting a hypothetical standard based on a good year. Instead, underlying market behavior would have to be examined, and the natural rate of unemployment consistent with nonaccelerating inflation would have to be determined. This was especially important, because the natural rate might change over time in response to various factors, such as demographic shifts. Indeed, the policymaker might not have the luxury of choosing any mix of unemployment and inflation to be found on the Phillips Curve: as a policy of increased inflation attempted to drive down unemployment, inflation might continue to rise much higher than expected. Most Keynesians eventually conceded this. They still argued, however, that some gains in employment could be achieved by accepting more inflation, and that the primary goal of economic policy should be to improve the inflation-unemployment tradeoff—i.e., reduce the unemployment rate associated with a given rate of inflation. This led to some of the incomes policy suggestions mentioned in Chapter 2.

Rational Expectations

The Friedman-Phelps hypothesis was extended and elaborated by Robert Lucas, Thomas Sargent, Robert Barro, and others whose contributions have generally come to be called the "new classical macroeconomics." Building on John Muth's studies of rational expectations, Lucas emphasized that economic agents (firms, workers, investors, consumers, and so on) tend to get confused in the very short-run between changes in relative and absolute prices. For example, they might easily mistake a general price rise caused by a surge in money growth for higher real wage rates or rates of return in particular markets.

This disagreement between Keynesians and new classical economists is in reality a dispute over the factors affecting the slope of supply and demand curves, the classic economic model — in this case, what economists call the "aggregate demand" and the "aggregate supply" curves.* The aggregate demand curve summarizes the relationship between price levels (or inflation rates) P, and real aggregate demand (real GNP) Y. As shown in Panel 1 of Figure 1, it is presumed to slope down and to the right. Underlying this simple diagram is a theory of the markets for goods and money, and the factors that determine equilibrium in each: planned saving equals planned investment in the market for goods and real money demand equals real money supply in the market for money. When the real money supply expands, either because the money supply expands or prices fall, interest rates will fall, thereby causing investment to rise. A new equilibrium is reached with higher real demand. Thus, as prices fall (or rise), real aggregate demand will rise (or fall), yielding the aggregate demand curve in Panel 1 of Figure 1.

A corresponding relationship can be developed between P and Y for the supply- or production-of-goods-side of the economy. This is the upward sloping relation also shown in Panel 1 of Figure 1. Just as the aggregate demand curve represents the markets for products and financial assets, so the aggregate supply curve represents the market for labor. The supply of and demand for labor determine real wage rates and employment. Given available capital and technology, this employment is translated, at a given point, into the production of goods and services. A change in the price level can affect both labor demand and supply. If prices rise, firms will find at a given wage rate that it is profitable to demand more labor. If the labor supply is unchanged, real wages fall and employment rises, thereby expanding output.

However, thus far I have assumed that the labor supply curve is unaffected by changes in the price level, given money wages. Thus, there is a sort of inflation illusion. Wouldn't higher economy-wide prices lower

---

* To facilitate the discussion and make minimal demands on the reader, this presentation is quite heuristic. However, those who are haunted by ghosts of economics courses past may skip the next few paragraphs and accompanying graphs.

FIGURE 3-1a   **Aggregate Demand and Aggregate Supply**

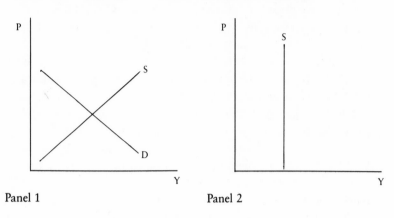

Panel 1   Panel 2

FIGURE 3-1b   **Effects of Expansionary Demand Management**

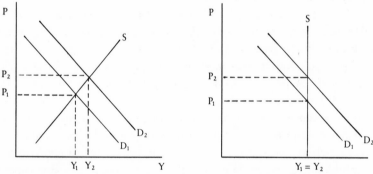

Panel 3: Keynesian Case: Both price   Panel 4: Classical and New Classical
level and real GNP (and employment)   Case: No effect on real GNP and
rise. Effect depends upon slopes of   employment; effect on price level
curves. Through time aggregate   only.
supply becomes more vertical.

P stands for price, Y for quantity, D for demand, S for supply.

real wages, thereby causing workers to supply less labor? If workers were
fully informed about price rises in the economy as a whole and had flexible enough contracts, they would reduce their supply of labor until the
initial real wage rate and employment were restored. If workers who supply

FIGURE 3-1c   **Two Caveats**

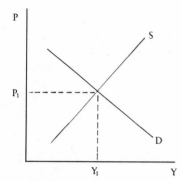
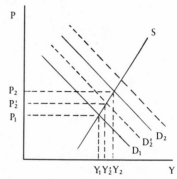

Panel 5: Ricardian Equivalence: No shift in aggregate demand curve.

Panel 6: Open Economy: Domestic demand effect may be curtailed or expanded by the effect of interest rate on exchange rates and net exports.

the labor react to the price level increase as rapidly as the firms demanding labor, the aggregate supply curve would be vertical, as in Panel 2 of Figure 1. But, if workers are bound by long-term contracts, they will not be able to adjust so quickly and the aggregate supply curve may indeed slope upwards for awhile.

This is where expectations are crucial. How long is "awhile"? How flexible are prices and wages? How quickly will markets clear? If wages are fixed less frequently than the price of most goods, workers may temporarily price themselves out of the market by overestimating the equilibrium wage. But will this pattern persist? While there will always be room for forecast or expectation errors, why should workers persistently make the same mistake and fail to learn from experience? Involuntary unemployment does not persist very long—wages and wage expectations will adjust to expand employment. In terms of the diagram, the short-run, upward-sloping aggregate supply curve quickly becomes vertical. Note the analogy to the monetarist position that the lasting effect of demand stimulation is on prices, because output tends to its full employment level. Finally, note that the Keynesians differ primarily due to their views as to how *long* it takes the economy to move back to a full-employment equilibrium, and that government demand management can be effective in boosting output during a recession because the short-run aggregate supply curve slopes upward to the right and would take several years to get back to its long-run vertical position (see Panel 3 of Figure 1).

These are important differences, but their nature, scope, and implications have been greatly exaggerated in both the popular press and political discourse. Most Keynesians no longer dispute the fact that the long-run aggregate supply curve is vertical and that output in the long-run can only be expanded by increases in productivity. Further, the rational expectation theorists argue, since all agents make economic decisions based on all information available to them — *including* their best guesses about future economic policy — they cannot be fooled for very long. Eventually they will incorporate expectations of countercyclical behavior on the part of monetary and fiscal authorities into their individual decision-making. Thus, much of the new classical macroeconomics attempts to make macroeconomics consistent with microeconomic analysis of individual optimizing behavior. It conflicts with Keynesian analysis in its judgment of the ease of market adjustments — the extent to which a full set of markets exist, whether markets clear quickly at competitive prices, the length of information and recognition lags, and the rationality of expectations.

Microeconomics was also undergoing major advances in the 1970s. From the current perspective the most important issues concern imperfect information, risk, insurance, and expectations. Often, different macroeconomic predictions and prescriptions stemmed from different assumptions on the nature of individual markets. Most Keynesians accept the notion that at least some very important markets exhibit substantial price stickiness (e.g., wages in labor markets) for considerable periods of time, and that this feature does not change rapidly. Economists have developed various microeconomic theories explaining *why* some markets might exhibit such characteristics. For example, in labor markets it may be quite costly to renegotiate a contract frequently. If labor contracts are staggered and of substantial duration — as part of the *efficient* contract setting in those markets reflecting various risks — wages may be sticky, and discretionary demand management *may* produce desirable results. The new classical macroeconomists tend to doubt that a long period is needed for markets to clear or that markets will not adjust, e.g., in the above example, to shorter contract lengths over time.

In the 1970s, the combination of rising inflation *and* unemployment, often called stagflation, exposed significant problems with simple Keynesian models, since Keynesian theory (through the Phillips Curve) posited an inverse relationship between inflation and unemployment. The assumption was that when one rose, the other would fall, and vice versa. But the appearance of rising inflation *and* unemployment revealed serious problems with this simple trade-off theory. It did not, however, discredit Keynesian theory completely, for the commodity and oil price shocks of the 1970s could still be interpreted as cost-push inflation in the Keynesian manner, though these shocks could not account for the principal part of the 1970s inflation.

This apparent failure of Keynesian theory to explain the major economic problems of the 70s brought forth new, more compelling analyses. Many of these stressed the important role that expectations and incentives play in the behavior of firms and households, and therefore, of the overall economy. Too often in economics there is a rift between those who look at the "short-run" and those who look at the "long-run." Often these two groups of researchers go merrily along their way, and the harder job of reconciling their studies is left unattended. Thus, intellectual gaps result. Obviously, the two must be consistent, since the long-run must emerge from a series of short runs. For this reason, the long-run natural rate hypothesis of Friedman and Phelps placed great pressure on macroeconomists to reinterpret short-run phenomena and data.

Focusing on expectations and the length of time horizons has important implications for both monetary and fiscal policy. For example, the idea that *anticipated* inflation is neutral in its effect on unemployment, and thus only *unanticipated* inflation can stimulate employment, focused attention on the expectations of consumers and firms not only for future inflation but also for the future course of economic policy. As Lucas notes, when an activist (Keynesian) demand manager uses a particular *short-run* macroeconometric model — call it Model A — to guide the choice of money growth over, say, a decade, it can only lead to trouble. "If we concede that Model A gives us an inaccurate view of the 'long-run,' then we have conceded that it leads us to bad short-run decisions because these decisions are sufficient to dictate our long-run situations as well." He adds, "This is not a hypothetical story of the 1980s, is it? It is a history of the 1970s."

Ricardian Equivalence

Simultaneously, Robert Barro developed an important attack on the efficacy of tax cuts, given government spending, to stimulate the economy. Barro developed a model of overlapping generations, where the well-being of a representative individual in each generation depends not only on his own lifetime consumption, but also on the consumption preferences of his heirs. Thus, *all* generations are linked because the parents are concerned about the well-being of their children, and *their* children's well-being in turn depends upon the well-being of their children. In such a view, when older generations leave substantial bequests to their heirs, a common practice in the United States, the result generally obstructs the efficacy of fiscal policy to accomplish certain goals.

Take, for instance, the belief that debt burdens shift when fiscal policy substitutes debt for tax finance. Older workers and retirees, it is assumed, get a break as the burden of paying for government shifts to younger workers. However, increased debt through deficits commits the government to increased future interest payments and possible repayments of principal. These must be financed by *future* taxes, whose present value approximates the value of the debt. Since those who are paying taxes currently shift the liability to future generations, they can undo this shift in tax burdens to future generations by spending less themselves and increasing their bequests. Such changes in private intergenerational transfers of income within families can offset the government's fiscal policy, thus aborting attempts to increase the wealth of present consumers. In the extreme, there will be no change in spending (see Panel 5 in Figure 1), and therefore, no stimulative effect from the fiscal policy.[1] Thus, demand management is called into question not only because of the shape of the aggregate supply curve, but also whether aggregate demand is affected in the first place.

Taxes and Incentives

Substantial research had also addressed the effects of taxes on incentives to work, save, and invest. The work of Martin Feldstein, Robert Hall and Dale Jorgenson, James Heckman, and myself, among many others, had revealed that the incentive effects of real after-tax returns on factors of production such as saving, investment, and labor supply, are far greater than had previously been thought.[2] Many of these studies focused in particular on the adverse incentives produced by a tax system not indexed for inflation. These studies gradually began to have some influence, and for the first time, relative prices, as opposed to merely short-run income flows, were included in some large econometric models.[3]

New Theories

Paralleling these developments in macroeconomics and fiscal and monetary policy, a new approach to the traditional microeconomics of government policies, especially those of resource allocation and income redistribution was emerging. Three sets of new developments cast further doubt on the efficacy of government policy in these areas. First, the theory of optimal taxation was used to determine the most socially beneficial design for the tax structure and transfer payments. Analysis revealed the desirability of low marginal tax rates. A rigorous model of social welfare maximization could not justify high and steeply progressive marginal tax rates, even if the disincentive effects of taxes are quite small.[4] These studies of efficiency and equity generally concluded that tax rates of one-third or less of income were optimal, and that the optimal level of transfer payments to the poor was on the order of one-third of average income. In short, the theory of optimal taxation laid a rigorous intellectual foundation for major changes in the tax structure and for changes in the level and nature of transfer payments.

Second, following much microeconomic study of externalities, or third-party effects causing market failure (as when commuters clog traffic, ignoring the cost they impose by slowing down other commuters), and a plethora of government programs to ameliorate them, a theory of government failure was developed. Based not merely on historical experience, but also on a reexamination of the incentives motivating government agencies, economists gradually began to see the relationship between imperfect market outcomes (such as externalities) and imperfect government mediation of the imperfect market. Often, the government seemed to have made matters worse, not better. Just as activist demand management *sometimes* helps but *often* does worse than nondiscretionary rules, so the case for government intervention to ameliorate market failure must be judged against the practical outcome, not the idealized textbook one. Milton Friedman, George Stigler, and James Buchanan were the economists most notable for bringing these issues to public attention.

Finally, economists started to study government itself as an industry, an institution responding to the self-interest of those who sought to use it for selfish ends, rather than as a purely benevolent, impartial arbiter and defender of the good. This public choice theory helped lay the intellectual basis for rejecting government action as the answer to social problems, in favor of a more direct and less romanticized version of government behavior. Again, Buchanan, Friedman, and Stigler played leading roles.

Inflation and Incentives

It became increasingly clear that money and inflation are not neutral when a tax system is not indexed for inflation. Martin Feldstein was the researcher most responsible for pointing this out. Indeed, he argued, many traditional measures of the tightness or looseness of monetary policy can be quite illusory when one looks only at the movements of gross before-tax nominal (i.e., without adjustment for inflation) interest rates, rather than real (inflation-adjusted) after-tax returns. For example, in the 1970s, real after-tax costs of capital were commonly negative—which is to say the after-tax interest rate was lower than the inflation rate. Feldstein notes this produced a drastic overestimate of the "tightness" of monetary policy. The negative real after-tax returns demonstrated that monetary policy in the seventies was much looser— and therefore more inflationary— than commonly supposed by those who focused solely on nominal before-tax interest rates.

A similar argument of "inflation adjustment" for fiscal policy has been advanced by Robert Eisner of Northwestern University. Since inflation decreases the value of the previously issued national debt, the "nominal deficit" may be a quite misleading guide to fiscal stimulus. In the high-inflation year of 1980, for example, the "large" deficit was less than the decline in value of the debt. Thus, fiscal policy, according to Eisner, was much tighter than commonly supposed, despite large budget deficits by the standards of the 1970s.

Note the key role that expectations, incentives, and time horizons play in these new theories. For example, in the Barro argument, the time horizon is extended from that of a single short period—say, a year, the traditional focus for current disposable income in Keynesian analyses— even beyond the lifecycle and permanent income considerations of Franco Modigliani and Milton Friedman, to more than one generation. The *expectations* of future taxes might encourage behavior (spending less and saving more to increase bequests) that would sharply reduce the perceived change in wealth of *current* consumers. Hence, deficit finance has little impact on aggregate demand.

For these reasons, analytical developments in economics during the 1970s caused serious doubts about the efficacy of attempts to manage aggregate demand through monetary *or* fiscal policy. The traditional concerns of being able quickly to identify or forecast economic fluctuations, of implementing policies soon enough so that they may mitigate rather than aggravate business cycles, and of judging the speed with which the economy reacts to the policies all waned in importance. In their place much greater emphasis was placed on expectations and incentives, and a correspondingly longer time horizon. Among these, special importance was given to expectations of the future course of economic policy.

Supply-Side Economics and Fiscal Orthodoxy

Thus, a second "revolution" against the orthodox Keynesian demand-management position was developed. This new revolution reflects the belief that the inflation of the 1970s was much more costly than had been thought. While a monetary expansion might temporarily reduce unemployment, a higher inflation rate could cause serious, long-term harm to the economy by reducing incentives for future efforts to produce income. The emphasis changed from short-term cash flows to relative prices, from aggregate demand (or spending) management to concern about the economy's potential to produce more output. Growing concerns about the productivity growth slowdown brought with them the name "supply-side economics."

There is nothing new about the central issues of supply-side economics. Since the time of Alfred Marshall in the late nineteenth century, economists have realized that supply and demand affect prices and output in both particular markets and the entire economy. However, the complexity of the effects of taxes, inflation, and other government policies on the factors of supply had been underestimated. Although supply-side incentive effects are large enough to be of major concern, they are neither so large nor so immediate that broad across-the-board tax rate cuts could increase supply enough to be self-financing. The major debate centered on *how large* these incentive effects were and *how quickly* they occurred: in other words, what policy would get the biggest bang for the buck.

Despite these limits, some advocates dramatically overstated the case for supply-side economics. They claimed that tax cuts would unleash such a frenzy of economic activity that they would be self-financing, eliminating the need to worry about first controlling government spending. The argument was often supported by the "Laffer Curve," which claimed to show that above a certain tax rate, further rate hikes would cause tax revenues to fall. While this is true in specific cases where savings or investment or work effort can be altered in the short-run, there was no evidence to suggest that it was true in general. Although these supply-side economists dramatically overstated the lessons to be learned from the serious supply-side studies, one must also note that the Keynesians argued from the other extreme that the relative price effects of the tax cuts could be safely ignored indefinitely. Experience taught us that both extremes were wrong: both the relative price effects and the size of the tax cuts were important.

"Consensus" Versus "Recipe" Economics

It is important to distinguish what might be called "consensus" economics from "recipe" economics. While disagreements raged over the cost and speed of disinflation, and the size and time horizon of incentive effects, these disagreements were based on scientific analyses, both theoretical and empirical. This intellectual ferment should have clarified the areas of dispute and agreement and led to tests of competing views, producing a consensus that contained some elements of each approach. Yet some extreme supply-side economists argued that *any* combination of ideas and estimates was sensible: large tax cuts would stimulate the economy and cause GNP to grow so rapidly that tax revenues would rise, while a credible Fed anti-inflation program could disinflate quite rapidly with virtually no recession. By using the most optimistic or exaggerated parts of each of these ideas and estimates as the alleged basis for Reaganomics and the original Administration economic forecasts, these extreme supply-siders conjured up a most implausible scenario and raised expectations to a level that could not possibly be met. Their strategy amounted to taking the good ingredients from various recipes, doubling them for good measure, and combining them in hopes that something desirable might result. They were responsible for giving the core of Reaganomics — good ideas based predominantly on sound economic principles — a bad name when it did not deliver instant, painless success.

A large group of fiscally orthodox conservatives, myself included, argued that it was essential that the government intrude less in the economy and be more cost-conscious. This argument extended to active attempts to "fine tune" the economy and manage aggregate demand, and to the general approach which, through the 1960s and 1970s, tended to shift aggregate demand away from investment toward consumption. It was also argued that over the long run, a balanced budget should be the rule rather than the exception. Thus, orthodox conservatives argued that the government should run surpluses in good times to cover its deficits in bad times, as Keynes himself had argued. These economists and politicians were never very happy with attempts to stimulate the economy by tax cuts or government spending increases, but sometimes the distinction between the short-run macro consequences and the appropriate size of the public sector became blurred. The practical manifestation of this distinction was that some conservatives focused on the size of deficits whereas others focused on the level of government spending as the major fiscal evil. In any event, a great debate ensued about the extent to which deficits really mattered, which was yet another attack on the activist fine-tuning of Keynesian demand management. The deficit debate is discussed in greater detail in Chapter 9.

The International Economy

At the same time, economic events were unfolding that would eventually change the thinking of virtually all U.S. economists, regardless of their school of thought. The shift from fixed to flexible exchange rates, the growth of world trade, the technological advances in information and communication that lowered the costs of international flows of capital in response to interest differentials or other factors, gradually forced economists — as well as businessmen, labor leaders, politicians, and the Federal Reserve — to realize just how open the huge U.S. economy was becoming. While foreign trade used to account for only one tenth of GNP on average, the United States is increasingly competing in a world-wide market for many goods, as well as short-run capital flows. This has striking implications. Consider, for example, a "Keynesian" attempt to stimulate an economy in recession via a large tax cut. The policy is likely to place upward pressure on U.S. interest rates. This in turn makes assets denominated in dollars (as opposed, say, to yen or francs) more attractive, driving up the demand for dollars and the exchange rate, thereby making U.S. exports more expensive and imports less so. Whatever Keynesian stimulus the tax cut produces will be offset, at least partly, by a decline in our net exports (see Panel 6 of Figure 1). Thus, in an "open" economy, Keynesian demand management is likely to be far less effective than traditional Keynesians assumed throughout the 1970s, quite apart from the issues raised by the new classical economists.

Further, if assets denominated in the currencies of the major world economies are at least partly substitutable for one another (e.g., a financial institution in country X may hold part of its portfolio in assets of country Y to achieve higher returns or lower risks), it follows that the monetary and fiscal policies followed in these other countries can have a major impact on the U.S. economy. As the dollar rebounded from a 1978 low, about 20 percent undervalued, some economists, such as Ronald McKinnon of Stanford University, argued that U.S. monetary policy ought to place increased emphasis on the foreign exchange value of the dollar, not just the domestic price level, and that the effect of monetary policy would be better understood by examining a weighted average of monetary growth in the major economies, not just domestic monetary growth.

Is There a Crisis in Economics?

The decline of theories that dominated economics since the 1930s has made it fashionable to say that the profession is undergoing a "crisis." This discussion, however, shows that is not true. Economics, like other intellectual disciplines, is a dynamic enterprise: its theories are subject to continual tests. When theories fail, they tend to be replaced or at least revised. If the word "crisis" has a place, it would seem descriptive of circumstances where the governing theories have fallen, but nothing has taken their place. This is not the case for the discipline of economics in the mid-1980s.

The economics profession and policymakers in general have moved toward a new set of concerns, influenced by various schools of thought — the monetarists, the new classical economists, the fiscally orthodox conservatives, and both the serious and popular supply-siders. They have shifted their attention toward a longer-term time horizon (and its potential impact on *short-run* decisions), toward expectations of the future course of the economy (including expectations of future government policies), and toward the critical role played by economic incentives. From this discussion of changes that took place largely before Ronald Reagan assumed the Presidency, it is clear that economists had increasingly come to agree on the following conclusions:

1. Reviving incentives to produce wealth would require a reduction in marginal tax rates, especially on investment, accompanied by slower government spending growth and disinflation;

2. Active demand management should be abandoned except when the economy is in extreme difficulty;

3. Inflation is far more costly than previously thought, eroding incentives to produce wealth both through its interaction with an unindexed tax system and by increasing economic uncertainty; and

4. *Gradual* disinflation might not be necessary if the economic policies of the Fed and fiscal authorities are credible. In this case, economists believe, people will quickly revise their expectations, thus sharply reducing the costs of disinflation in terms of lost output and higher unemployment. Further, the disinflation would help reduce the rise in effective marginal tax rates caused by the interaction of inflation and the unindexed tax system.

How rapidly the disinflation could occur, exactly how large the loss in output and rise in unemployment would be (even if much less than orthodox Keynesians were predicting), and how long it would take to restore productivity growth, let alone recoup any reasonable fraction of the revenues lost by a general tax cut—these questions were still subject to debate. But by 1980, even most Keynesians were coming to agree qualitatively with these points. This intellectual ferment—which by no means constituted an intellectual crisis—combined with the deterioration in economic performance of the 1970s led to Reaganomics. Economists generally agreed that disinflation would be necessary; a smaller public sector would be necessary as well as desirable; the tax structure would have to be changed, focusing on reduction of marginal tax rates, especially those on investment. This would lay the foundation for an economy with a better chance for relatively stable growth. Since these new ideas implied different responses of the economy to monetary contraction and tax cuts, the 1980s would provide a partial, if imprecise, test of the competing claims. The *structure* of the Reagan program was quite closely tied to these ideas and events. Its specific implementation as amended by Congress was much less so.

♦ *Chapter 4* ♦

Reaganomics 1981–84

President Reagan's economic program is often misdescribed, if only because what the President submitted to Congress in 1981 was not exactly what he advocated during the election campaign, and what Congress ultimately adopted was a different program than the one he proposed. In addition, Congress made several changes which the Administration opposed, at least initially, and the Administration accepted other changes in order to get its basic program through. Finally, the Federal Reserve's monetary policy, which the Administration generally supported, was neither as stable nor as responsive to some concerns as the Administration would have liked.

Although the economic policies of 1981–86 are not entirely the program of President Reagan, together they have been described as the "Reagan economic program." As implemented, these policies were the product of multiple compromises that are normal to a democratic political process. That process gave the Administration most of its original tax proposal, the first four years of its defense buildup, and some of its proposed spending cuts. The Administration was less successful, however, in controlling other areas of spending. The original tax cut turned out to be much larger in real terms than had been anticipated, partly because Congress added substantial additional tax cuts in 1981, and partly because the inflation rate declined more rapidly than had been predicted.[1] This combination produced a string of substantial structural deficits.

The Reagan economic policy evolved further between 1982 and 1986, reflecting both the original goals and subsequent political and economic events. In this chapter and the next I describe the basis of the Reagan policies for the years 1981–84 and 1985–86 respectively; in subsequent chapters I evaluate them. Two remarkable fiscal facts indicate the enormous changes that occurred during the overall period: the top marginal tax rate in the individual income tax has been reduced from 70 percent to 28 percent (our *top* rate is lower than the *bottom* rate in many countries, e.g., the United Kingdom), and the national debt has more than doubled. Clearly, the Reagan economic program sought and wrought — sometimes inadvertently — very great structural changes in economic policy.

This chapter will explore the Reagan economic program in several different stages. To begin, I review the primary goals and policy instruments of Reaganomics and trace the important policy initiatives undertaken on several fronts. These include the Economic Recovery and Tax Act of 1981, the fiscal year 1982 budget revisions, and the initial Social Security proposals. The 1981–82 recession, widening deficits, and the political need to compromise led to some important modifications in administration policies. This chapter traces these developments through the important policy proposals of 1982–84 — including budget proposals, Social Security reforms, the Tax Equity and Fiscal Responsibility Act, the gas tax, the Deficit Reduction Act, and monetary, regulatory, and trade policies. The next chapter will discuss the policy initiatives of 1985–86, including the Tax Reform Act of 1986, budget initiatives and stalemates, structural changes in the budget process (such as Gramm-Rudman-Hollings), monetary and exchange rate policy, and the battle against protectionism. The final section of Chapter 5 will discuss the overall nature of economic policy from 1981–86, with special emphasis on what was novel about the Reagan economic policy. At the end of Chapter 5, a chart highlights the chronology of policy initiatives — implemented or rebuked — and provides an overview of the scope and depth of the Reagan program.

Major Economic Themes

It is clear that the economic themes of the Reagan Administration are based on the economic events and policies of earlier years. As discussed above, the U.S. economy in the 1970s experienced high and fluctuating inflation, lagging productivity growth, increased regulation, and stifling of economic incentives. Federal spending on transfer payments had grown rapidly, while defense spending as a proportion of the budget and of GNP had fallen. Economic policy, in its attempts to respond to problems in the earlier period, had been erratic and ineffective. Policy during this period had been a weathervane rather than a compass: a series of attempts to focus first on one, then another economic problem, with little serious coordination among various components of economic policy and little recognition of the potential interrelationships among these various policy instruments and their economic outcomes.

When President Carter took office in 1977, the economy was recovering rapidly from a severe recession, the unemployment rate was falling, and the inflation rate had fallen well below its double-digit levels of 1974. Despite these indicators of improvement, the new Administration still pressed for an expansionary fiscal policy. The President focused on unemployment to the exclusion of all other problems, advocating expansion of public service jobs as the solution. As a result, the inflation rate ratcheted upward in a series of episodes, and by late 1978, President Carter declared inflation as the real enemy, replacing unemployment. At best, the Administration's attempts to reduce unemployment more rapidly than it would have fallen through the private sector's natural expansion had only a minor impact on employment; unfortunately, this policy had a pronounced effect on the inflation rate. In fact, attempts to control inflation through the Council on Wage and Price Stability, other forms of jawboning, and regulation of wage and price contracts had little effect on the inflation rate.

In January 1980 President Carter issued his fiscal year 1981 budget, calling for $616 billion in spending and $600 billion in revenues, leaving a deficit of $16 billion. With inflation running at an annual rate of about 18 percent for a couple of months, there was a clamor for a balanced budget. Incredible as it may seem from today's perspective, President Carter was forced to recall his fiscal year 1981 budget, somewhat like an automobile manufacturer recalling a defective part, and reissue a balanced budget. Unfortunately, his reissue occurred on the eve of a sharp, but brief, recession, thus invalidating all of his budget projections. This soon forced him to issue yet another budget—his third for FY81 in the course of a few months.

Economic policy seemed to possess little direction or vision; it simply responded to each crisis as it emerged.

The Reagan economic program was designed to set a new course. In the President's own words:

> My economic program is based on the fundamental precept that government must respect, protect, and enhance the freedom and integrity of the individual. Economic policy must seek to create a climate that

encourages the development of private institutions conducive to individual responsibility and initiative. . . . My program — a careful combination of reducing incentive-stifling taxes, slowing the growth of federal spending and regulations, and a gradual slowing of the expansion of the money supply—seeks to create a new environment in which the strengths of America can be put to work for the benefit of us all.[2]

The economic agenda of the Administration placed high priority on the following issues:

1. **Disinflation.**   A gradual reduction of inflation to a level where it was no longer a major factor in economic decisions; i.e., no more than low single-digit levels, was considered desirable in and of itself, and a *necessary prerequisite* to restoring incentives to produce income and wealth.

2. **Restoration of Long-term Productivity Growth.**   Restoring long-term productivity growth to something like its historic level was seen as desirable in general and also likely to be a more effective way to assist low-income people than an ever-growing government welfare system.

3. **Stronger National Defense.**   While President Reagan's advisors were divided between those who stressed economic problems and those who stressed defense, all of them concurred with the conclusion reached by the Carter Administration itself toward the end of its term that our defenses had been neglected for many years, and that increased spending was necessary to restore them to acceptable levels.

4. **Increased Individual Freedom of Choice and Decentralization in Economic Affairs.**   Enhancing an individual's command over his own resources and encouraging smaller units of government to provide public services were seen as desirable.

5. **Preservation of a Humane Social Safety Net.**   The Administration was committed to maintaining sufficient funds to preserve a humane "safety net" for the disadvantaged, but believed the government's role in redistributing income and maintaining welfare programs should be limited to those at, near, or below the poverty line.

These goals shared widespread acceptance inside and outside the Administration. The only debate was over exact priorities and necessary trade-offs. To address these goals, the Administration committed itself to a four-pronged policy:

1. **Control of Federal Spending and Transfer of its Composition Toward Defense.**   Control of spending was to be accomplished by main-

taining a social safety net for the truly needy, while tightening eligibility standards in transfer payment programs; eliminating waste, fraud, and abuse; and shifting substantial responsibility from the federal to state and local governments, "together with the resources necessary to finance them." In addition, spending was to be reallocated toward defense.

2. **Tax Rate Reduction and Tax Reform.**   Marginal tax rates for individuals were to be reduced by 30 percent over three years. Tax brackets would be indexed. The depreciation system in the corporate income tax would be both accelerated and simplified. In 1980, numerous asset classes existed. The Administration proposed consolidating these into three classes.

3. **Slow, Steady Monetary Policy.**   The Administration desired steady money growth consistent with non-inflationary economic expansion. The President reiterated his support for the general nature of the anti-inflationary policies begun in late 1979 by the Federal Reserve Board, though from time to time the Administration was to complain about the specific implementation of the Fed's monetary policy.

4. **Continued Deregulation.**   This would lower costs of various activities by reducing the number of regulations, taking economic effects into account in evaluating the desirability of "social" regulations, and increasing competition in economically regulated industries.

In addition to endorsing these explicit policies, the Administration expressly rejected the notion of fine-tuning the economy. Instead, the policies stressed long-run stability and sought to unleash the inherent strengths in the economy. Monetary policy was to be set through a nondiscretionary monetary growth rule, consistent with disinflation. The tax system was to be set on a path toward sensible reform over a few years. Government spending was to be rationalized, made more efficient and effective, and reduced.

Each of these policies made sense individually. The truly novel aspect of the Reagan plan was its vision of vigorous growth—the assumed result of the tax and deregulation policy—accompanied by falling rates of inflation. Typically, disinflation has been accompanied by a period of reduced output and rising unemployment, only thereafter followed by a period of economic expansion. The Reagan Administration, in contrast, more or less ignored this intermediate phase of the cost of disinflation. Ultimately this placed severe strains on the consistency of the policies and raised questions about the program's fairness. But although the strains caused by recession and other factors forced some policy modifications in later years, the main elements of the program have remained largely intact.

Following is a description of the important initiatives, and the evolution of particular policies.

Major Policy Initiatives—1981

The Administration entered office with a comprehensive set of economic plans. Its most fundamental goals were to reduce inflation and encourage growth of real incomes—in hopes that the combination would be sufficient to balance the budget in 1984. A balanced budget was to be the *result* of dealing with more fundamental economic ills, rather than *the* goal to which other goals would be sacrificed. To achieve these objectives, the Administration in 1981 made policy proposals along several fronts. These included significant reductions in FY82 spending, general reduction and reform of taxes (which became the Economic Recovery and Tax Act), and a plan for Social Security reform (later retracted). The Administration also made some preliminary moves toward deregulation and endorsed the Federal Reserve's handling of monetary policy.

Revisions to Fiscal Year 1982 Budget. In early 1981, soon after assuming office, the Administration proposed revisions to President Carter's FY82 budget. As expected, the revisions emphasized reduction in the rate of federal spending growth and reallocation of the budget towards defense.

President Carter's budget for FY82, issued in January 1981, proposed outlays of $739 billion, receipts of $712 billion, and a deficit of $27 billion. President Reagan proposed increased defense spending of $6 billion and nondefense reductions of $48.6 billion. His total proposed outlay was $695 billion. On the revenue side, President Reagan proposed tax reforms projected to lower revenues by approximately $53 billion in fiscal year 1982. Thus, projected revenues were $650 billion and the deficit $45 billion. Since actual fiscal year 1981 receipts and outlays were $599 billion and $657 billion respectively, the Reagan plan represented an 8.3 percent increase in receipts and a 5.8 increase in outlays. President Carter's program, by contrast, proposed a 17.8 percent increase in receipts and a 12.5 percent increase in outlays over fiscal year 1981 levels.

As noted above, reducing overall growth in federal spending was one of the central themes in President Reagan's economic plan. From 1974 to 1980, federal outlays grew at about 14 percent per year, while nomi-

TABLE 4-1   The Spending Control Gap: Reagan Administration's
             Original Plan for FY85 vs. Actual Outlays for FY85
             (Outlays as % of GNP)

	Actual 1981	March 1981 target for FY85	Actual FY85	Actual–Target Difference
National Defense	5.5%	6.5%	6.6%	+ 0.1%
Benfit payments	10.8	10.0	10.7	+ 0.7
Grants	1.9	1.0	1.4	+ 0.4
Other	2.3	1.2	1.5	+ 0.3
Net interest	2.3	1.5	3.2	+ 1.7
Undistributed cuts	—	- 1.0	—	+ 1.0
Total	22.8%	19.2%	23.4%	+ 4.2%

nal GNP grew 11 percent per year, and inflation averaged 7.6 percent. Thus, federal outlays grew at almost *twice* the rate of inflation. Moreover, by 1980 the share of government spending in GNP was close to record levels. The Administration hoped to reduce the growth of federal outlays to about 7 percent per year in nominal terms, thereby reducing the budget as a percent of GNP from 23 percent in 1981 to 19 percent by fiscal year 1985. The detailed blueprint of this is shown in Table 1. Reduced budget growth, coupled with other Administration policies—and unreasonably optimistic forecasts—led to a projected balanced budget by fiscal year 1984, with small surpluses in fiscal years 1985 and 1986.

The Administration also proposed reallocating the budget in important ways. It planned to reverse the steady decline in the share of the budget and GNP going to defense, slow the growth of nondefense spending while preserving a "social safety net," and transfer responsibilities to state and local governments. Since about three-quarters of federal spending was going to defense, Social Security, Medicare, and net interest on the debt, the percentage cuts in the remaining programs had to be large. Interest on the debt obviously had to be paid; and the President had committed himself to a defense buildup somewhat larger than President Carter had already committed the nation to in international agreements. Social Security and Medicare, together the largest and most rapidly growing items in the federal budget, were left virtually untouched (the Social Security fiasco is discussed elsewhere in this chapter).

Consequently, large reductions in the remaining programs were necessary to reduce the overall spending growth. For example, the percentage of the budget devoted to all programs other than defense, the safety net, and interest on the debt was to decline from 29.5 percent in fiscal year 1981 to only 18.4 percent in fiscal year 1984, a reduction of more than one-third. The social safety net actually grew as a percentage of the budget and in real terms. The social safety net is defined to include basic Social Security benefits (retirement, disability, and Medicare); unemployment benefits; cash benefits for dependent families, the elderly, and the disabled; and income support and medical benefits for veterans. In addition, Headstart, summer youth employment, and subsidized nutrition programs to low income families were left untouched. These programs were projected to grow at 9 percent per year in *current* dollars through 1984.

Real defense spending was to rise at about 8 percent per year through 1986. It is important to note that the proposal for increased real defense spending began under President Carter, who proposed a more modest increase (from 24.9 percent to 27.7 percent of the budget between 1982 and 1985). Many recent comments, especially in the popular press and unfortuntately to some degree encouraged by the Reagan Administration, imply that the defense buildup was exclusively President Reagan's idea. This is misleading. Although President Reagan called for a more rapid defense buildup than his predecessor—indeed, the largest buildup in peacetime history—both presidents agreed about the importance of defense as a budget priority.

To achieve the necessary spending cuts, the Administration expected all other domestic programs to accept cuts, and proposed the following guidelines:

1. Reduce subsidies to middle and upper income groups;
2. Apply sound economic criteria to subsidy programs;
3. Recover costs that could be allocated to users, e.g., by substituting user charges for tax finance;
4. Reduce overhead and personnel costs of the federal government;
5. Impose fiscal restraint on all other national programs;
6. Stretch and retarget public-sector capital investment programs; and
7. Consolidate grant programs to the states into block grants.

As guidelines, these made a lot of sense. However, as I will show in Chapter 7, they were neither implemented as fully as the Administration had hoped, nor honored consistently under the pressure of political commitments. These guidelines did lead to several reductions in the FY82 budget. Among the most important, entitlement programs were revised to eliminate *unintended* benefits.[3] This meant, primarily, tightening eligibility standards — for instance, lowering student Social Security benefits or lowering the eligibility level of food stamp recipients. This was projected to reduce outlays by $5.8 billion. Welfare programs such as Medicaid, Aid to Families with Dependent Children, and school lunches, were to be reduced by $5.5 billion. Large reductions in grants-in-aid to state and local governments were proposed. There were to be cuts in subsidies to agriculture (which were inadvertently reversed in the payment-in-kind program subsequently proposed), energy, and other industries. Federal civilian employment was to be cut by 83,000, and a revised pay comparability scale with the private sector was proposed. These proposals are highlighted in Table 1, which shows actual 1981 budget expenditures by various categories, the Administration's March 1981 target for fiscal year 1985, and the actual 1985 results. The difference between the two is partly the result of congressional refusal to approve several major cuts, and partly the result of the defense buildup. One percent of GNP in cuts was left unspecified, to be decided upon later; naturally, not many of these cuts materialized.

Congress accepted, with minor modifications, about three-quarters of the Administration's spending cuts. This was widely hailed as a tremendous victory for better management of the federal government. How modest these actual spending reductions would prove to be was ignored in the general euphoria over the passage of the budget.

Economic Recovery and Tax Act. Tax reform and reduction was also a centerpiece of the Administration's economic plan. The Economic Recovery and Tax Act of 1981 (ERTA) contained several important revisions of the tax code. The two most important were the three-year, across-the-board reduction in income tax rates, and the accelerated depreciation of capital investment, following closely the proposal by Congressman Kemp and Senator Roth.

The tax reform was motivated by several concerns. First, the Administration placed great weight on the potential incentive effects of lower taxes. Reducing tax rates would increase incentives to work, save, invest, and innovate, and the tax cuts therefore would lead to greater output. Extreme supply-siders contended that the tax cuts might even be self-financing, i.e., that no loss in revenue would occur. This required the tax base to increase more than proportionally to offset the rate reduction. For a broad,

across-the-board rate cut such as the proposed personal income tax reduction, this contention was preposterous. Some revenue would be recouped,
and in some cases targeted reduction of very high tax rates might well
produce more revenue, as apparently the 1978 reduction in capital-gains
taxes had done.[4] However, as discussed in Chapters 2 and 3, it was overwhelmingly evident that the labor supply, saving, and other responses,
while significant, were nevertheless too small and slow to allow the tax
cuts to be self-financing.

The second motivation was that the general population considered
taxes too high and government spending too large. Moreover, some individuals in the Administration argued that the tax rate reduction would
force spending reduction via deficit-phobia or a starvation theory of public
spending, while others argued that marginal rate reductions were important because marginal tax rates had risen greatly for the general population, as described in Chapter 2.

ERTA was proposed in early 1981. Over the period 1981–84, it called
for reducing individual income tax rates approximately 30 percent—at
10 percent increments per year—while leaving the top marginal rate at
50 percent. This would lower the top rate from 70 percent to 50 percent
over three years, and thereby eliminate the differential in top-bracket tax
rates between labor earnings and investment income. While the President
wanted to lower the top rate from 70 percent to 50 percent immediately,
he was persuaded not to take the lead on this issue because it would be
called unfair and used against his tax plan. In fact, as so often happens
in politics, the President got someone else—in this case, the House
Democrats—to propose what he wanted. Under the proposed tax bill,
a family of four with an adjusted income of $20,000 would have their
tax burden reduced 28.7 percent by 1984.[*]

The proposal for Accelerated Cost Recovery emphasized stan-
dardized, simplified, and faster depreciation of assets. Structures were to
be written off in ten years, other machinery in five years, and light equipment in three years. This would replace a myriad of asset classes and provide more rapid tax recovery. To some, this merely offset the erosion of
depreciation incentives due to inflation; to others, it was the major vehicle by which an increase in investment demand, i.e., demand for new cap-

---

[*]The difference between 28.7 percent and 30 percent arises because the latter refers to the
decrease in rates, whereas the former refers to tax liabilities. Since various features of the
code were not indexed for inflation, the value of these features (personal exemptions, for
instance) produces the difference.

ital goods, would increase the investment rate and future productivity. Despite the econometric evidence that suggested a rapid increase in investment would increase productivity only gradually, great emphasis was placed on the ability of these so-called supply-side effects to increase output rapidly.

Much controversy ensued over the revenue impacts of the tax cuts — both over what the impacts would be and what the Administration said they would be. In a February 18, 1981, document the White House claimed, "These tax cuts will contribute importantly to raising the levels of economic activity materially above those which have been attained under present law." They did *not* claim that the individual income tax cuts would be self-financing. Instead, they noted, "the reduction in marginal tax rates will reduce individual income tax liabilities by 27.3 percent for 1984." Since a 30 percent income tax rate cut would lead to a 27.3 percent reduction in tax revenues, this suggested only a minute response of labor supply and earnings over the period 1981–84 — not exactly the extreme supply-side response that some in the Administration claimed.

Congress accepted ERTA with only minor modifications. The Democrats, led by Congressman James Jones (D-OK), developed an alternative to President Reagan's tax plan, as well as to his budget plans. The most important difference between the two plans was that Congressman Jones tied the third year of the tax cut to achieving spending reduction goals, thereby limiting the possibility of burgeoning deficits. The Administration opposed this idea on grounds that there would be no pressure placed on spending reduction unless the third year of the tax cut was actually passed. When Congress eventually passed the bill, the 10 percent per year plan had been changed to 5 percent, 10 percent, 10 percent, and, as noted above, the top rate was reduced to 50 percent immediately, instead of over three years, at the insistence of the Democratic-controlled House Ways and Means Committee. President Reagan signed the bill in August 1981.

ERTA contained several other important provisions besides tax cuts for individuals and accelerated depreciation. It provided for indexing of individual rate brackets starting in 1985, thus eliminating bracket-creep, and the automatic inflation-kicker in revenue. It also allowed all charitable contributions to be deducted regardless of whether the taxpayer itemized. Capital gain taxes on the sale of principal residences were deferred if a new residence was purchased within two years. Individual retirement accounts (IRAs) were made universal, regardless of whether

TABLE 4-2a   Decomposing the Projected Deficit Into Policy Changes

	1985	1989
Budget deficit		
1981 Policy continued		
% of GNP	2.1	-0.2
Tax cuts (net)	3.0	3.8
Defense Buildup	0.9	1.4
Nondefense spnd. cuts	-1.4	-1.5
Interest	0.5	1.7
8/84 Projection	4.9	5.2
Actual 1985	5.4	—
2/86 Projection	—	2.8

Source: CBO, August, 1984 and February, 1986, and OMB, January, 1986.

the employee already had a private pension plan. A research and development tax credit was adopted "temporarily."

Each of these items was potentially important in various ways. While the purpose of this chapter is to describe only the main elements of the program and the 1982 and 1984 tax laws revising part of ERTA, it is instructive to examine the likely long-run impact of ERTA on revenues, and the provisions of ERTA on the structure of marginal tax rates. Panel A in Table 2 shows the estimates of long-run revenue by the Congressional Budget Office, and Panel B gives estimates of differences in marginal effective tax rates across assets and industries. Clearly, ERTA returned hundreds of billions of dollars of tax revenue to the general population. Even after the TEFRA tax increase (discussed below), the tax cuts account for more than half of the 1985 deficit. This implied a substantial increase in the ratio of deficits to GNP for many years *unless* government spending was substantially controlled.

By lowering tax rates and simplifying corporate taxes, ERTA made an important contribution. Nevertheless, the Accelerated Cost Recovery System, the Investment Tax Credit, and the capital gains differential led to a huge growth of tax shelters, inadvertently causing substantial inefficiencies. Needless complexities continued to plague the tax system,

TABLE 4-2b   Effective Tax Rates By Asset Type
(selected major categories)

Asset	pre-1981	ERTA	ERTA/TERFA
EQUIPMENT			
Autos	17.0	-32.8	9.6
Office, Computing, and Accounting Equipment	2.3	-49.4	11.9
Trucks, Buses, and Trailers	10.1	-45.2	11.3
Service Industry Machinery	20.3	-28.5	8.3
Electric Transmission and Distribution Equipment	29.2	3.2	24.2
Enginges, Turbines	31.8	16.3	30.2
All Equipment	17.2	-18.8	11.4
STRUCTURES			
Industrial Structures	49.6	38.4	38.4
Commercial Structures	46.8	35.6	35.6
Farm Structures	41.1	35.8	35.8
All Structures	40.8	30.0	36.1

Source: Jane Gravelle, "Capital Income Taxation and Efficiency in the Allocation of Investment," *National Tax Journal,* 1983.

which was to lead eventually to one monumental and two important reforms.

The Social Security Dilemma.   In early 1981, the President submitted a plan to revise Social Security, a plan that met with hostile opposition. In September, 1981, the President withdrew the plan and formed a bipartisan commission on Social Security reform. After the 1982 elections, the commission issued its report, which formed the basis for the 1983 Social Security amendments. Although these were hailed as solving the Social Security problem, in reality they deferred many of the problems for future solution.

Social Security is the largest domestic spending program, and though it is also the most popular, it is increasingly beset by three interrelated sets of problems: it is inequitable, inefficient, and financially insolvent in the long run. All are major problems, but hard to see — or rather, easy to ignore — because the program has a huge number of beneficiaries. It provides substantial income during retirement to 36 million Americans — but it is also the source of the single-greatest tax burden to a majority of the more than 100 million taxpayers.

The program is inequitable because many wealthy retirees are receiving many times what they and their employers have paid in, plus interest, while it is heavily financed by taxes paid by low- and middle-income workers. In addition, it redistributes the benefits from low- and middle-income, two-earner couples to wealthy one-earner couples. It is inefficient in that it does not target benefits as well as it should to those who need them the most. Moreover, it impairs incentives to continue to work in old age and to save for retirement. Finally, on the problem of solvency, the old-age and disability and survivors insurance fund at the beginning of the 1980s had an enormous long-term unfunded deficit of $1.8 trillion, the excess of projected benefits over projected tax revenues over the next 75 years (adjusted for inflation and discounted to the present). An even larger deficit was projected in the Hospital Insurance (HI) section of the program. These deficits meant that large tax increases or benefit reductions would ultimately be required.[5]

It is possible that none of these issues would have been sufficient to bring Social Security reform to the fore in 1981 had there not been a short-term cash flow problem as well. The high inflation of the 1970s, lagging productivity, and recession had created a situation where, by mid-to-late 1983, tax receipts would not be quite sufficient to cover promised benefits. Despite alarm that Social Security was "bankrupt," the truth was simply that it was going to be a couple of percentage points short of being able to issue its checks on time. Either a very minimal tax increase or a very small benefit cut would have to occur, or benefit checks would have to be delayed for a few days each month. This situation undoubtedly heightened the pressure to find a Social Security solution as soon as possible. In any case, reform of the Social Security system was a major agenda item for the Reagan Administration.

In February of 1981, Health and Human Services Secretary Richard Schweiker proposed reforms in Social Security benefits which would eliminate minimum benefits, phase out student benefits for some beneficiaries, place a cap on disability benefits, and sharply curtail benefits for persons retiring before age 65. For example, an individual retiring at age 62 would be cut from 80 percent to 55 percent of full benefits. There were a variety of other proposals. Of special note, the plan did *not* raise the retirement age, did *not* raise Social Security taxes, and did not require any general revenue finance.

The Administration's proposals in many regards were similar to the proposals developed by the Social Security Subcommittee of the House Ways and Means Committee under the Chairmanship of Congressman Jake Pickle (D-TX). His bill, which was working its way toward the full committee and the House floor, would have raised retirement ages gradually and accomplished many of the same things that the Administration was attempting to do, although more gradually and not as fully. Indeed, it is hard not to conclude that the Administration rushed its proposal to beat the Democrats to the punch.

The hostility to the Social Security bill revolved around the enormous reduction in benefits for early retirees. This proposed reduction meant that 61-year-olds planning to retire at the age of 62 would face an immediate one-third cut in their benefits if they did. In response the Senate quickly passed a resolution against the President's Social Security proposals by a vote of 98 to 0.

The Administration later withdrew its proposals, to avoid losing momentum gained on tax and budget items, and the general overall sense of victory and accomplishment in 1981. Then, to depoliticize Social Security, President Reagan proposed a bipartisan national commission—the National Commission on Social Security Reform—with five members appointed by the President, five by the Majority Leader of the Senate, and five by the Speaker of the House. It contained an eight to seven Republican majority, and its members included prominent House and Senate committee members who dealt with Social Security legislation and other related issues. It was chaired by the eminent economist Alan Greenspan.

Monetary Policy.   The Administration recognized monetary policy as a key ingredient in its economic program—one of the four important components of the Reagan economic package (with tax, budgetary, and regulatory reform). Though nominally out of the Administration's control, monetary policy does respond to policy pressure from the Administration and other economic policies, as well as to economic conditions.

The Federal Reserve is a quasi-independent agency, and before President Reagan's election it had embarked on a course of targeting money growth at steadily declining rates to disinflate the economy. On the other hand, Presidents usually get the monetary policy they want, even if they do not admit it. The Federal Reserve is often used as a lightning rod to take the blame for bad economic outcomes. The Reagan Administration relied on the Federal Reserve to disinflate the economy, while concentrating on reducing the size of the public sector and tax, budgetary, and regulatory reform. As detailed in Chapter 6, monetary policy was much more erratic than what monetarists, and many in the Administration, would have liked. As a result, occasional disagreements became more vocal as the recession of 1981–82 worsened.

Regulatory Reform.   Another important Administration goal was to reform federal regulation of business, both for its potential cost-cutting and incentive effects and as a part of a broader campaign to streamline government. A task force known as the "Bush Commission" (after its chairman, Vice President George Bush) was created to identify regulations that could be eliminated or reformed.

In other actions along the same lines, the President in 1981 accelerated decontrol of the domestic oil industry, put a freeze on the "midnight" regulations issued by President Carter's outgoing staff, and tried to strengthen presidential oversight of the regulatory process. Under the leadership of Assistant Attorney General William Baxter, the Antitrust Division of the Justice Department re-examined outmoded notions of anticompetitive behavior. Bigness *per se* was no longer to be opposed and foreign competition was to be taken into account. This ultimately led to the dismissal of the antitrust case against IBM and the breakup of AT&T.

The Administration emphasized cutting the private sector's compliance and administrative costs of conforming to regulations—which CEA Chairman Murray Weidenbaum, as noted in Chapter 2, estimated to be on the order of $100 billion per year. This continued a commitment to economic deregulation that began under President Carter. An early sign of some accomplishment was the reduction by one-third of new pages in the federal register. But the volume of new pages was still enormous.

In all, there were high hopes and good intentions, but the problems were so numerous and diffuse, it was unclear how much could be accomplished.

Economic Events and Policy Changes, 1982–84

For economic, political, and other reasons, a variety of changes, both additions and deletions, were enacted in the Administration's program between 1982 and 1984. Just as the initial Reagan program was a response to events of the 1970s, so its program in later years adapted somewhat to political and economic events. But although significant changes were made, the main thrust of the program remained the same.

In recalling these events, it is important to remember that the economy went into a prolonged recession from mid-1981 to late 1982. The ensuing recovery was robust at the outset and lengthy. It also became apparent that deficits, enormous by historical standards, were to accrue for the indefinite future, *even at relatively full employment.* That is, the recovery itself would not eliminate the large deficits (large as a fraction of GNP and of private saving). Moreover, the combination of the recession and high real before-tax interest rates, despite ACRS and other tax incentives, led to a sharp fall in an already low rate of investment during the recession.

Spending and Tax Initiatives.   The most widely discussed economic issue of the Reagan Administration has been the federal budget deficit. General public awareness of and debate over the "deficit problem" began in 1981–82 for two reasons. First, the Administration had forecast a deficit of $45 billion for FY82. The recession and other factors increased outlays by $30 billion and decreased revenue by $23 billion and thus raised the $45 billion deficit to $98 billion. This was large in absolute dollars, but not particularly large as a share of GNP during a recession. Second, it was clear that not all of the deficit was due to the cyclical downturn. Instead, a rather large deficit was likely to persist in the future, even as the economy returned to full employment.

These factors led both congressional critics and friends of the Administration to press for deficit reduction packages. As a result, beginning with the FY83 budget, deficits and deficit reduction strategies became primary economic issues. Obviously, there are only two ways to reduce a deficit—increase tax revenues or reduce spending. In general, the Administration opposed tax increases and thus forced itself to look for solutions exclusively on the spending side. Given its spending priorities, its options were severely limited.

The *FY83 budget* proposals reflected both the new concern about deficits and faithfulness to the original Reagan program. The budget called for a one percent increase in real spending and a 3 percent increase in real tax revenues. Spending limitations, combined with increased economic incentives through tax and regulatory policy, were counted on to balance the budget. However, the target date for a balanced budget was moved from FY84 (in the original budget) to FY87. More striking was the Administration's continued dedication to reallocating the budget. Defense spending was still scheduled for 8 percent annual real growth, while non-defense spending was scheduled to *fall* by 2 percent. Nondefense spending, excluding net interest on the debt and entitlements, was projected to fall 8 percent annually *in real terms.* In fact, in FY83 alone, discretionary social spending was slated to fall 20 percent in real terms. On the revenue side, the President rejected the notion of raising income taxes on a contingent basis. He continued to call for better management initiatives, massive user charges, and further application of the guidelines issued in 1981. A few corporate taxes were raised.

Another important introduction in the FY83 budget was the proposal for a "New Federalism," which represented a shift in government functions away from the federal to state and local levels. While this proposal seems not to have gone very far, it appears that some federal government spending reductions, especially in social safety net programs, have been picked up by the states. The New Federalism had as its major feature further consolidation or reduction in grants to state and local governments (about $10 billion in FY83 compared to FY82). Beginning in FY84, the President proposed a swap and turn-back program, in which the federal government would assume responsibility for Medicaid and return AFDC to the states. The federal government was to give the states responsibility for $30 billion worth of current programs financed by federal grants.

Congress responded by passing the *Tax Equity and Fiscal Responsibility Act* (TEFRA), which was signed into law in September 1982. The bill was designed to raise an additional $99 billion cumulatively through 1985. It increased tax enforcement and eliminated some loopholes. It left undisturbed the individual income tax cuts passed in 1981, the indexing to be implemented in 1985, and many of the provisions of the corporate tax policy enacted in ERTA. However, it repealed the further acceleration of depreciation scheduled for 1985–86 under ERTA. Roughly speaking, TEFRA "took back" about 25 percent of the tax cuts in ERTA. The net impact by fiscal year 1988 was still to be a $215 billion tax reduction.[6]

In the *FY84 budget,* the dominant issues were the current and projected deficits and the traditional Reagan themes of increased defense spending, caps on social spending, and resistance to individual income tax increases. The budget for fiscal year 1984 proposed outlays of $849 billion—a $43 billion increase over FY83. This represented a 5 percent nominal increase and virtually no real increase. Proposed receipts were $660 billion, an increase of about 10 percent in nominal terms—5 percent real. The deficit was projected to be $189 billion, and it had become obvious that future deficits, even with substantial spending restraint and modest tax increases, would remain large for the remainder of the decade unless drastic action was taken.

The major features of the FY84 budget include acceptance of almost all the recommendations of the Social Security Commission, including several Social Security taxes. These were projected to raise $23 billion. All other indexed programs would be frozen for six months. The scheduled July 1983 tax cut and tax-bracket indexing in 1985 were to proceed as scheduled; and, as usual, a continuing reallocation of the budget away from social spending toward defense was proposed.

Another major feature of the FY84 budget was a contingency tax program for three years if FY86 deficits were not less than 2.5 percent of GNP. The potential contingency taxes included a tax surcharge of 5 percent on all individual and corporate tax liabilities and a $5 per barrel (12 cents per gallon) excise tax on gasoline. The contingency tax would raise revenue by approximately $49 billion in FY86–88 *provided* the deficit was not less than 2.5 percent of GNP, the President's spending program was enacted, and the country was not in a recession.

The *FY85 budget* reflected two major themes: protecting the military buildup and what was left of the 1981 tax cuts, as well as acceptance of 1984 as an election year. The proposed FY85 budget projected outlays of $926 billion and receipts of $745 billion, and thus a deficit of about $180 billion. Similarly, FY86 and FY87 deficits were projected to run about $180 billion, with a slight decrease in projected deficits through FY89. The Administration proposed surprisingly few budget reforms.

The major features of the FY85 budget included protection of the military spending buildup and tax cuts from previous years; a continued clamp on social spending; and no change at all in proposed Social Security programs. It continued to press for realignment of the federal budget toward defense and away from social spending. There were proposals to raise $33 billion in revenues over the next three years, but these mainly involve closing loopholes, for instance eliminating the growth of tax-exempt industrial development bonds. All of the actual tax proposals were minor. Congress passed the Deficit Reduction Act of 1984, which enacted some of these proposals and others, thus raising a minor amount relative to the deficit.

Between the FY83 and the FY85 budgets, several rounds of tax increases and additional spending changes occurred. The most important were the partial elimination of some provisions in ERTA by TEFRA in 1982; highway tax increases, with 85 percent of the funds earmarked for rebuilding infrastructure; and a large number of miscellaneous items. On the spending side, the President's policies were continued: increased defense expenditures and curtailed social expenditures other than Social Security, Medicare, and net interest on the debt. One might well sum up FY83–85 as a standoff, or a slight reversal from the Administration's 1981 proposals for FY82. Most additional spending cuts were too difficult to get through Congress, especially since Social Security and Medicare were off limits for political reasons. The President begrudgingly signed some tax increases, which partially offset his 1981 tax reductions.

Other Policies.   Monetary policy also changed because of economic events and other considerations. For example, the Federal Reserve formally abandoned its strict monetary growth targeting, and adopted "flexible" targets, reflecting its concern with the changing definition of money due to financial market deregulation. Certainly, the Federal Reserve launched a major monetary expansion, which was one of the reasons the economy came out of its recession so quickly. Indeed, for many months the money supply grew at an annual rate of 15 percent. This partly compensated for the unexpected decline in the velocity of money, and undoubtedly was partly a reaction to the Third World debt crisis. I discuss these issues in more detail in Chapter 6.

The Bush Commission on regulatory reform issued its report in 1983, but the consensus is that progress has been slow on general deregulation. There have been some successes and some setbacks. As noted earlier, the IBM case was dismissed and AT&T broken up to allow for greater competition in the long-distance market, pursuant to important technological advances which no longer rendered AT&T a "natural" monopoly.

As part of the desire of the President to make the government more cost-effective, a Commission on Private Sector Initiatives produced literally thousands of recommendations for reforming accounting, pay, and program decisions. Chaired by Peter Grace, what came to be known as the Grace Commission claimed over a trillion dollars in federal spending could be saved over several years. The Congressional Budget Office argued, however, that only 10 to 20 percent of the Grace Commission's claims would really lead to any savings; most of the rest, the CBO argued, actually involved cuts in programs or were exaggerated estimates because they did not allow for compensating items—for example, making military pensions less generous might lead to a need to increase military pay scales.

The Social Security amendments of 1983 were passed and embraced by both parties. Everyone breathed a collective sigh of relief that Social

Security would not be an issue, at least for a while. The Social Security amendments made several important changes by:

1. Accelerating previously scheduled tax increases;

2. Extending coverage to new federal workers and employees of non-profit institutions not then covered;

3. Making Social Security benefits taxable above $32,000 for a family and $25,000 for a single individual under the income tax, with the proceeds credited to the Social Security system (this is the first use of general revenue for Social Security, but it did move in the direction of tilting the benefits away from excess benefits to the very rich); and

4. Gradually raising the retirement age first to 66 in the year 2005 and then to 67 in the year 2022. Congress added this last provision, which the National Commission did not explicitly recommend. Congressmen Jake Pickle and Dan Rostenkowski, among others, deserve credit for insisting on this sensible provision and pushing it through despite opposition from the House leadership.

These proposals will solve Social Security's short-run cash flow problems through this decade. They are *not* full solutions to its long-term financial insolvency.[7] Furthermore, the proposals do nothing to redress the questions of equity and inefficiency.

Finally, it is important to note what the Administration expressly *rejected* throughout this period. The Administration consistently resisted the demand for large tax increases in the middle of the recession. It steadfastly, even if on occasion tartly, defended the Federal Reserve's policy of disinflation. It expressly refused to consider massive public works programs in the midst of the recession, and in principle, it rejected an industrial policy or national economic planning. The broad economic themes and the intent of policy initiatives in the Reagan Administration remained rather stable throughout the President's first term. The President campaigned on the themes of reduced government, reduced taxes, strengthened national defense, and a credible disinflation. His 1981 proposals made important steps in these directions. However, political and economic events slowed the pace of further progress towards these goals. The policy initiatives in fiscal years 1983–85 did *not* achieve further substantial inroads in spending cuts or tax reductions or deregulation. The retreats, when they occurred, were minor, and the Administration stood firm on major issues such as disinflation.

Perhaps the biggest policy accomplishment has been the change in what is considered appropriate economic policy. The Administration has firmly avoided fine-tuning the economy, and "quick-fix" programs, and has instead stressed increased reliance on the private sector, a federal system of government, and longer-term policy. However, as implemented by Congress, the policies have also led to large and ongoing budget deficits that have lowered national saving and caused serious problems.

♦ *Chapter 5* ♦

Reaganomics 1985–86

President Reagan's economic policy in 1985–86 reflected a variety of additional changes in the economic and political environment: sharply reduced inflation, the dilemma of long-term structural budget deficits, the President's resounding electoral victory in the 1984 presidential election, and a massive trade deficit (caused partly by an overvalued dollar), which threatened both output and employment, and imposed substantial hardship on specific industries and sectors that either exported or competed with imports in the economy. A key debate during the 1984 presidential campaign concerned whether it was necessary or desirable to raise taxes. Walter Mondale correctly argued that large budget deficits would have to be dealt with sooner or later, and probably better sooner than later. The economy was booming in 1984, well out of the severe recession of 1981–82—in fact, it was getting close to traditional measures of full employment. The investment rate had increased substantially, partly reflecting the success of the investment incentives in the earlier tax reforms and reductions.

The President continued to insist that domestic spending could be reduced while simultaneously continuing a defense buildup and avoiding tax increases. The President thus stood firm on the importance of reducing the size of the nondefense federal government in the scope of its activities and the level of its expenditures. By 1984, however, the noninterest, nondefense, nonSocial Security component of the budget had already been reduced substantially, and many people were dubious about further cuts. Still, the President's commitment to charge people for various services directly received from the federal government, to eliminate programs that were either ineffective or did not properly belong in the domain of the public sector, and to transfer various activities (including selling some assets to the private sector) remained resolute.

In 1984, the President requested the Treasury Department develop a set of proposals for fundamental reform of the tax system. This tax reform was to become the President's top domestic priority during his second term. Reflecting legitimate economic and political concerns and perhaps also to deflect criticism from the deficit, the Treasury was to issue its report shortly after the election. The Administration refused to talk about tax reform—other than the general need for lower rates and closing loopholes—until after the election. Thus the carrot of tax reform was held out, while deficit reduction, if desirable, still was only to be dealt with on the spending side of the budget.

In placing the 1985–86 policy initiative in perspective, it must be remembered that the robust recovery of 1983–84 was continuing, but its pace had slackened. The recovery, as of this writing, is well beyond that of typical postwar business-cycle upturns in duration, but it is sluggish and its continuation is in question. The second quarter of 1986 had a real GNP growth of 0.6 percent, after a fairly strong first quarter; overall growth in 1986 was a modest 2-plus percent. Opinions are divided as to the future course of the economy. Few expect it to be as robust as the Administration's official forecasts of more than 4 percent GNP growth for 1987, and some even consider a recession likely. There are various conflicting forces operating on the economy, and it is not unusual, even well into a recovery, for the subsequent course of events to become much less obvious than in its early stages.

In 1986, the United States ran a $150 billion trade deficit, despite a free fall in the dollar's exchange rate of almost 40 percent by January 1987 from its peak in early 1985. Usually, the trade balance changes a year or so after a shift in exchange rates. Enormous protectionist pressure was building. The collapse of oil prices harmed both domestic production and exploration (and thereby total national investment). It brought substantial real income gains to consumers of energy, since the United States is still a large net importer. Nominal interest rates crept down, and with inflation at low levels, real interest rates were still high but falling. Despite the sluggish pace of GNP growth in 1985–86, unemployment remained under 7 percent of the labor force. It became increasingly clear that the structural changes in the U.S. economy, particularly the United States' role in the world economy, combined with various policy actions, had created a situation where different parts of the country, different industries, and different segments of the population were faring differently. Obviously, at a time of major structural change, it is unlikely that everyone will fare equally well across-the-board, and those faring poorly do place increased pressure on the political process for assistance, especially for protection from foreign competition.

Thus, government policies for the period 1985–86 dealt with sustaining the recovery, cementing the President's budget priorities, encouraging fundamental tax reform, and speeding the growth of the economy, while at the same time keeping inflation at low levels, and keeping unemployment from rising and turning the corner in the battle against the ever-growing budget deficit. The period 1985–86 will be remembered for two remarkable fiscal reforms: the Gramm-Rudman-Hollings Balanced Budget Act; and the most fundamental tax reform in decades.

Spending and Tax Initiatives

The most widely discussed issue continued to be the large and potentially growing federal budget deficit, which the Congressional Budget Office predicted would continue to rise. Not only has the nature of budgetary outcomes changed radically between the first and second Reagan terms in office, but there is now a balanced-budget act placing added pressure on the Administration and Congress to reach an accord. By understanding what the President continues to propose and what Congress continues to oppose, one may appreciate the enormous clash over national priorities. The President wants a continued defense buildup, cuts in domestic spending, and no tax increase. Congress refuses to cut domestic spending substantially, has brought the defense buildup to a halt, and wants to raise revenue without being blamed for it. It is worth appreciating in some detail the many specific proposals made by the President and rejected by Congress, in order better to evaluate whether it was possible to cut nondefense spending. The fight has not been just over broad priorities, but over dozens of specific initiatives.

The Administration's FY86 budget proposed reducing the deficit by lowering spending by $364 billion (compared to the Congressional Budget Office's baseline budget projection) over the next five years. According to CBO projections, under the Administration plan defense spending would rise $43 billion, and therefore nondefense spending would have been cut by $406 billion, a remarkable goal. Adoption of the President's budget would stabilize the deficit at around $190 billion in the subsequent five-year period, and with real GNP growth, the deficit would finally fall as a fraction of GNP. The President's own budget estimates relied heavily on the assumption that interest rates would drop considerably, producing deficits substantially lower than CBO projections by 1990.

Assuming there are no changes in current laws, the CBO estimated the deficit would grow from $215 billion to $302 billion between 1985 and 1990, with the public debt growing from $1.5 trillion to $2.8 trillion. The President's budget proposed a $43 billion increase in defense spending, a $43 billion decrease in net interest costs (from lower interest rates and a slower buildup of debt), and a $363 billion decrease in nondefense, noninterest spending. The cut was to be composed of a cumulative $144 billion cut in entitlements, a $187 billion cut in discretionary nondefense spending, and a $32 billion increase in user fees and offsetting receipts. Under the President's plan, national defense would rise as a percentage of GNP from 6.3 percent in 1985 to 7.8 percent in 1991, whereas nondefense discretionary spending would fall from 4.6 percent to 2.9 percent over the same period. Social Security and Medicare would remain unchanged at 6.6 percent of GNP, whereas other entitlements and mandatory spending would fall from 4.7 percent to 3.1 percent of GNP.

The key difference between the CBO's deficit projections and the President's revolved around the Administration's prediction that interest rates would fall gradually to 5 percent by 1990, whereas the CBO anticipated much higher interest rates. The CBO also had somewhat less robust assumptions about real growth, but both the CBO and the Administration assumed growth in the 3–4 percent range each year. It is now clear that this was not achieved in 1985 nor in 1986, and this slowdown will add substantially to the deficit if it continues. The proposed increases in the defense budget were to be concentrated in research and development, which would grow at about 18 percent in real terms, and rise from less than 11 percent of the defense budget in late 1985 to almost 14 percent by 1990.

The Administration assumed it could reduce spending on Medicare and Medicaid by $44 billion, farm price supports by $32 billion, general revenue sharing by $24 billion, and federal employee retirement by $12 billion in the 1986–1990 period. No cuts were proposed in Social Security, unemployment, or veterans' benefits. Also proposed were a one-year freeze on Cost of Living Allowances in all federal employee retirement and disability programs. General revenue sharing was to be eliminated, and the farm price support decreased by 50 percent. Student loans were to be reduced and targeted more carefully to the needy, housing subsidies slashed, and urban mass-transit assistance cut in half. The strategic petroleum reserve would no longer be allowed to grow, and the funding for Export–Import Bank lending would be eliminated. For nondefense discretionary spending, more than half of the five-year outlay savings were to be in this category, although it comprised only 17 percent of federal spending. Federal credit programs were to be tightened, and subsidized lending cut back in agriculture, export financing, housing, electricity, and general business. There would be a slight increase in loan guarantees, but direct lending would be slashed substantially.

Congress, however, approved a budget resolution and appropriations bills which differed radically from the President's fiscal year 1986 budget proposals. Some minor savings were achieved in domestic spending, but Congress abruptly halted the defense buildup. Real defense spending actually fell. It is not widely recognized, but this halt is a key juncture in the development of President Reagan's budget priorities.

The Gramm-Rudman-Hollings Balanced Budget Act

While Congress refused most of the President's domestic initiatives, and the President stood firm on the issue of tax increases and the need for substantial real defense spending, a rider known as the Gramm-Rudman-Hollings Balanced Budget Act was attached to an otherwise routine debt-ceiling increase bill. The Act developed a procedure whereby the budget would be brought into balance by 1991, requiring automatic spending cuts if Congress could not produce sufficient deficit reductions itself. It is one of the most important pieces of legislation in recent memory, and it will be discussed in more detail in Chapter 7. While one part of the Act requiring the Comptroller General and the General Accounting Office to trigger the automatic cutback to meet the five-year, phased-in deficit-reduction targets was declared unconstitutional by the Supreme Court, backup provisions are contained in the legislation and are likely to be implemented by Congress.

Gramm-Rudman-Hollings is an example of deficit phobia forcing substantial pressure for spending reduction. Whether the process will work will be seen in the next few years. The first year, $11 billion was sequestered. The amount involved was so small that only a small disruption occurred. In subsequent budgets the amounts become increasingly larger, and it is unclear whether they can all come from the spending side.

Already there are calls for substantial tax increases to meet these targets. It is also clear that the President will oppose tax increases. Gramm-Rudman-Hollings requires Congress to come up with budgets that meet the targets: given these circumstances a fiscal stalemate is bound to occur.

In the FY87 budget, the Administration proposed spending programs and revenue packages that would produce a $143.6 billion deficit, just under the $144-billion limit set by law. Under Gramm-Rudman-Hollings, the deficit is projected to shrink to a $1 billion surplus by FY91. However, the Congressional Budget Office estimates the deficits at $159.7 billion in FY87, shrinking to $40.1 billion in FY91; obviously, the differences will have to be reconciled if Gramm-Rudman-Hollings targets are to be met. If the President's budget is adopted, the deficit reduction will be accomplished primarily by raising revenue slightly above current services projection and cutting nondefense spending dramatically. Defense would rise relative to the current services budget. The Administration estimates that its proposals will reduce deficits over five years by $374.5 billion, whereas the CBO estimates the savings at $221.4 billion. The Administration proposes 6 percent real growth in defense in FY87, and 3 percent annually through FY87–91. This increases defense spending by $120 billion over baseline projections in the five-year period.

The CBO baseline projections switch from the historical growth rate and/or a variant of the Administration's program to *no real defense growth*, since this was what was adopted in the previous year. This leads to a tremendous change in the outlook for the budget deficit. Under the baseline economic assumptions, no real growth in defense would by itself be sufficient for deficits to fall in absolute dollars as well as a share of GNP. The proposals project IRS staff initiatives to raise $19 billion; an extension of the cigarette tax, $9 billion; and an increased federal employee contribution to civil service pensions, $6 billion. Nondefense outlays include a $115-billion cut in entitlements, of which $45.6 billion is in Medicare and Medicaid. $22 billion would be saved by eliminating general revenue sharing, and again, there would be no reduction in Social Security, unemployment, or veterans' benefits. $124 billion was projected to be saved in discretionary spending, including $17 billion in transportation programs, $15 billion in the Farmers Home Administration, and $14 billion in housing assistance. $45 billion was projected to be raised in higher offsetting receipts, including $18 billion in higher premiums charged participants in Part B of Medicare.

Clearly, the reduction of the deficit and the public debt would result in a substantial savings in interest payments, estimated at $24 billion. The

Administration also proposed to cut federal direct lending over the five-year period by one-quarter, with restrictions on eligibility and smaller subsidies for guaranteed loans. The Administration forecast a growth rate of 3.8 percent, whereas CBO forecast 3.4 percent. Again, the Administration forecast much lower interest rates than the Congressional Budget Office—4 percent in 1991, versus 5.4 percent, for T-bills. Other than defense, only international affairs (increased protection of U.S. diplomatic missions), general government (IRS staffing), and general science, space, and technology (NASA) have higher than baseline-proposed spending levels.

The House and Senate negotiators agreed upon a framework for the FY87 budget that is again in sharp contrast to the President's proposals. The framework gives the President the military spending increases he desires *only* if he proposes revenue increases or proposes other cuts, and actually cuts President Reagan's request by $28 billion, leaving it at roughly this year's level. Thus, after four years of a rapid defense buildup, the buildup would halt for two years, a dramatic setback for the President. Congress rejected the President's plan to terminate programs in all but two of forty-four cases. It rejected the sale of government assets and refused to make deep cuts in domestic programs. The proposed increase in defense spending would not even cover inflation. Defense spending would be $100 billion less than the President proposed. Foreign aid would be 10 percent below the current level and far below the President's request. Congress would approve the termination of Conrail and revenue sharing. Very small cuts in Medicare have been approved, compared to the large cuts proposed by the President.

Clearly, we are at an impasse. Whatever the economic effects of deficits (see Chapters 6 and 9), a law now requires us to move toward a balanced budget. This law could be ignored or reversed, or the timetable delayed (witness the Humphrey-Hawkins Act) but if implemented, it means that either spending cuts or tax increases must be made. The President has refused to raise taxes, except in very minor amounts from minor revenue sources. Congress has called an abrupt halt to the defense buildup and threatens to make real cuts rather than the real increases called for by the President to achieve the cuts required by Gramm-Rudman-Hollings. Whether and how deficits will be reduced is still an open question. The ground rules of the budget process have been changed, but the conflicting goals of the Administration and Congress still remain. The Administration's subsequent budgets will probably continue to call for privatization, reduced domestic spending, and increased fees for government services, plus substantial real defense growth. Similarly, Congress will undoubtedly try to reduce defense spending and perhaps demand tax increases, while protecting domestic spending. Gramm-Rudman-Hollings may create the pressure necessary to break this stalemate.

As this volume goes to press, the President has submitted his FY88 budget. It calls for $1,024 billion in outlays and $917 billion in revenues, and meets the Gramm-Rudman-Hollings target with a $107.8 billion deficit. But most of the program cuts, asset sales, and user fees have been continuously rejected by Congress. Indeed, to meet the previous year's Gramm-Rudman target, Congress cut over $34 billion in spending, but only about one-third of this total were real program cuts. Various gimmicks were used to "meet" the target. For example, the pay day for the military was moved from the last day of the month to the first day of the following month, thereby shifting one pay period into FY88, "saving" $2 billion for FY87. Numerous other temporary measures, which cannot be continued indefinitely, were adopted. Thus, while some pundits pronounced the President's budget as dead on arrival, Congress increasingly must face up to real program cuts or an unpopular tax increase. Since virtually all of the cuts in the 1981–84 period came in the 30 percent of the budget other than defense, Social Security, and interest, finding major spending reductions in these areas will require eliminating many small programs with powerful and concentrated constituencies.

Tax Reform

The President announced his desire for fundamental tax reform in November 1984, calling for lower tax rates and a broader base. The Treasury presented three volumes of proposals and justifications, calling for the most sweeping individual and corporate income tax reforms in U.S. history. This became known as Treasury I. Corporate and personal tax rates were to be cut substantially, and the number of brackets was to be reduced to three: 15, 25, and 35 percent. Over the succeeding five years, well over $100 billion of tax burdens would have been shifted from the individual income tax to the corporate income tax. Note that this is not the same thing as saying that it would be shifted from individuals to corporations: only people pay taxes. The increased corporate tax was to be paid by some combination of shareholders, workers, and consumers; however, a howl went up against the features of the Treasury program that discouraged capital formation, or investment and saving.

The President's subsequent proposal to Congress of May 1985 reflected this concern for encouraging capital formation. Depreciation was accelerated, and there was less concern than in Treasury I with indexing various features of the tax code except for the tax brackets. Within the constraints enunciated by the President, as well as various practical matters, Treasury I attempted to define, measure, and tax real (inflation-adjusted) income as comprehensively as possible. But such a taxation of income involved a double taxation of saving and investment, first when it is earned as part of income and then when it earns a return. TEFRA and ERTA particularly were successful in stimulating investment, and the President was concerned that this would be totally reversed.

The proposals were taken before the House under the leadership of Congressman Rostenkowski, where, despite greater concern with budget deficits than with tax reform, the tax reform process continued. Facing almost certain defeat on the House floor—when House Republicans succeeded in getting sufficient support from some House Democrats to defeat the Ways and Means proposals—tax reform survived when the President interceded "to keep the process going." The House bill reduced many of the capital formation incentives in the President's proposals, had a higher top rate (38 percent versus 35 percent), raised corporate taxes more than the President's plan, and had higher bracket rates starting at lower incomes. The House proposal also slowed depreciation substantially for equipment, partly indexed depreciation allowances when inflation was above 5 percent, and contained a large number of special features (see Chapter 8).

The process then continued on to the Senate Committee on Finance, where after much negotiation and the imminent possibility of failure, a radically different tax package was developed. Instead of the four rates in the House bill or the three in the President's, the Senate came up with two tax rates, 15 percent and 27 percent (along with a surcharge, which was like a third tax rate over a certain range of income). All of these proposals sought to remove the poor from the tax rolls, thereby increasing the equity of the tax system at the lower end of income distribution. The Senate bill called for full taxation of nominal capital gains as ordinary income, speeded depreciation of equipment, slowed depreciation of structures, cut the corporate tax rate to 33 percent, sharply curtailed deductibility of individual retirement accounts (IRAs), which were made universal as part of the President's 1981 tax reform, and other saving incentives.

When the new tax law was finally hammered out in Conference Committee between House and Senate conferees, approved by the Congress, and signed by the President last fall, it proved to be the most fundamental reform in decades. It is discussed in substantial detail in Chapter 8. Its most important features are the reduction in the number of rates, and the broadening of part of the tax base for personal income tax, the shift of a substantial amount of the tax burden from the individual to the corporate tax, the elimination of the investment tax credit (common to all the reform proposals), slower depreciation, a reduced corporate rate of 34 percent, and a maximum personal rate of 28 percent. Capital gains are taxed in full as ordinary income. A stiff alternative minimum tax is included, especially for corporations, to insure that no corporation which reports current profits to its shareholders will avoid paying taxes, despite having a history of losses for its investment program. The tax preferences of IRAs and other retirement accounts have been curtailed, and industry-specific tax preferences or special features have been reduced or eliminated, especially for financial institutions, the real estate business, and defense contractors.

The reform is so complex that a major technical corrections bill will undoubtedly have to be passed, governing a substantial part of how the tax bill affects short-run economic behavior. This tax reform is monumental, and was the President's major domestic priority for his second term. Whether it will go down in history as a wise tax reform will depend heavily upon subsequent events, including how the deficit is dealt with. Many people believe that tax rates will eventually be increased to lessen the deficit. If so, the major advantages of this monumental tax reform will be lost. Lowering tax rates was a major step in the direction toward the President's original set of tax reforms in 1981, although the reduction of capital-formation incentives was a step backwards. One thing is certain: future tax reforms will follow.

Other Policy Initiatives

Several other policies deserve mention in this general overview of the 1985–86 period. The Administration, faced with hundreds of protectionist measures in Congress, generally defended free trade but occasionally compromised. The number of goods imported without tariff into the United States from developing countries was sharply reduced in 1984. One Administration tactic to defuse the momentum for general protection was to grant trade restrictions on some products, such as textiles, autos, specialty steel, and even mushrooms. In 1984 alone, over 200 petitions for protectionist relief were filed with the International Trade Commission. These individual exceptions seem minor, but when taken together add up to a substantial increase in protection. To defuse protectionist pressure, the President promised actions to open up foreign markets, while simultaneously threatening to veto protectionist legislation. He has been partially successful in this effort—for example, the steel and textile policies enacted were only mildly protectionist, and were left much to his discretion. In 1985 he promised to veto the first of 300 protectionist bills that provided import quotas for textiles. This is considered an important test case, since the textile industry mobilized a strong coalition of labor and management, a coalition that claimed foreign competition resulted in 200,000 lost jobs and 250 plant closings in the last four years and threatens the jobs of 2 million Americans, or almost 10 percent of the manufacturing work force.

In late 1985, Reagan applied substantial pressure on foreign countries to open their markets to the United States, citing trade restrictions on insurance in South Korea, computers in Brazil, tobacco in Japan, and subsidies on canned fruits in the EEC countries. A round of recriminations with the EEC, which began with import quotas on EEC pasta exports in response to alleged discrimination against U.S. citrus exports and was followed by the EEC taking action against U.S. walnuts and lemons, ended when a U.S. trade representative reached a negotiated settlement. There is growing concern that U.S. dedication to the General Agreement on Tariffs and Trade (GATT) and multilateral trading principles is being eroded not only by the rising tide of protectionism but also by the subordination of trade policy to the needs of foreign policy in various bilateral trade agreements, such as the Caribbean Basin Economic Recovery Act. The Administration claims that these are steps to pressure a new round of GATT negotiations. Eventually, Congress sustained the presidential veto of the textile bill and various other protectionist legislation in a ringing, if only temporary, victory for quasi-free trade. But by late 1986, in retaliation for restrictions on U.S. feed-grain exports to Spain, the United States threatened a 200 percent tariff on liquor and cheese products.

As the trade deficit soared to over $100 billion a year and the dollar was 30 percent overvalued, Treasury Secretary James Baker arranged for the five major central banks (the "Gang of Five") to coordinate a depreciation of the dollar. Since their dollar holdings are quite small relative to the total, their influence could nudge the dollar down only about 5 percent. The continued decline in the value of the dollar is more likely the

TABLE 5-1 Charting President Reagan's Economic Policy

Year	Budget	Tax	Monetary	Other
1981	FY82 cuts; plan for drastic reorganization of priorities; defense buildup; domestic cuts	ERTA; ACRS; 1st yr. of personal cut; top rate reduced from 70% to 50%	Supports FED disinflation via slower monetary growth	Deregulation
1982	Defense buildup; domestic cuts; huge deficits emerge	TEFRA: partly rolls back corporate depreciation in ERTA; 2nd yr. of personal cut; miscellaneous increases	FED adopts "flexible" targets	New antitrust doctrine
1983	New Federalism proposed; basic themes continue, with limited success on domestic spending cuts; contingency tax proposed; agriculture spending zooms	3rd yr. of personal tax cut	FED expands	Social Security Amendments; Bush Commission deregulation report; Grace Commission
1984	Basic themes continue; limited success on domestic spending cuts	Deficit Reduction Act; miscellaneous revenue enhancers; Treasury I		Trade deficit and protectionist pressure worsen; free trade defended rhetorically, but partially compromised
1985	Congress abruptly halts defense buildup; minor domestic cuts; Gramm-Rudman-Hollings	President's Tax Reform Proposals; Ways and Means Bill (HR3838)	FED increasingly focuses on exchange rates; Gang of 5	Baker LDC plan; Press for new round of GATT
1986	Defense growth proposed, but rejected; minor domestic cuts; asset sales proposed, but rejected; basic thrust of President's proposals reversed; budget gimmicks to meet Gramm-Rudman-Hollings targets	Senate Finance Bill Tax Reform Act of 1986	Rapid monetary expansion; international coordination proposed	Massive protectionist legislation defeated as Congress sustains Presidential veto; Retaliatory tariffs for EEC grain restrictions threatened.

result of declining interest rates in the United States, corresponding expansionary policies by the Federal Reserve, and a sluggish overall macro environment, rather than interventions, by the "Gang of Five." Secretary Baker also proposed new lending policies, heavily focused on private-sector participation, to help ailing less-developed countries (LDCs) still in the midst of a tremendous debt crisis and growth slowdown. Baker emphasized the need for expanded loans to these countries and a growth-oriented policy environment.

Monetary policy sharply exceeded the target range announced by the Federal Reserve (see Chapter 6). The money supply grew at rates which cannot be sustained indefinitely without rekindling inflation. Still, inflation subsided as commodity prices continued to be weak and fiscal policy turned increasingly restrictive, since defense-spending cuts and reduction of the deficit are likely to occur. The Federal Reserve paid increasing attention to exchange rates, and has now come full circle: from its 1970s policy of targeting interest rates, to its famous conversion to monetary growth targets in 1979, through its adoption of flexible targets in early 1980s, to a more flexible approach today, focusing on exchange rates and international monetary coordination. The Fed is attempting to coordinate policy with the German Bundesbank and the Bank of Japan, among other central banks, to get the world economy moving.

A Perspective on the Program

The Reagan economic program, or Reaganomics, has been subject to praise and ridicule, in whole and in part. The program thus far encompasses major budget initiatives, several historic tax reforms, and much more. Its scope is detailed in Table 1, which presents a chronology for each major policy area from 1981–86. What was so novel about the program as originally conceived, marketed, and amended? I speak here of the goals and instruments of the program, not of its ultimate economic effects, to which I will return in the chapters that follow. To appreciate the difference of Reaganomics, a good place to start is an examination of the major components of the program: reduced growth of government spending, reduced tax rates, reduced government regulation, and slow, predictable money-supply growth. Was this really a tremendously novel plan, compared to previous policy proposals, especially those of conservatives?

Reduced government spending and tax rates were basic themes of the Republican party for decades, as was reduced government regulation. As noted above, President Carter — and even Senator Edward Kennedy — were on the reduced regulation bandwagon prior to President Reagan's election. Slow and predictable monetary growth had been elevated from academic treatises to Federal Reserve policy by 1979. Indeed, former CEA Chairman Herbert Stein concluded that the Reagan revolt was not really a revolt, and in fact, the major novelty resided in the extravagant claims that were made for its policies. Though the claims made were extravagant, placed in its historical context this four-pronged policy had a revolutionary meaning. By 1981, reduced government regulation was likely to bear much greater economic benefits at the margin than in 1971 or 1961. The domestic budget had burgeoned to the point where reduced growth in government spending meant a fundamental reversal of national priorities. Redistributive outlays permeated the budget, beginning with the New Deal, continuing through the Kennedy–Johnson era, and growing ever-larger with President Nixon's enormous across-the-board boost in Social Security benefits (and their subsequent indexing for inflation).

Reducing the growth of government spending in the Eisenhower Administration, when six out of every seven dollars spent by the federal government was on purchases of goods and services, had a vastly different meaning than reducing the growth of government spending in 1981, when a large percent of the federal budget was spent on income transfers. Reagan and Eisenhower may have stood for the same thing, and perhaps even for some of the same reasons, but their policies had radically different implications, given what had happened in the period between their administrations. Reduced tax rates also were encouraged by previous presidents, and the supply side of the economy had even become the focus of a historically bipartisan Joint Economic Committee under Senator Lloyd Bentsen (D-TX) in 1979 and 1980, when for the first time ever, it issued unanimous reports urging that our most important goal be that of increasing productive capacity, rather than managing aggregate demand and redistributing income.

The discussion in Chapter 2 stressed the enormous increase in the marginal tax rates on the general population. It is true that the top marginal tax rate on labor income had been decreased to 50 percent, although it remained at 70 percent on investment income. But the proportion of the population subject to high marginal tax rates, say 40 percent, had quadrupled between 1965 and 1980. Hence, reducing marginal tax rates — leaving people more income, after taxes, for working that extra hour or making that extra investment — was a doctrine that would now benefit the general population, not just the wealthy. Thus, intervening

economic and demographic events, from real income growth, to inflationary bracket creep, to the growth of two-earner families, made the Reagan plea for reduced tax rates more generally applicable than that of any
prior administration.

Finally, support for the Fed's disinflation policy, which was to be
accomplished gradually via steady and predictable declines in the rate of
monetary growth, was somewhat novel. As discussed in the introduction,
most previous presidents had responded to inflation in erratic, erroneous, and even bizarre ways. Richard Nixon, a conservative Republican
president, assumed office saying that he would never freeze a wage or a
price, nor impose wage and price controls. By the time President Reagan
took office, inflation had gone back to double-digit levels. It appeared
to be going out of control, and this could not be blamed exclusively on
oil prices (as the mostly erroneous claims for the 1973–74 inflationary
episode did). The inflation President Reagan inherited had gone on for
a much longer period than the inflation of his predecessors, and that meant
that inflationary expectations were that much more entrenched, and possibly that much more difficult to eradicate as a necessary prerequisite to
reducing inflation.

The real novelty in the Reagan program was not only its *scope* and
size, but also its sense of urgency: the belief that our economic and political vitality and future were at stake. Spending growth was not just to be
slowed, it was to be reduced substantially in many categories and
redirected from domestic spending, especially transfer payments, to
defense. The defense buildup was to be large, reflecting the needs of a
decade or more of neglect. Tax rates were to be reduced *substantially,* and
government regulations reduced *radically.*

The over-marketing of what could be accomplished, how quickly,
at what cost, were not necessarily a unique feature of the Reagan program—after all, previous administrations have felt compelled to make
extreme promises for their policies in order to win elections, encourage
optimism, or divert blame for bad outcomes. While in many of its basic
themes the Reagan program was more or less standard Republican economic doctrine, its size and scope was much larger than the size and scope
of the policies of any previous new administration since FDR.

Another important difference between standard Republican doctrine
and Reaganomics was the populist emphasis of the latter compared to
the former. This is most clearly visible in the tax policy. The 1981 tax
act included very large cuts in personal tax rates, as well as enhanced business investment incentives. When changes were made in 1982, they curtailed a substantial fraction of the business tax cuts, but *not* the personal

tax cuts. More importantly, the 1986 Tax Reform Act goes still further in this direction. While containing many desirable features (and some not-so-desirable ones), this allegedly revenue-neutral bill is in reality a large additional personal tax cut financed by a large corporate tax increase.

This is not simply a case of the Democrats beating the Republicans in Congressional bargaining. Democrats generally focused their efforts on tax relief for lower- and middle-income persons, but not on reduction of *marginal* tax rates. Rather, they often enacted special legislation designed to help one group or another deemed worthy of a tax break. The populist, supply side of Reaganomics focused on reducing marginal tax rates (even while removing some deductions) in order to reduce the personal tax burden. Indeed, as I will show in Chapter 8, the likely effect is a further shift toward consumption at the expense of saving and invest-ment, an unusual twist in tax policy for a Republican administration (and a major reason why the primary Congressional opposition came from Republicans). It has traditionally been the Democrats who pushed tax policies to stimulate personal consumption, even if at the expense of busi-ness investment.

The marketing of the program led to promises — rapid growth, no recession, a balanced budget by the end of 1984 — that were even more overblown than those of previous administrations. Thus the expectations of the public and the press were raised to a level that no serious econo-mist believed could possibly be fulfilled. Whether this was sensible poli-tics, necessary to get the original program passed in hopes that more could be done later, or pie-in-the-sky dreaming, remains to be seen. All of it should be viewed in the intellectual and historical context delineated in previous chapters. While I am sympathetic to the goals and policies pro-posed, the inconsistencies and overly optimistic projections and prom-ises have already come back to haunt the Administration. The lesson to be learned is that unnecessary elevation of expectations from reasonable economic policies can ultimately discredit those policies and drive us toward worse policies. We shall see in the discussion of the exportability of the Reagan program in Chapter 12 and the unfinished agenda in Chap-ter 13 that separating extravagant claims from realistic hopes is impor-tant in order to evaluate which components of Reaganomics should be kept or expanded and which should be abandoned. But that is getting ahead of the story. I will now evaluate the policies as they affected and were affected by economic outcomes, such as inflation, recession, trade, and growth. Many of the initiatives highlighted in Table 1 will be discussed in greater detail.

◆ *Chapter 6* ◆

Inflation and Recession:
Macro Policy in the Reagan Era

Ronald Reagan's first six years in office were marked by several remarkable developments in macroeconomic performance. A pronounced disinflation occurred in 1981–82, accompanied by a sharp recession. A rapid recovery began in 1983–84 and continued, although somewhat sluggishly, into 1987. Inflation remains relatively low. Major changes occurred in Federal Reserve policy and fiscal policy. What was accomplished, and at what cost? Are we likely to be better able to deal with inflation and recession in the future?

It is commonly believed that the recession of 1981–82 was the worst in the United States since the Great Depression of the 1930s. Was it necessary in order to reduce inflation from double-digit to relatively manageable levels? In 1980, a number of prominent economists argued that the cost in lost output and increased unemployment would be simply too great to offset the benefits gained from reducing inflation. Others, such as Barry Bosworth and the late Arthur Okun, argued that most of the costs of disinflation could be avoided by adopting a formal "incomes policy," which they believed would eliminate inflation gradually without the cost of a recession. James Tobin argued that inflation was not very harmful to the economy, and others argued that it might even be helpful in reducing unemployment.

It was often asserted that the recession was primarily due to President Reagan's budget and tax policies, and his support for Federal Reserve policy. Actually, the Fed's disinflation policy was begun well over a year before President Reagan assumed office, under the leadership of Chairman Paul Volker. International economic developments were gathering momentum to induce a world-wide recession, and President Reagan's "loose" fiscal policy did not become loose until 1983. While the Administration issued an unduly optimistic forecast and downplayed the possibility of a recession, its policies were not the primary cause of the recession, though they probably extended it somewhat. Even if the President had wanted a much more expansionary monetary policy, it is unclear that it would have prevented the recession by the time it could have been enacted.

Those who argued that we should learn to live with inflation — because reducing it would cost too much in increased unemployment and lost output — relied on the estimates of Keynesian economists such as George Perry. The late Arthur Okun, former CEA chairman established a rule of thumb that 3 percent of a year's real GNP (spread over several years) would have to be given up for each percentage point rise in unemployment. The Phillips curve estimates suggested each percentage point decline in inflation was associated with as much as a three percentage point rise in unemployment. Hence, each percentage point fall in inflation might result in as much as a 9 percent fall in real GNP! In fact, as painful as the recession was, it was not nearly as bad as these estimates, which predicted enormously increased unemployment and lost output. Even so, was the campaign to reduce inflation worth it? What did it cost in lost output and jobs? Was there a less-costly way to disinflate? Should we have caved in and learned to live with inflation? And if so, would this have prevented future recessions? Can we implement monetary and fiscal policies that are conducive to stable, noninflationary growth?

Dealing with Inflation

During the 1980 election, many economists argued that the public was overly concerned with double-digit inflation, and that the costs of reducing it by conventional deflationary means would exceed the benefits. Therefore, they argued, it would be better either to employ an incomes policy — a watered-down version of controls — to limit inflation, or simply to live with it by indexing various institutions and contracts. With an incomes policy, the government would use taxes and subsidies to coerce business and labor to keep wage and price increases down. Proponents claimed these policies would have no significant negative side effects, and held the promise of reducing inflation without a corresponding temporary rise in unemployment. Such policies have been tried more extensively in Europe, where unemployment and inflation have often been worse than in the United States. Proponents of these policies argued that without them, the strong momentum associated with inflation could only be broken over *many* years, with very high unemployment rates. This implied an economic downturn which, if as severe as predicted, was clearly an unthinkable cost.

While attention focused primarily on the extravagant claims of the extreme supply-siders in the Administration during the recession, the real news was being made at the Federal Reserve. Its announced conversion to monetarism in late 1979 brought about a tight but erratic money growth. Combined with an even tighter money growth rate in other major economies, the Fed's policy produced a deep recession. The inflation rate plummeted much more rapidly than had been anticipated. While the recession was bad, it was nothing approaching the predictions of Perry, et. al., whose estimates of lost output and unemployment to reduce inflation to the 3 percent level were much larger than actually occurred. While these Phillips Curve estimates had substantial ranges of error, Philip Cagan notes that the actual cost was only one-half of the estimate based on "Okun's law."[1] Equally important, many recent estimates of this output loss assume an optimistic full employment output growth. The late William Fellner made some telling criticisms of these simple extrapolations.[2] Without going into them all, the *actual* trend of output from the early 1970s on slowed substantially, as lower productivity growth and reduced capital formation took their toll (these are discussed more fully in Chapter 11). Using this lower actual trend lowers the output cost to much less than one-half of the Okun's law estimates, about 12 percent of a year's GNP for the 6 percentage points decrease in inflation by Cagan's estimates, compared to 24 percent to 60 percent by the pessimistic estimates.

Comparing these predictions with the actual outcome is important to correct the record, since we are likely to be faced with similar choices in the future. While the Reagan Administration and the Federal Reserve appear to agree on the goal of modest monetary expansion and growth, there is always pressure on the Fed to lower interest rates. If inflation starts to rise, renewed attempts to impose wage and price controls or incomes policies are possible. Bad ideas rarely die; they simply wait to be revived. Therefore, to evaluate seriously the claims of those who advocate incomes policies to deal with inflation, one must take a careful look at the actual performance of the economy during the recession: what caused the recession, what could have been avoided, and what was a necessary price to pay for the disinflation.

Presidents, like quarterbacks, get too much credit when things go well and too much blame when things go poorly. It was never a "Reagan"

FIGURE 6-1   Growth of Real GNP, 1980–1986 (1982 Constant Dollar)

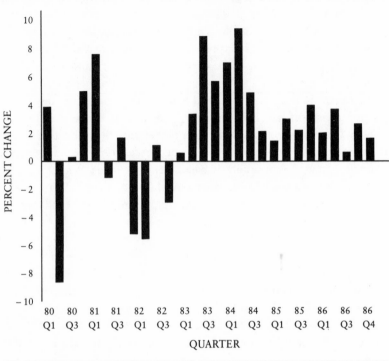

Source: Economic Report of the President, 1983–1987

recession: the rest of the world went through one too, and its seeds were sown well before the President took office. Nor was it exclusively a "Reagan" recovery, although the third year of the tax cut and the defense buildup, which were implemented for other reasons, probably helped somewhat. We must look back on the process of disinflation, recession, and recovery to be able to evaluate various approaches to dealing with inflation and recession and separate the wheat from chaff in alternative policy proposals.

Inflation, Recession, and Recovery through 1986

As the recovery from what is often called the worst recession in 40 years continues, unemployment has fallen to 6.8 percent, employment has risen

FIGURE 6-2   **Inflation Rate**

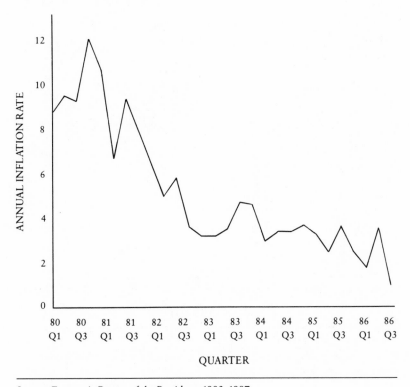

Source: Economic Report of the President, 1983–1987

to an all-time high, and inflation holds steady at 3 percent. Figures 1 through 5 highlight the course of real GNP, inflation, employment, and unemployment for the past several years.

Most economists, myself included, predict a modest increase in inflation in 1987, due partially to the depreciation of the dollar and partially to an end to the fall in oil prices. I also see some improvement in the trade balance, modest growth, and perhaps a slight decline in unemployment. With so much tension in foreign trade, the dollar is likely to remain volatile and we may even see some modest protectionist legislation, designed in part to forestall major protectionist legislation that could launch a serious trade war and worldwide recession.

By 1980, inflation was running at double-digit levels, and it was clear that the economy needed to disinflate to provide a *long-run* restoration

FIGURE 6-3   **Employment**

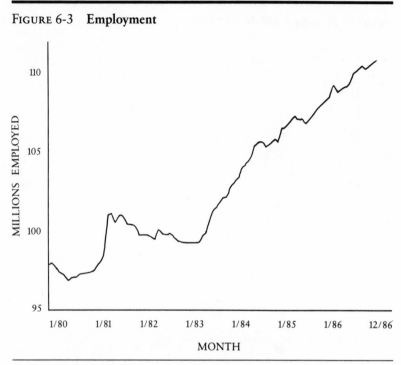

MONTH

Source: Economic Report of the President, 1983–1987

of stability and growth. The likely short-term cost of doing so was downplayed, but the real question is whether there was an alternative. As Figure 2 reveals, during the Reagan Administration's first term, inflation as
measured by the GNP deflator fell by about 6 percentage points, from
about 9 percent to about 3 percent. Other measures of inflation, such as
the Consumer Price Index, fell even more, about 9 percentage points, from
12 to 3 percent. Ronald Reagan was the first president to appreciate inflation's *long-term* economic cost. As the economy of the 1970s proved, high
and fluctuating inflation, especially when combined with an unindexed
tax system, produces uncertainty which discourages investment.[3] President Reagan backed the Federal Reserve's disinflation policy, and resisted
its abandonment, which most predicted would occur at the first sign of
higher unemployment.

How often did one hear that the higher and the longer-lasting the
inflation, the more costly it would be to reverse? That is because infla-

FIGURE 6-4   **Employment Rate**

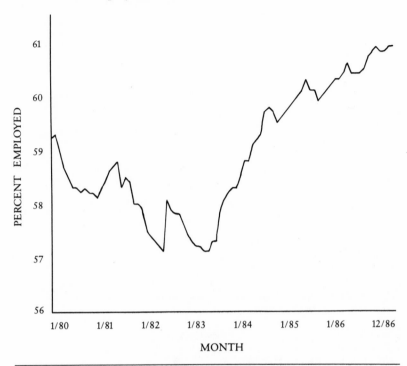

Source: Economic Report of the President, 1983–1987

tionary expectations become more widespread and more deeply embedded in our economy. But ever since inflation began to heat up in the latter-1960s, presidents have preferred inflation to the short-term costs of curtailing it. Presidents usually get the monetary policy they want, at least to some degree, and so with President Reagan. While the Fed's policy was certainly much more erratic than the President would have liked, the President gave the Fed's disinflation policy credibility for the first time. Even this was a limited credibility, since the Fed had changed gears and reaccelerated money growth — and subsequently, inflation — so often in the past.

Comparing President Reagan's stand on inflation with those of his predecessors, it is astonishing to realize that President Nixon imposed wage and price controls in 1971 when inflation was at about 4 percent.

FIGURE 6-5   **Unemployment Rate**

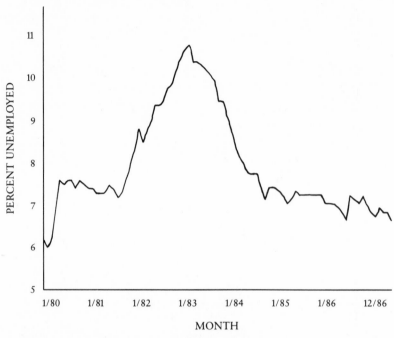

MONTH

Source: Economic Report of the President, 1983–1987

Currently, inflation is considered to be more or less under control. The Nixon controls suppressed inflation temporarily, but also worsened it profoundly. Princeton economist Alan Blinder estimates that the controls added one to 1.5 percentage points to the subsequent rate of inflation.[4] Inflation rose to double-digits in 1973–74, prompted by the Arab oil embargo and the subsequent increase in energy prices, and finally declined to 4.8 percent in 1976, following the severe recession in 1974–75. President Ford's primary anti-inflation actions were to ignore monetary policy, veto as much additional spending as possible, and call summit meetings among business, labor, and government groups, issuing "Whip Inflation Now" (WIN) buttons.

When President Carter assumed office, attention turned away from inflation. Unfortunately, it began to accelerate. President Carter's initial policy was an expansionary budget program. Through a series of spending increases, public service jobs, and other measures, Carter attempted to reduce unemployment more rapidly than the private sector would have done. These policies may have had a minor impact on unemployment, but it was unlikely to be long-lasting. By 1978, President Carter shifted gears, and issued a five-point anti-inflation plan. Unfortunately, it had little to do with inflation.[5] Several of the points were constructive (such as continued deregulation of business), but his only reference to the Federal Reserve was that he hoped the Fed could keep interest rates down. Later, President Carter moved to incomes policies, jawboning, and proposals for tax-bludgeoning businesses to influence pricing policies. Toward the end of the Carter Administration, the Fed abruptly changed course and began a serious policy of tightening the growth of money in an attempt at gradual disinflation. We shall return to the Fed's policy in a moment.

Is inflation licked? The answer to this question is definitely no. Certainly inflation has stayed at low and stable levels for longer in this recovery than others. But while great progress has been made, the progress has been overstated for several reasons. To begin with, the Consumer Price Index, for technical reasons, overstated inflation somewhat in 1979–80, and it is probably slightly understating inflation now.[6] Second, the long overvalued dollar (discussed in detail below) meant that import prices were substantially lower than normal. As the dollar returned to purchasing power parity—as real interest rates declined in the last year or two—our price level will experience a *one-time* increase of about 2 percent, with a lag of a year or two (relative to what the price level would have been, not necessarily relative to what it is now). When this happens, probably in 1987–88, it is important not to confuse this *one-time* price increase, related to adjustment in the value of the dollar, with a general reacceleration of inflation, caused by excessive monetary growth. A misunderstanding of this distinction could lead the Fed to step on the monetary brake and throw us unnecessarily into a recession. And it is possible that the Federal Reserve itself could rekindle inflation through excessive monetary growth (more on this below). And, of course, events in other parts of the world could trigger price increases in the United States unless we have the will to deal with them.

It is important to keep in mind how inflation, especially a gradually creeping inflation, can undermine long-term growth and doom us to a severe recession to correct it.[7] The most striking thing about recent discussions on inflation is how inured we are to inflation rates of 4 percent or so, and how rapidly interest in wage and price controls, or incomes policies of various types, have become disreputable. The President gets high marks for helping to change public attitudes — for making the dis-inflation his top priority, and sticking to his guns despite enormous pres-sure to abandon this goal in the face of recession.

How Bad Was the Recession and What Caused It?

The recession of 1981–82 is often called the worst since the Great Depres-sion. The official statistics certainly recorded a substantial amount of lost real output, increased unemployment, and an increase in the number of bankruptcies. While the recession caused substantial suffering, its seeds were sown well before President Reagan's economic policies were pro-posed, let alone enacted. The recession was not as severe as the official statistics record, and as I have shown, it was not nearly as severe as had been predicted considering the drop in inflation. I do not mean to mini-mize the suffering and disruption caused by the recession, but it is impor-tant to understand what really happened, rather than rely on misleading statistics and analyses.

The recession cost the economy billions of dollars of lost output, and at its worst, the unemployment rate rose to 10.7 percent — an increase of about 4 million unemployed workers. Total unemployment reached about 11 million workers (see Figures 1 and 5). To understand the full meaning of this in human terms, it is important to realize that in a mod-ern economy, a great deal of unemployment is due to the normal course of events in the labor market, and not to severe economic disruptions. For example, much unemployment is due to the entry and re-entry of per-sons into the labor market as they take some time to find jobs. A lot of unemployment occurs as people quit their jobs to look for better ones, and no one would regard this type of unemployment as undesirable. It is a natural part of the process by which people improve their job opportunities — by which workers and jobs are most effectively and efficiently matched. The undesirable type of unemployment occurs when workers lose their jobs because of a sharp reduction in aggregate demand or shift in demand away from their activities. It is especially unfortunate if the loss is permanent.

Even from this perspective, while the increase in unemployment in the 1981–82 recession was severe, it rapidly abated in 1983–84, and con-tinued to improve in 1985–86, as Figure 5 indicates. Moreover, the most striking thing about the performance of the American economy is that a substantial number of jobs — ten million in all — were added over the last

FIGURE 6-6   **Growth of Employment, 1980–1985**

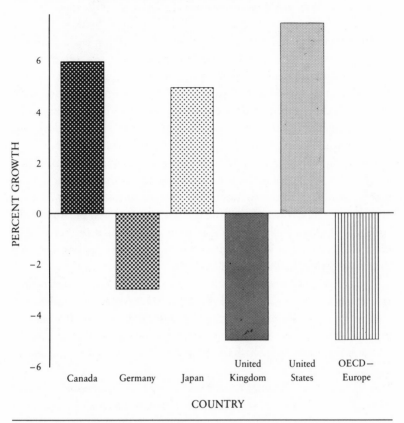

Source: Economic Report of the President

several years (see Figure 3). While 10 million jobs were added from 1979–86, 12 million were added in the service sector and 2 million lost in industry. This decline in industrial employment occurred worldwide in advanced economies, but probably was worsened in the U.S. by the overvalued dollar, discussed below. This contrasts with the performance of most of the other advanced economies, particularly those of Western Europe, which have had substantial problems generating new employment and where severe unemployment has become a *chronic* problem. Figure 6 presents some comparisons of recent gains or losses in employment in other countries. The position of the United States is enviable in relation to the European members of the Organization for Economic Cooperation and Development, especially France, Germany, and the United Kingdom. Indeed, some British economists put the rate of unemployment necessary to avoid accelerating inflation at 11 percent. The mismatch between skills and jobs, as well as the labor market inflexibility, are more severe in Europe than the United States.

The ability of the U.S. economy to generate new employment is particularly impressive in light of the nearly 20 million workers added to the labor force during the decade of the 1970s, due to the enormous increase in the number of women working in the labor market as well as the home, and new young workers entering the labor market following the maturing of the baby-boom generation. Absorbing such a large influx of new workers was a startling achievement, and the subsequent growth of employment is particularly impressive on top of this base. As Figure 4 reveals, the employment rate—the fraction of employed persons to the total population of relevant age—is at an all-time high of over 60 percent. Of course, the increase of employment in the recovery has not matched, job for job, the loss of jobs during the recession. Structural shifts, continued sluggish demand in some industries and regions of the country, and other factors prevented the impressive increase in employment from helping everyone who lost a job during the recession. While many have gone back to work, many are working in new jobs. The adjustment of the labor force to such sharp changes is impressive but not instantaneous.

In early 1987, unemployment is running at 6.8 percent of the labor force. Two decades ago, such unemployment would have been considered unacceptable. Today, most economists consider it fairly close to full employment, for reasons largely related to the demographic factors mentioned above. These include the change in the age structure of the population and the increase in families with two potential earners. In the latter case, when unemployment hits one of them, hardship is mitigated not only by unemployment insurance, but by a second income as well. This allows the family more time to search for a second job. For these reasons, the high unemployment rate is not really comparable to historical rates of unemployment. The 4 percent unemployment rate considered full employment in the 1950s and 1960s corresponds to a rate of around 6 to 6.5 percent today.

Viewed from perspectives *other* than unemployment, the 1981–82 recession was not particularly severe in relation to other postwar recessions. For example, the percentage decline in real output during the recession of 1981–82 (see Figure 1) was much less than that during the 1973–75 recession, and about the same as during the two recessions of the 1950s. Another important but potentially misleading statistic is that of bankruptcies, which hit a post-depression high in the 1981–82 recession. However, in the same period there was a record number of new startups. This paradox can be explained by a variety of factors, including major changes in the bankruptcy laws that made it much easier and more attractive to file for bankruptcy. Certainly, many businesses suffered extreme hardship, and there were many legitimate failures. But, again, the statistics are not comparable to those in prior periods, because their meanings have changed.

Besides lost output, which may not have been unavoidable (see below), the most important question about unemployment and bankruptcies is whether they lead to *permanent* disruptions and scars. Will the people who were temporarily unemployed suffer much more in the remainder of their work career? Will the firms be able to recuperate and reorganize? Will the capital be efficiently and effectively reallocated? While evidence on these questions is hard to get, it is clear that some industries were hurt sufficiently to suffer residual damage.[8] Still, it is also clear that the long-term damage of the recession is much less than the statistics might historically suggest.

Many factors caused the recession, but the most important was the Federal Reserve's reduction of money growth, combined with an unanticipated, severe drop in the velocity of circulation of money, and the effects of even tighter monetary policies in the rest of the world. Especially in Japan and Germany, monetary policy was even tighter than in the United States. The recession was *not* caused by the federal government's budget deficits (the "Reagan" deficit), as is often alleged.[9] Those who argue that a clash between tight money and loose fiscal policy drove up interest rates and caused the recession are simply mistaken. Federal fiscal policy did not become loose until late 1982. The Reagan tax cut in 1981–82 merely offset bracket-creep and previously scheduled payroll tax increases, and the defense buildup was in its very early stages. Hence, fiscal policy turned "expansionary" in the third quarter of 1982, under the usual Keynesian short-term analysis of these effects, as the cyclically adjusted budget deficit rose sharply. The expansionary effect of tax cuts (and spending increases) was felt in the second half of both 1982 and 1983. They probably assisted the recovery, but had little to do with the recession in 1981–82.

A more subtle anti-deficit argument is that were it not for the prospect of these very large deficits, the Federal Reserve could have followed a somewhat more gradual policy. While one cannot be sure what policy the Fed would have followed, it is also unclear whether that policy would have reduced inflation nearly as much as what was actually achieved. The Fed was clearly taken by surprise by the large drop in money velocity, which made its monetary targets much more restrictive than it had thought. It also was not paying attention to what was going on abroad — for example, the much tighter money policies in Japan and Germany. Taking these problems together, it seems clear that the Fed's policy turned out to be much more restrictive than it had intended.

In addition to the Fed's and other countries' monetary policies, the sharp overvaluation of the dollar by 1980 was another important precursor of the recession. Overvaluation of the dollar meant a decline in exports and an increase in imports, as foreign goods became cheaper. A very interesting but often overlooked fact about the recession is that about half of the decline in real GNP came from the decline of net exports. Net exports, as well as residential construction and business investment, are very sensitive to changes in interest rates because interest rate differentials tend to cause changes in relative values of currencies and hence relative prices of exports and imports, an effect discussed further in Chapter 9. The sectors most hurt by the overvaluation of the dollar and the subsequent recession were those industries exporting and/or competing with imports, such as automobiles and agriculture. But the decline these interest-sensitive industries experienced was more than offset during the recovery by expanding consumption, and the generally unforeseen expansion in investment resulting from the delayed impact of the 1981 business tax cuts.

By 1982, people were wondering why the investment tax credit (ITC), accelerated cost recovery system (ACRS), and other "supply-side" tax cuts had not worked — that is, had not prevented the recession.[10] The answer is that the recession was in place well before these policies were enacted, and foreordained by the factors mentioned above. In fact, once consumption picked up and unused productive capacity started to decline, businesses began to invest in new plants and equipment. Thus, the impact of the ITC and ACRS changes was substantial. Although investment increased more than the average percentage increase from post-war recessions, it was rebounding from a post-World War II low, and there is substantial concern whether investment will remain at levels consistent with historical experience and future needs; indeed, as Figure 7 reveals, investment spending has fallen sharply in 1986 — due in part to tax reform uncertainty and the retroactive repeal of the ITC. This delayed effect of the ITC and ACRS poses another dilemma: they are available only on investment in the United States, which surely helps increase *domestic* investment.

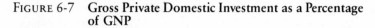

FIGURE 6-7   Gross Private Domestic Investment as a Percentage
              of GNP

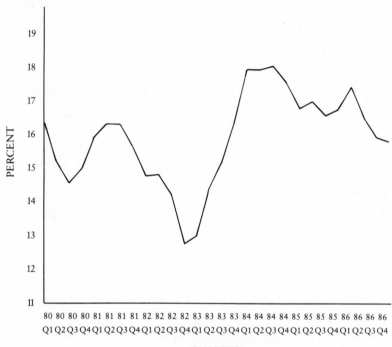

Source: Economic Report of the President, 1983–1987

Since they were removed in the 1986 tax reform, more U.S. investment
would be directed abroad, and net capital imports—which are composed
of foreign assets flowing into the United States less U.S. assets flowing
abroad—would decline. Thus, the deficits might exert more upward pressure on interest rates.

In any event, for both supply-side and demand-side reasons, the Reagan fiscal policy, which was enacted for reasons having nothing to do with
fine-tuning fiscal policy, fortuitously assisted the recovery. The tax cuts
were enacted without anticipating a recession, and the defense buildup
was instituted for other reasons. There was a large increase in the cycle-
adjusted deficit in mid-1982 and mid-1983—about $80 billion in the
former and almost $40 billion in the latter.

The recession, which was worldwide, thus had its roots well before President Reagan took office, and was a necessary consequence of the disinflation process. Any incomes policies to mitigate the recession side-effects of the disinflation almost certainly would not have worked, and would have imposed other kinds of substantial costs.

How severe were the costs of the recession compared to those predicted? The decline in output often quoted in analyzing the early 1980s disinflation is about $220 billion per point of inflation.[11] Reducing inflation 6 or 7 points would reduce output by between $1.3 and $2.0 trillion, implying an enormous rise in unemployment. This is about twice what actually occurred. The economy is now not very far from an unemployment rate of 6.5 percent. Estimates of the loss in output, compared to output in an economy with a steady employment of 6.5 percent, are about $800 billion.[12] Thus, even if the unemployment rate could have been kept at 6.5 percent with a different mix of monetary and fiscal policy — a proposition I believe is mistaken — or if we could have successfully disinflated with incomes policies, the loss in real output is about half that predicted by conventional "Okun's law" and Phillips Curve analyses.

Many economists and politicians blame President Reagan's policies for this loss in real output and the corresponding loss in jobs. But another way of looking at it is to say that President Reagan and the Fed *saved* the economy hundreds of billions of dollars of lost output and several points of increased unemployment by making the disinflation more credible *compared to* standard predictions. I personally agree with former CEA Chairman Herb Stein when he says that ". . . there is not much evidence to support the standard Democratic argument that a different mix of fiscal and monetary policies would have yielded the gains on the inflation front with less recession."[13]

Why did Keynesian economists overestimate the cost of disinflation in their "inflation-unemployment tradeoff"? There are undoubtedly many reasons, but I believe the single most important is that Fed policy, backed by the Administration, was considered much more credible than in the past. One strand of the rational expectations school of thought discussed in Chapter 3 implies that the output cost of disinflation would be reduced substantially with such a credibility effect. This appears to have occurred, at least partly.[14] People believed both that the Fed was serious and that President Reagan, unlike his predecessors, would not succumb to the political temptation of a monetary expansion to avoid the temporary cost of a recession. Reducing inflation is one of President Reagan's most important accomplishments, although he must share the credit with the Federal Reserve. Opinions about exactly why the President placed such a high priority on disinflation and stood firm in his commitment vary widely, but without this commitment, the costs of disinflation would have been much higher, and political pressures almost certainly would have aborted it — as so often in the past.

This discussion suggests that neither a "Reagan recession" nor a "Reagan recovery" occurred. The President's support of the Fed helped make the disinflation less costly than had been anticipated, and his fiscal policy, begun in 1981 — although planned for other reasons — helped in the 1983–84 recovery. In broadest terms, the inclination of many people to evaluate Reaganomics in terms of recession and recovery conflicts fundamentally with the Administration's explicit rejection of fine-tuning. The Administration believed that monetary and fiscal policies should follow a more stable course, and that government intervention to heat up the economy during a recession is often ultimately counter-productive, bringing at best temporary benefits outweighed by long-term costs.

The Recovery

The recovery from the trough of the business cycle has been impressive. By 1984, the increase in total output was 10.9 percent, larger than the first six quarters in any postwar recovery (past recoveries ranged from 8 percent to 10.1 percent). While the rate of real GNP growth has been more modest in 1985–86, as Figure 1 reveals, by the end of 1986, there had been four years of economic expansion. Even more impressive is the fact that despite this impressive recovery, inflation has stayed at around 3 percent, for a full six years after its peak in 1980.[15] To place this in perspective, it is good to recall that when the inflation rate dropped from 12.2 percent in 1974 to 4.8 percent in 1976, it quickly rose back to 9.0 percent by 1978. Other important features of the recovery include a boom in gross domestic private investment during 1983–84. Investment was higher in the second quarter of 1984, for example, than at the corresponding point in any postwar recovery. I attribute much of this to the 1981 tax incentives. However, these incentives were due to be exhausted by now, and the new tax law actually eliminates many of them. The retroactive repeal of the ITC to January 1, 1986 is undoubtedly part of the explanation for the recent investment slowdown. Productivity growth has rebounded, although it is still unclear whether this is only a typical cyclical phenomena. In addition, the U.S. trade balance continues to hinder

FIGURE 6-8   **Trade and Current Account Deficit as Percent of GNP in 1982 Constant Dollars**

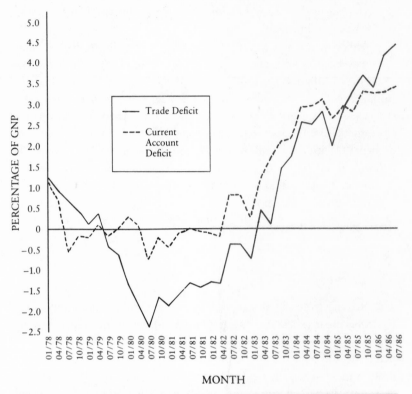

MONTH

Source: Economic Report of the President, 1983–1987

economic performance, which causes some to call for protectionist trade restrictions (see Figure 8 for the recent performance of our trade and current account deficits).

Separating the recovery into supply-side, Keynesian, or monetarist influences is not an easy task: everyone wants credit for it. Certainly, the investment tax credit and ACRS have given a big boost to investment in the United States.[16] There certainly was a substantial fiscal stimulus in traditional Keynesian terms in mid-1982 and mid-1983 (see Figure 9). However, more importantly, during this recovery there has been a larger increase in the real money supply (adjusted for inflation) than in any previous post-World War II recovery. My view is that both forces were at work,

FIGURE 6-9   Full Employment Deficit as a Percent of Trend GNP

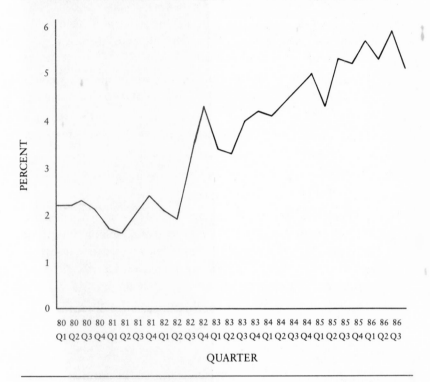

Source: Survey of Current Business, various issues

but that monetary expansion probably had the larger short-term impact. An the rational expectations/credibility view appears to have been partially correct in predicting less lost output in the disinflation.

Will the recovery continue? Unfortunately, as mentioned above, economies are subject to periodic shocks that result in recessions. Sometimes these are exacerbated by policy mistakes. We have no guarantee that the recovery will continue beyond 1987, but it is extremely misleading to suggest, as some have, that the deficit is the primary factor threatening the recovery. No doubt there are reasons to be concerned about the deficits, but they mostly reflect long-term growth issues rather than short-term stabilization ones, assuming the Fed will offset any contractionary pressure from decreased government spending which may be enacted under Gramm-Rudman-Hollings. These will be discussed in substantial detail

in Chapters 8 and 9. In fact, to see how tormented the reasoning seems
to get on this issue, consider a typical position concerning deficits:

1. The recession was made more severe by President Reagan's poli-
    cies, as large deficits forced the Federal Reserve into very restric-
    tive monetary policies; therefore,

2. A different policy mix (i.e., a more expansionary monetary policy
    and a smaller deficit) would have reduced inflation with much less
    unemployment; still,

3. We had a Keynesian-style recovery—that is, a recovery fueled by
    large budget deficits; but,

4. The recovery will be aborted because of the effects of the large deficit
    on interest rates.

More than one economist and politician voiced this sequence of statements.[17] Unfortunately, if you follow the chain of reasoning, it suggests
that deficits first caused the 1981–82 recession, then caused the subsequent
recovery, and are now about to cause another recession. Deficits may cause
various problems—occasionally they may even do some accidental
good—but this contradictory chain of reasoning is somehow unper-
suasive.

The Future

Has the boom and bust cycle that typically afflicts economies been halted?
Can any economic policy insure us against economic fluctuations? Have
we eliminated the frequent tendency of fiscal policy and monetary policy to aggravate economic fluctuations, even while attempting to combat
them? The answer to all these questions is no. We have made a start,
though in many ways it is intangible, because there are at present no
institutionalized budget procedures or monetary policy rules codifying
the terms of increased stability.[18]

The single greatest achievement of the Reagan economic program
probably has been to turn the debate about economic policy away from
short-term management to broader, longer-term issues bearing on the
proper role of government in the economy—issues such as the relationship between the public and private sectors, and how to promote long-
term growth and stability. It is astounding to any serious economic
historian that in the depths of what was called the worst recession since

the Great Depression, Congressional demands for action were limited to spending a few billion dollars on highway construction and other related "job creation" programs.[19] Only a few years earlier, such calls for public service jobs would have demanded ten times that amount. The Reagan Administration gradually dismantled public service jobs in the very midst of a recession. The muted response in Congress reflects a broad change in thinking about the appropriate role of government in macroeconomic policy. Economists now understand that the government cannot fine-tune the economy. Some, especially the rational expectation theorists discussed in Chapter 3, argue that government economic policy in general is neutral with respect to the economy's performance, and that the notion that government really makes much difference is a delusion. While I think that is only partly true, government intervention to deal with economic fluctuations should be limited to extreme, long-lived problems, which may respond to major intervention with only minimal long-range effects. Such circumstances are few.

The Possibility of a Crisis

While the probabilities are small, it is worth noting several possible scenarios for a major economic crisis. So far, we have discussed recession and recovery, double-digit inflation, and disinflation. By historical or international standards, these are not extreme economic events. Could we slide into a crisis as bad as the Great Depression or reaccelerate inflation, if not to Latin American levels, to levels as high or higher as their postwar peak? I believe the answer to these questions is yes, but the most likely outcome is that we will muddle through with only modest economic problems. While the potential sources of crisis are many, and events not currently anticipated could precipitate one, there are several problems already causing concern. For example, the recent trend toward protectionism could degenerate into trade wars of tariffs and quotas that could plunge the world economy into a recession. The LDC debt problem could worsen if real interest rates rise so far as to make the burden of interest payments a more severe strain on the debtor nations. Several defaults by major debtor nations could threaten the stability of the banking system. The FDIC has modest assets as well as standby borrowing authority at the Treasury. If the Fed did not react to a liquidity crisis, a run on the banking system could escalate the dimensions of the disruption. In a $4.5 trillion economy, the default on even a large amount of debt need not cause

a major recession, but it could if the Fed and Treasury made major policy blunders. Similarly, many savings and loans are technically insolvent,
and the FSLIC is warehousing bad loans. Again, without merely raiding
the Treasury, the regulators can avert a run on the thrifts. Finally, the
United States has shifted rapidly from a position of the world's largest
net creditor to the world's largest net debtor. This carries with it the temptation to inflate in order to pay back our debts to foreigners — our external debt — in dollars of lesser value.

Each of these situations — trade tensions, the LDC debt problem, the
financial stability of the thrifts, and the temptation to inflate to "pay off"
external debt — could be the problem that precipitates a crisis, whether
of deep recession or high inflation. But each would also require major
policy blunders to escalate into a full-blown crisis. While we should not
underestimate the capacity for such policy blunders (recall the Smoot-
Hawley tariff), these crises can be averted. In fact, they probably will be,
and the press and the polity may not even realize how close we came.
Again, my best guess is that a modest, hopefully temporary, rise in inflation will occur in 1987 and that while there are several non-traditional
potential sources of shocks to drive the economy into recession, we will
most likely avoid one in the near term.

The Future of Monetary and Fiscal Policy

Whether Reaganomics will leave a legacy in regard to inflation and
recession — macroeconomic policy — depends on how we continue to
believe that the government should not be activist in monetary and fiscal
policies while the economy is moving within tolerable boundaries.

Monetary policy has been erratic during the Reagan Administration,
but it did accomplish the disinflation. Some observers advocate a fixed
nominal GNP growth rule for the Fed, rather than the classical monetarist
commitment to a fixed money growth rule. My colleague Robert Hall
argues this point persuasively, and the 1983 *Economic Report of the President* considers the idea. The Fed moved to the monetarist position in late
1979, but has abandoned it on numerous occasions — whether because
conditions warranted it, or because it saw fit to do so, depends upon one's
point of view. Indeed, money growth was often far outside the Fed's target range (see Figure 10). We have no guarantee that a Federal Reserve
policy based on either a fixed money growth rule or a nominal GNP
growth rule will lead to a smooth course of *real* GNP and relatively sta-

FIGURE 6-10   **Target Ranges and Actual Growth of M1, 1980–1986**

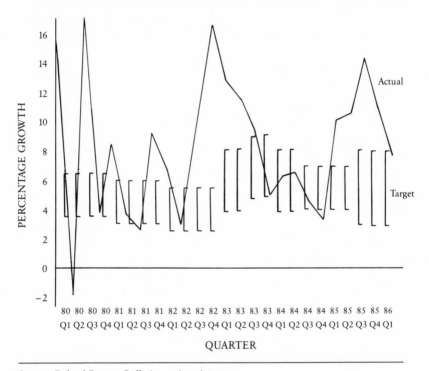

Source: Federal Reserve Bulletin, various issues

ble prices. The assumption is that following either rule will reduce the extra uncertainty that widely fluctuating monetary policy and fiscal policy can have on the economy, thus encouraging long-term investment and perhaps reducing the likelihood and severity of economic fluctuations. But applying a rule mechanically could cause deep trouble under extreme circumstances. For example, with an unexpected, dramatic drop in velocity, a money-growth rule might lead to a severe downturn. Because velocity has fluctuated so dramatically in the last several years (see Figure 11) relative to its previous impressive stability (as indicated in the discussion of the monetarist position in Chapter 3), a nominal GNP target is probably preferable to a money-growth rule.

The Fed, both under the pressure of recent events and with the advent of new Reagan appointees, now appears to have moved not only away

FIGURE 6-11   **Percentage Change of M1 Velocity 1980–1986**

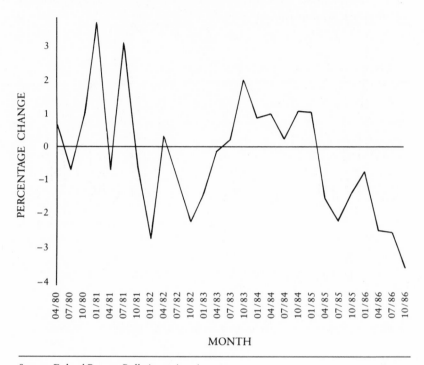

MONTH

Source: Federal Reserve Bulletin, various issues

from the strict money growth rules of the 1979 period, but also away from the flexible multi-faceted targets for money and credit of the 1982–84 period. It now seems to be operating *de facto* on an economic activity (GNP) target. So long as inflation remains modest, this should augur well for the next few years. But will inflation remain low? There are several concerns — rapid monetary expansion, dollar depreciation, the specter of enormous public and private debt — that leave much uncertainty in forecasts of further inflation.

It is possible for the Federal Reserve to adopt procedures that would increase its efficiency in meeting its targets, and move toward a more stable targeting.[20] This should be a high priority for macroeconomic policy, yet it is unclear whether the Reagan Administration considers it so. From time to time, there has been a discussion of making the Federal

Reserve part of the Treasury, as is the case in many other countries. This would allow the Fed to follow more closely the government's desired monetary policy, and at the same time perform its regulatory duties consistent with other Administration goals. While there are advantages in having a policy of rules rather than discretion, placing monetary policy under much greater political control could be dangerous, as we have in innumerable instances witnessed in other countries. In fact, there are some countries in which inflation averages as much per week as it does per year in the United States. My belief is that we should first try increased pressure and institutional reforms in Federal Reserve operating procedures to encourage the Fed to live by nondiscretionary rules—whether fixed money growth, nominal GNP growth, or some related variant.

Fiscal policy also needs more stability. Creation of the Congressional Budget Office and budget committees was one attempt to bring this about, but the goals of the 1974 Budget Reform Act have not been fulfilled.[21] The new budget process has not tied spending and taxing decisions more closely together, as it was meant to do. Again, institutional reform should be a high priority. Though some progress has been made, not only with the Gramm-Rudman-Hollings Balanced Budget Act but with numerous other attempts to change the structure of decision-making, spending and deficit control are still very uncertain. The early rounds of spending cuts under Gramm-Rudman (other than defense cuts) have been mainly accounting gimmicks. Whether serious programmatic cuts will be made, taxes increased, or a balanced budget goal abandoned or postponed remains to be seen. We will discuss this more fully in the chapters on budget policy and the agenda for the future.

What is clear is that the large structural budget deficits contributed to the trade and current account deficits. The severe imbalance between our national saving—the private sector's saving less the government's borrowing—and our domestic investment has caused us to import vast amounts of foreign capital to finance the difference. The sharp appreciation of the dollar (see Figure 12) was caused in part by these deficits (other factors included the safe-haven nature of U.S. investment, the investment incentives in the tax law, and high real interest rates caused previously by tight monetary policy). This in turn severely worsened our trade balance (recall Figure 8), slowed the growth or real GNP, and reduced inflation. The recovery was thus quite unbalanced with the traded goods sector suffering relative to the rest of the economy. The cry for protection from foreign competition led to an attempt to devalue the dollar against other currencies via coordination of monetary policy, jawboning, and interven-

FIGURE 6-12   Multilateral Trade-Weighted Value of the U.S. Dollar
               (Quarterly, March 1983 = 100)

Source: Economic Report of the President, 1983–1987

tion in foreign exchange markets. Apparently, the inability to get our budget deficit under control has created a cruel dilemma for the free-market Administration — outright, and costly, protection passed by Congress, or exchange-rate intervention to try to force the dollar lower and faster than it would have fallen in the natural course of events. These effects of budget deficits will be discussed more fully in Chapter 9.

The Reagan Administration helped pull off something that few thought possible: a substantial and rapid disinflation with much lower costs in terms of lost output and jobs than had been anticipated. The Reagan Presidency has also helped transform the debate about the appropriate role of government in aggregate macroeconomic policy away from continual fine-tuning of short-term demand toward setting broad objectives in a framework that might increase the stability of monetary and fiscal policy, and thus of the general economy. Taken together, these represent a large and impressive first step, even acknowledging their costs. These signs of progress do not guarantee better outcomes in the future, but they do improve the prospects, and our goals are probably considerably more realistic than they were even a few years ago.

President Reagan will go down in history as having been the only president willing to take the heat to disinflate the economy. When the time again comes to face inflationary pressures — and it certainly will — one can hope that this experience, and the tremendous change in views concerning the appropriate policies to deal with inflation, will have a substantial impact on how we respond. The President will also go down in history as having allowed a huge increase in the national debt, generated the most fundamental tax reforms in decades, and partially achieved a major reorientation of budget priorities. To these issues I now turn.

♦ *Chapter 7* ♦

Budget Policy

Although President Reagan was determined to reduce sharply the role of the federal government in the economy, federal spending as a share of gross national product has gone up substantially during his Administration. He did achieve a major restructuring of budget priorities during his first term, away from domestic spending—especially grants-in-aid to state and local governments and means-tested entitlement programs—toward defense. Since then, the defense buildup has been halted, and additional domestic spending cuts have been hard to come by.

This is not for lack of effort. The President has repeatedly proposed a wide range of sensible initiatives to reduce government spending, and therefore cut the large deficits. He has argued consistently that high-priority programs should be adequately funded, unnecessary programs eliminated, and other programs reduced to a more appropriate scale. He believes that programs which could be better done by the private sector should be shifted, and services better provided by state and local governments should be transferred. He also believes that federal programs should be better managed, and user fees should be charged for government services where individuals receive a clear, direct benefit. Such a set of priorities could and should concern *any* president whether conservative or liberal, Republican or Democrat, when attempting to balance the budget, let alone when attempting to reduce large deficits.

Congress, however, has a tremendous difference of opinion on how to implement these goals. What should government produce, finance, or sell? What responsibilities should be shifted to state and local governments, rather than kept at the federal level? Who should be charged user fees for what? Which programs should shrink and which be eliminated? Unfortunately, these questions not only face conflicting interpretations as to their answers, but also face the vagaries of the political process, the concentration of interest for a particular program, and the regional interests in certain subsidies or programs. Everyone wants someone else's benefits reduced or services eliminated, and wants his or her own continued, preferably financed by someone else. This dilemma confronts all administrations, and all democracies.

Chapters 4 and 5 show how the Reagan Administration developed its budget and tax priorities over its first six years in office, what succeeded, and what failed. This chapter provides the background to the Reagan budget policy, restates its goals, and discusses the major problems encountered in attempting to achieve them. It discusses whether budgetary choices should be constrained via constitutional means to balance the budget and/or limit spending, and discusses the viability of the Grace Commission's more than two thousand proposals to streamline the government, reduce costs, and manage the federal government more effectively. The potential redistributive effects of these budget cuts are discussed in more detail in Chapter 10.

Background to Reagan Budget Policy

The large and growing role of government in the United States must be understood against a backdrop of changing economic events, and particularly in light of American institutions and customs. While total government spending as a fraction of GNP is somewhat less in the United States than in the advanced welfare states of Western Europe, it has grown very rapidly (see Figure 1 and Table 1), and recently its composition had shifted markedly from government purchases of goods and services to transfer payments to individuals. Debates over the budget are continually played out against a backdrop of dispute over which level of government (federal, state, or local) is most appropriate to do the spending or raise the revenue. Further, the federal government has a budget which is neither comprehensive nor comprehensible: a very large amount of government spending occurs off-budget and in a variety of indirect forms. No doubt this is true of most other economies, but budgetary reforms in the U.S. Congress in the mid-1970s created a situation where this "other" budget has grown much more rapidly than direct government spending.

FIGURE 7-1   Total Government Outlays as a Percent of GNP

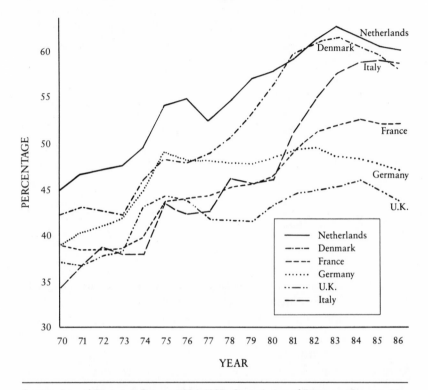

Source: Annual Economic Report, 1986–1987, Commission of European Communities

A half-century ago only one dollar in ten passed through government coffers, and three-quarters of that was at the state and local levels; today, that amount exceeds 40 percent, with about two-thirds at the federal level.[1] Excluding interest on the debt, more than one-half of federal outlays is for transfer payments today. As recently as a quarter-century ago, only one dollar in seven of the much-smaller absolute and relative size of the federal budget was spent on transfer payments. The remarkable growth of these transfer payments in the United States in the 1960s and 1970s is both a great accomplishment and a source of concern: an accomplishment because it helped substantially reduce the incidence of poverty in the United States, but a concern because it also created a situation where the marginal tax rate on the earnings of the typical American family grew

TABLE 7-1   Continued Growth of Federal Budget Outlays, 1966–84

Fiscal Year	Outlays as a % of GNP
ave. 1966–70	20.2
ave. 1971–75	20.4
ave. 1976–80	21.7
1981	22.7
1982	23.7
1983	24.3
1984	23.1
1985	24.0
1986	23.7

Source: Budget of the United States, FY87.

dramatically. These programs have been neither cost-conscious nor target-effective, and often transferred billions of dollars to individuals who by no means could be considered poor, or even below the median income of the taxpaying population.[2] A myriad of overlapping programs—unfortunate gaps between them for some needy people—were developed to transfer income in cash and in kind. These include what is generally referred to as welfare, Aid to Families with Dependent Children, and such items as food stamps, housing allowances, and medical care for the indigent.

It is such entitlement programs which have received the most attention in recent attempts to slow budget growth. However, when all of these programs are taken together, they account for only a small fraction of the budget. The truth is that the attempt to get domestic non-defense spending under control ran aground because of the inability to deal with Social Security, now the second-largest and most rapidly growing item on both sides of the federal government budget. It annually transfers over $200 billion of resources from the current generation of workers to the current generation of retirees, disabled persons, and a few other groups.

Social Security is not income-tested: benefit payments are made irrespective of need. A retired millionaire may receive substantial Social Security benefit payments above and beyond what he or she, matched by employer, paid in, plus any reasonable real rate of interest; yet these are

FIGURE 7-2   **Federal Budget Outlays by Major Category**

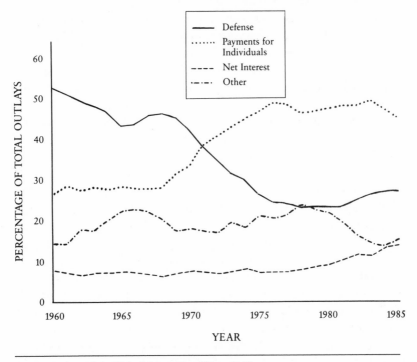

YEAR

Source: Budget of the United States, Fiscal Year, 1987.

considered entitlements because some "earmarked" taxes were paid. The illusion persists that Social Security benefits are being paid out of some sort of trust fund which accumulates large enough reserves on a person-by-person basis to be paying the benefits. Actually, if such a calculation were made, benefits would be exhausted in the third or fourth year of retirement. Social Security and its Hospital Insurance component comprise almost a quarter of the federal budget.

Another important trend to note was the substantial decline in the relative share of the budget and the GNP devoted to defense spending, which fell, from 1960 to 1980, from about 50 percent and 9.1 percent respectively to under 25 percent and 5.3 percent (see Figure 2). Whatever one may think of the necessity for particular arms programs, or the dangers of various tensions and conflicts in the world, it is clear that the

United States systematically reduced its military capability in a variety
of ways, and that by 1980 there was a genuine consensus in the United
States that some sort of improvement in our defense system was desirable. Debates, of course, rage over the extent of any military buildup, and
exactly how throwing dollars at the problem could solve it.[3] However,
it is important to note that the bulk of military expenditures are personnel costs, not new weapons systems, and when a new weapon system is
approved, it takes three to four years before substantial expenditures occur.
Therefore, very little reduction can be made in a *current* budget deficit
by canceling one or another procurement program. That reduction in the
projected deficit could only be made several years later.

The state of the economy as a whole also had a strong influence on
the nature of government spending and its method of financing such
spending. During this period the United States, as well as several other
major countries, suffered the worst economic performance since the Great
Depression. I am referring not only to the 1981–82 recession, but to a
series of recessions and sluggish economic growth, discussed in Chapter
2, which marked the U.S. economy from the late 1960s when the growth
of productivity began to slow. In brief, the U.S. economy suffered
extremely slow rates of growth during the 1970s, after the rapid growth
of the 25 years after World War II. While other economies — for example, that of Japan — slowed from rapid to modest growth averaged over
the decade, the U.S. economy saw virtually no gain whatsoever in the level
of real GNP per worker. Although total GNP figures showed growth in
real per capita income, virtually all this growth represented large additions to the labor force, primarily women and those of the post-World
War II baby boom generation. These additions have added about 30 million workers to the labor force since 1970. After making adjustments for
inflation and the rise in tax rates, it is clear that in 1980 the typical taxpaying American family was not much better off, if at all, than it was in
1970.

This background of events explains a series of major changes that
occurred at roughly the same time: the *role* of government changing from
provider of goods and services to redistributor of income; the federaliza-
tion of this role; the sluggish economic performance; the high and wildly
fluctuating inflation by U.S. standards; the substantial increase in typical marginal tax rates facing the middle class; and the slowdown in standard of living gains relative to the previous twenty-five years. To
summarize, Americans were getting more government for a higher price,
and doing more and more things at a more remote government level, while

their own private incomes were hardly growing at all. These changes, I
believe, explain better than anything else the enormous discontent with
government spending that surfaced in a variety of tax revolts against various levels of government. Somehow, the political process had encouraged
public services for which the private sector was not prepared to pay. It
would be no easy thing to restore or stabilize this pattern, since a variety
of virtually automatic spending increases have been built into the legislation in the 1960s and early 1970s, at a time when the economy was
expected to grow much more rapidly than it actually has. Only against
such a background can current budgetary policy be understood as more
than just ideological confrontation over the appropriate role of government in the economy.

President Reagan's Budget Policy

At the beginning of its first term, the Reagan Administration committed
itself to the following goals for spending and tax policy:

1. Reduce the relative role of government in the overall economy;
2. Change the composition of federal spending away from transfer
   payments toward purchases of goods and services, especially military spending;
3. Transfer some responsibilities for various services, together with
   the resources necessary to finance them, to state and local
   governments;
4. Gradually phase in reductions in tax rates;
5. Index the tax system;
6. Balance the budget by 1984.

   It was an ambitious program, but one broadly supported by virtually all parties. The debate predominantly concerned matters of degree:
the extent of the military buildup, the size and speed of the tax cuts and
their relative effect on corporate and personal taxes, the menu of responsibilities to be returned to state and local governments under the new federalism, and the size of reductions in the growth of non-military spending.

   The Administration policies were only partially implemented, and
the severe recession from the middle of 1981 to the end of 1982 caused
substantial problems in meeting some of the above goals, raising questions about their compatibility. Before I discuss this, it is worth pointing

FIGURE 7-3   Comparison of Spending Composition as Proposed by
              Presidents Carter and Reagan in FY82 for FY85

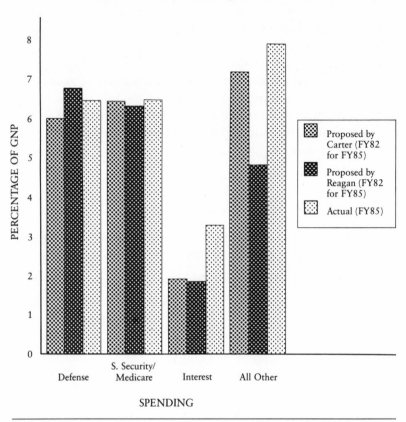

Source: Budget of the United States, various years

out that Congress failed to enact the Administration's budget proposals
fully and cut taxes much more than the Administration recommended.

The Administration asked for, and received, major reductions in projected spending relative to the proposed Carter Administration budget,
and a major tax cut and reform called The Economic Recovery and Tax
Act of 1981 (ERTA). But Congress added about $175 billion of additional
tax cuts to those originally proposed by the Administration. The Congressional additions not requested by the Administration amounted to
about a quarter of the total tax cuts enacted. The size of the tax cut was
further increased, as we shall see in a moment, by a very sharp reduction

in inflation in the United States. This reduction made the real tax cuts much larger than originally anticipated, since the personal tax cuts had been originally intended only to offset bracket-creep due to inflation and previously legislated payroll tax increases.

On the spending side, President Carter was already committed to a gradual military buildup in real terms. President Reagan only proposed a more rapid and extensive buildup. Figure 3 compares the composition of Carter's FY82 budget proposal and Reagan's FY82 proposal for FY85. Further, it was clear that many government transfer payment programs were transferring income to those who were by no means needy. Eligibility standards had become lax in a number of entitlement programs, thus creating subsidies for middle-class families as well as the poor.

The Administration attempted in 1981 to reduce Social Security, by far the largest transfer payment program, by issuing proposals similar to recommendations made by Democrats on the House Ways and Means Committee. The only major difference was that the Administration's plan would have reduced benefits for early retirement (i.e., at age 62) to only 55 percent of full benefits, available three years later. Nevertheless, this proposal touched off such a tremendously negative reaction that the Administration was forced to create a bipartisan commission to deal with it.

With Social Security exempted from cuts, and military spending increasing, spending cuts had to come almost entirely from two remaining sources: means-tested transfer programs (which are aimed specifically at the poor) and aid to state and local governments. State and local governments were already hard-pressed by various tax and spending restrictions that voters placed on them in the 1970s. Military spending was growing rapidly; Social Security and Medicare (most of which is covered under Social Security) continued to grow. Interest on the debt also increased substantially as both the deficit mounted and real interest rates grew to unprecedented levels. Figure 4 shows the figures as *then* projected by President Carter in his FY82 budget and President Reagan in his FY85 budget, as well as the actual FY85 outcome. Thus, comparing Figures 3 and 4, we see how Reagan's proposals changed during his first term.

Many readers will be surprised to learn that real government spending has grown faster under Reagan than under Carter. This is especially significant since spending under Carter was already a substantially greater share of GNP than in most other peacetime governments in the United States. Partly because of the recession, federal government spending as a percent of GNP increased from its traditional 18 to 20 percent average

FIGURE 7-4   Comparison of Spending Composition as Proposed by
President Carter in FY82 and President Reagan in FY85

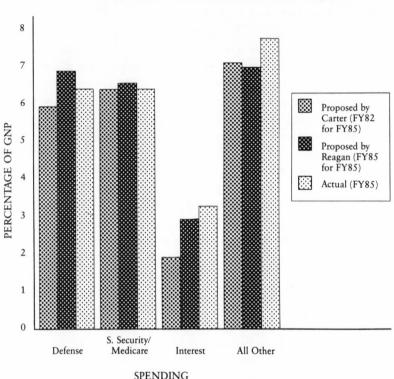

Source: Budget of the United States, various years

to between 24 and 25 percent—up several percentage points from the
Carter years and up about one-fifth in the last two decades. Although the
federal share has fallen by a percentage point or so with various cost-
cutting provisions and a more robust economy, federal spending will
remain in this neighborhood unless major program cuts are enacted.

President Reagan's goal to return some program responsibilities to
state and local governments was achieved. The federal revenue needed
to fund them did not follow, despite claims that it would. On the other
hand, many of these grant-in-aid programs were inefficient, encouraging
state and local governments to spend money on projects regardless of their
value.

The Administration's cuts in means-tested programs have been criticized, though to some extent unfairly. The Administration avoided simple across-the-board cuts, instead paying careful attention to program effectiveness in targeting cuts, so that efficient programs were cut the least and inefficient ones the most. Public service jobs, for example, were virtually eliminated because they had little success in moving people to permanent private sector jobs, and certainly were not helping the poorest in our society. Obviously, the recession created extra burdens on programs that were cut back, and the near-poor, as well as some people made poor by unemployment, found it more difficult to receive aid. As a result, poverty climbed substantially during the recession, from 11 to 15 percent by 1982, according to official estimates. However, these figures do not take into account the value of in-kind transfer payments such as food stamps, housing allowances, and subsidized medical care, which, when included, show a real increase in poverty from about 5 to 9 percent.

The Social Security Dilemma

Social Security is deservedly the most popular and important social program, preventing poverty for millions of elderly Americans. But it also suffers from major problems. Its benefits are not targeted effectively: much goes to wealthy retirees who do not need support. It has adverse incentives on retirement, savings, and insurance decisions.[4] Most important, it faces a potentially huge long-run deficit. In 1982, revenues were estimated to fall short of outlays over the next seventy-five years by trillions of dollars, primarily because of longer life expectancies and the retirement of baby-boomers.

Though legislative attempts to reform Social Security failed in 1981, pressure for reforms increased as the recession and several other factors brought on a short-run cash crisis in the trust fund. It was anticipated that by July 1983, Social Security's revenues plus its reserves would not have been able to cover outlays. While this is not equivalent to bankruptcy—at worst, it would have required a very small benefit reduction, or a delay of a couple of days each month in payment—it would have imposed hardship on the most needy recipients, who depend exclusively on Social Security for support.

Under such pressure, and with Social Security already a political hot potato, a bipartisan commission, chaired by Alan Greenspan, was appointed to recommend solutions. The commission's recommendations, amended and supplemented by Congress, produced some major reforms in 1983:

1. Taxation of half the benefits for individuals and families with incomes above a certain substantial level;

2. A very small and gradual increase in the retirement age during the twenty-first century;

3. Extension of mandatory coverage to new federal employees and tightening of the option of withdrawing from Social Security for some other groups;

4. Acceleration of some previously legislated tax increases;

5. Increase of taxes for the self-employed; and

6. Possibly some very small benefit cuts, such as a delay in implementation of cost-of-living increases.

These proposals were designed to solve the short-run funding problem in OASDI (the retirement and disability programs) by raising $165 billion for the balance of the decade. Under the intermediate demographic and economic assumptions, these proposals would be sufficient to get OASDI through the remainder of the 1980s, barring a major recession.

Unfortunately, the short-run funding problem is not limited to the retirement and disability program. The Medicare part of Social Security, hospital insurance, will begin to run a deficit in the 1990s. Therefore, the 1983 amendments will not be sufficient to keep Social Security as a whole solvent for very long, even if the economy performs well. Obviously, if the economy performs worse than predicted, we will again face the choice between a tax increase or benefit cuts.

The most interesting part of this compromise is the estimated reduction in the program's long-term deficit. First, and most important, the overwhelming bulk of the long-term deficit is due to the Hospital Insurance portion of Social Security; its deficit is three times as large as that of the retirement and disability portions. That is why even if the 1983 changes remain in effect—a question to which I will return in Chapter 9—the 1983 amendments solve only 25 percent of the long-term problem.

Second, a large part of the reduction of long-term benefits is to come from taxes to be levied on half the benefits of *currently* wealthy recipients. Congress has set high *nominal* cutoff levels on the income of individuals and families before Social Security benefits are taxed, and currently very few of the elderly have such income. However, since these levels are not indexed for inflation, the final result, assuming continuing real income growth and inflation, will be that virtually all of the elderly will eventually be taxed on one-half of their benefits. The original commission proposal, which Congress watered down, had estimated that almost one-third of the deficit could be eliminated in this way. But can we really expect Congress, whose intent was to tax the benefits of the wealthy, to sit idly by while middle-class retirees are taxed on half of their benefits? In addition, assuming nothing is changed, this proposal will have little effect on the long-term deficit, because even on the limited basis with which it purports to deal with the long-term funding problem, it will be grossly inadequate.

Third, savings that result from raising the retirement age are probably overestimated. The proposal phases in a higher retirement age, since it would be unfair to change the age abruptly for those who have made plans based on the existing structure and are close to retirement age. However, in many other societies, especially in Western Europe, there has been a growing trend toward making modest disabilities — those that do not prevent people from working even though they may be unpleasant and uncomfortable — the basis for receiving pre-retirement benefits. Raising the retirement age will certainly create incentives in this direction, and therefore, if we also experience an increase in disability claims and payments for people who would otherwise retire at a later age, the long-run cost saving projected from raising the retirement age will turn out to be less than expected. In this case the 1983 amendments will not solve even the OASDI deficits, which represent only a quarter of the total long-term deficit.

The final, and politically explosive, complication will result from the growing OASDI surpluses projected for the years 1990–2020 when the baby boomers are in their peak earning years, a surplus that is predicted to rival the regular national debt in size. Figure 5 displays projections over the next seventy-five years of the annual surplus and deficit in Social Security, including and excluding hospital insurance, each as a percent of taxable income. As can be seen there is substantial surplus projected to accrue for the next twenty-five or thirty years. It will reach a peak almost as large as the regular national debt if it actually is accrued. But we have never accrued such a surplus in the past, and it will be a tempting target to bail out Hospital Insurance, to finance other government spending programs, to postpone or eliminate the prospective increase in retirement age in Social Security, and/or to index the exempt amount of the Social Security benefits taxed. Each of these would reduce the short-run surplus and dramatically worsen the long-run deficit portrayed in Fig-

FIGURE 7-5   Projected Social Security Finances

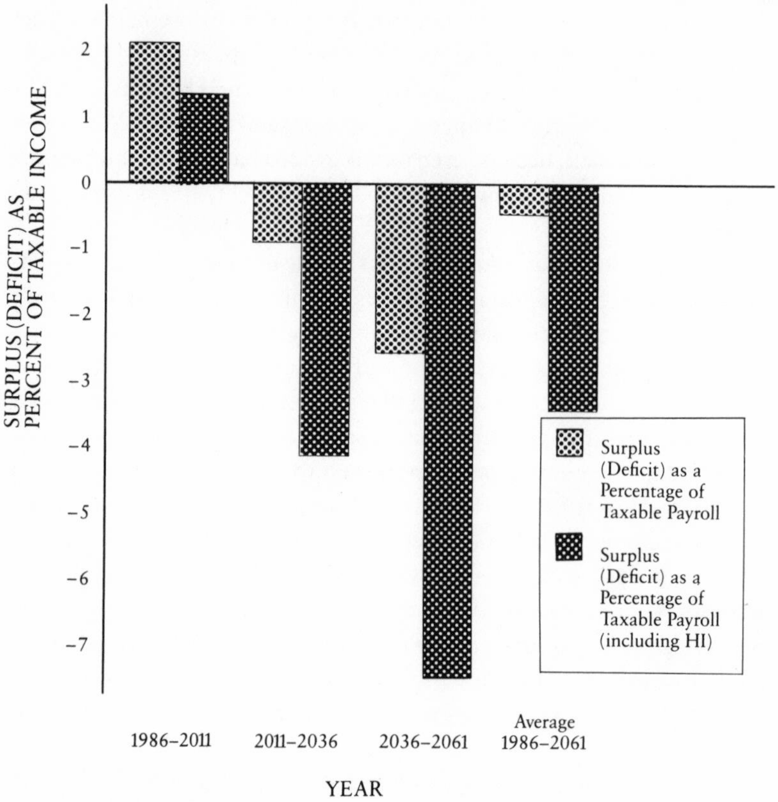

Source: Annual Reports of the Trustees of Social Security, 1986.

ure 5 and Table 2. The deficit could become much worse if these surpluses are dissipated or worse yet, used to raise benefits. Dealing with the long-run Social Security financing problem will be one of the great political and economic problems facing our society in the decades ahead. *Only* an acceleration of real wage growth will ease the intergenerational tensions substantially; sensible structural reforms in Social Security, such as those I have proposed elsewhere, can help somewhat.[5] But an increase of half a percentage point in real wage growth over that projected would substantially improve the system's long-run finances as well as the real income of future generations of Americans. In spite of these problems, and although the amendments do almost nothing about the immense ine-

TABLE 7-2   Projected Social Security Finances

	1986–2010	Period 2011–2035	2036–2060	75 Year Average 1986–2060
Surplus (+) or deficit (–) as percent of taxable payroll — Retirement & Disability only	2.12	-0.89	-2.56	-.044
Retirement + Disability, including Hospital Insurance	1.34	-4.14	-7.48	-3.43

Source: *Annual Report of the Trustees of Social Security,* 1986.

qualities and mistargeting of Social Security benefits, the 1983 amendments did give us time to deal with the problems of financial insolvency and the inequitable and inefficient benefit structures of Social Security.

Neglected Items

Many government programs serve narrow special interests. Farm subsidies, for example, have grown enormously, and most of them go to the owners of large corporate farms, not poor family farmers. Maritime subsidies aid yacht owners, which hardly helps the destitute. The rural electrification program, originally designed to help poor people in rural areas, has been transformed into a massive giveaway to middle- and upper-income owners of rural land. Transportation subsidies, urban development action grants, community development block grants, postal subsidies, and a host of other special programs originally designed to assist the needy or to serve a genuine social purpose have grown far beyond their original intent. All of these could be sharply curtailed, and some could even be eliminated.[6] Each of these programs, plus many others, pits the concentrated interests of the beneficiaries against the broad, diffuse interest of taxpayers.

Many of these programs should be reduced, streamlined, or eliminated *even if there were a balanced budget.* But the urgency of reform
is even greater in the face of the huge deficit. The Reagan Administration
has reduced the growth of many non-defense, non-Social Security, and
non-Medicare programs. But there are a variety of others whose very exis-
tence needs to be justified continually. After all, needs change and information on the effectiveness of programs accumulates. A program's life
should not be automatically extended, or its budget increased for inflation, simply because that is the easy thing to do. Unfortunately, Congress
is often so overwhelmed with work on appropriations bills that it frequently does so.

The problem, of course, is that every program has beneficiaries,
which become a political lobby far stronger than any lobby that favors
rethinking programs. Many of these programs serve legitimate purposes,
if inefficiently. Often, Senators and Congressmen vote on programs only
because they are likely to help specific individuals in their own districts.
These decisions give short-run satisfaction, but often do not take into
account any sense of the public good. Careful evaluation of these programs is an urgent priority. A two-year budget cycle would allow much
more careful evaluation of the existing programs than is currently possible. Other options include institutional reforms such as zero-based budgeting and sunset legislation. Adopting more sensible accounting, control,
and budgetary procedures would improve the budget process, and though
this would not always mean less spending on every single program, it
would provide more target-effective and cost-conscious spending even in
the few individual cases where it might actually *increase* spending. The
Reagan Administration has been in a unique position to accomplish these
ends, due to its popularity and commitment to reduced government. But
achieving them will take many years of hard work beyond Reagan.

The Grace Commission

In response to charges of mismanagement in the federal government, the
President's Commission on Private Sector Initiatives was established to
mobilize the help of prominent private sector managers in seeking ways
to improve efficiency and reduce waste. Commonly known as the Grace
Commission after its chairman J. Peter Grace, the commission organized
an army of volunteers to pore over every aspect of government operations,
including accounting and program policy. The effort produced more than

2,000 recommendations for changes in spending, cash management, and program administration, as well as suggestions for program consolidation. The final report noted "the overriding theme of the recommendations in these task force reports is there are significant deficiencies from a managerial and operating perspective."

The Commission points to a major defect in the structure of the federal government itself—a lack of centralized financial and administrative management, as well as government-wide information. Combined with a lack of continuity in high level positions, the result is a nightmare of administrative problems. The Commission recommended that an office of federal management be established in the executive office. The new management agency would be responsible for policy and programs throughout the government, and would combine financial management information systems, coordination of reporting policies and procedures, effective management of human resources, and planning and budgeting. This office would subsume the Office of Management and Budget, the General Services Administration, and the Office of Personnel Management.

The Commission produced an ambitious list of 2,470 cost-cutting, revenue-enhancing recommendations, which it claimed would save nearly a quarter of a trillion dollars without raising taxes and without harming necessary social welfare programs or the defense buildup. However, despite the value of many recommendations, the savings projected are enormously exaggerated. Most of the savings are based on policy or program reforms that are difficult to achieve. The Congressional Budget Office study of the Grace Commission recommendations found less than one-third of the savings claimed. Part of the problem comes from the Commission's definition of savings. Most economists believe many of the Commission's recommendations would have to be offset by compensating payments elsewhere. A good example is the recommendation to lower military retirement benefits to make them equivalent to private sector retirement benefits. The military has long used lucrative retirement benefits as a recruiting, promotion, and retaining device in personnel management. While some reforms are probably possible, a sharp reduction in military retirement benefits almost certainly would need to be accompanied by a substantial increase in current wages for military personnel. The generous pension program is simply delayed compensation. I do not mean to suggest that no savings are possible, but it is examples such as this that have led the CBO and many economists to believe that the Grace Commission's case is dramatically overstated.

TABLE 7-3   The Off-the-Books Credit Budget
             (Total Outstanding in Billions of Dollars)

Year	Loans	Guarantees	Enterprises
1960	23	67	9
1965	33	91	15
1970	51	126	38
1975	50	189	85
1980	92	299	196
1983	105	364	309

Source: M. Boskin and B. Barham, "Measurement and Conceptual Issues in Federal
    Budget Treatment of Loans and Loan Guarantees," CEPR Discussion Paper
    No. 11, Nov. 1983.

This is unfortunate, because it has had the effect of discrediting all of the Commission's recommendations. Many of them would produce significant savings and are worth adopting. Perhaps they could only be implemented slowly; still, there is no excuse for mismanaging the single-largest business in the world, especially when it has severe budgetary problems. It is unfortunate that there seems to be no compromise between those who argue that all 2,470 proposals should be implemented, regardless of their programmatic effects, and those who dismiss the entire study outright.

In rethinking the budget process, we must start by fundamentally restructuring the federal government's accounting procedures. The fact is that congressmen today are receiving irrelevant and inaccurate information about everything, from the level and growth of federal spending to the nature of costs in the various programs. They are also being excluded from a variety of hidden appropriations in credit programs (see Table 3). We must improve the budget *process* to improve budget *outcomes,* and this will almost certainly depend on improving budget *information.* The Reagan Administration's FY87 budget message is a welcome call for such reforms.

Distributive Effects

Virtually every regulatory, tax, spending, and monetary policy decision that government makes alters the distribution of income. For example, tariffs may provide very little revenue and may not appear to be vehicles for redistributing income, but nonetheless they may substantially increase the incomes of some groups — often those who are already well off. Such effects often occur as unintended consequences of programs that are not designed to affect income distribution but do so anyway. On the other hand, some programs specifically designed to help the poor produce the opposite effect and end up hurting them. An example is the minimum wage, which probably worsens the lot of low-skilled workers, especially minority teenagers.

In the United States, the largest impact on income distribution in the late 1970s and early 1980s resulted from severe recessions, the growth of various aid programs (such as extended unemployment benefits), the sharp reduction in inflation and the capital gains and losses this created (e.g. in the housing market), and the structural tax and budget reform policies. Since I believe, as I have already mentioned, that the 1981–82 recession was unavoidable, even if it could have been partially mitigated by a different Fed policy, I shall focus here on the much more direct effects of the Reagan administration's budget changes on income distribution.

The Reagan Administration's economic program attempted to limit income redistribution to a social safety net. The program proposed to turn us away from a partly unintentional trend that was transforming the government's fiscal machinery into a system for redistributing income. The Reagan Administration explicitly rejected using the tax system to tinker with the distribution of tax burdens. Its policies have focused instead on restoring economic incentives to produce income and wealth and to raise the *absolute level of* average income. The hope was that the resulting environment would maximize opportunities for mobility by low income people and minorities, while also raising their absolute income levels through general economic growth. Underlying this program was the belief that when economic growth is sluggish, the poor face the greatest difficulty improving their lot, and those who need public support will also face deteriorating political support for the taxes to finance social programs. In a stagnant economic environment, the poorest may be doomed to suffer the most.

While there is not enough evidence to make definitive judgments about the success or failure of the Administration's long-term policies, it is clear that the overall objective of restoring historical growth rates required restoring incentives to produce income and wealth. And this in turn depended on our ability to control the exploding growth of government spending, including spending for transfer payment programs.

It is also clear that in trying to maintain a social safety net, some would fall through the cracks. The growth of many means-tested programs had relaxed eligibility standards to the point where the programs were subsidizing middle-class families. The subsidized school lunch program is an example, since malnutrition is not a problem for middle-class families. But even if these programs were subsidizing more people than they should have, tightening eligibility standards has imposed a painful transition process on those who are not very well off but are nevertheless well above the poverty line. The Administration originally hoped they would make up what they had lost by working harder or more, but this has not occurred in many cases, owing in part to the slack labor market during the recession. Whether their distress will continue is uncertain, and is discussed more fully in Chapter 10. Despite the problems these cutbacks have caused for some families, there are good reasons for believing that as the economy grows, rising incomes will mitigate these hardships. The important thing is to ensure that the safety net is indeed sufficient to support those who cannot help themselves.

The greatest irony is that the reduction in means-tested benefits payments has been more than offset—in both absolute dollars and growth rates as a share of the budget and GNP—by growing benefit payments in programs that are not means-tested. The most obvious example of the latter, of course, is Social Security: we are not only preserving, but actually increasing, massive middle-class subsidy programs, partly at the expense of the poor and near-poor. There is no doubt that there is a need to tighten eligibility standards for means-tested programs. But there is also no doubt that our inability to control the very large and rapidly growing programs that are not means-tested is a disgrace.

Unfortunately, the debate on these issues has been sadly oversimplified by overzealous opponents. Those who argue that virtually every item in the Reagan policy disproportionally hurt the poor are wrong. But so are those Administration supporters who claim that no one has suffered during this transition. A balanced assessment shows that over the past quarter century poverty has been greatly reduced in the United States, although recently there was an unfortunate rise due to the 1981–82 recession and the growing number of households headed by single women. Enormous costs have also been incurred in building the myriad of overlapping anti-poverty programs. Most analyses of the distributive effects of the Reagan budget changes focus on short-run current income. If this is the end of the story, the Reagan Administration has, indeed, reduced the short-term *current* income of some near-poor families. But this is not the end of the story; there is much more to it than that, as discussed in Chapter 10.

Constraining Budget Options

The growth of government taxes and spending, combined with poor economic performance, has produced a national movement devoted to limiting federal governmental discretion over taxes and spending. Some elements in the movement advocate a constitutional amendment mandating a balanced budget; others wish to limit spending to a certain fraction of GNP. Each proposal contains a multitude of variations. In the United States, thirty-two states have now gone on record, in one way or another, in support of a constitutional convention to pass some sort of balanced budget amendment to the U.S. Constitution. Although it may seem somewhat ironic in view of the record deficits, President Reagan supports the balanced budget amendment.

One of the many problems that plague these amendments is the technical limitation in current budgetary information. For instance, in the official federal government accounts for the budget, not all government spending and taxes are included, and no separation is made between capital and current accounts. These problems make it difficult to find an adequate measure of spending, taxes, and deficits. For such reasons, implementing a simple balanced budget act will require extremely detailed amendments, to make them as loophole-proof as possible.

Proponents of a balanced budget amendment claim it would provide greater long-run flexibility than a spending limit, by allowing changes in spending relative to GNP. Such flexibility could be important to accommodate change in demography or other exogenous events. They also contend that although Congress does not at present feel constrained by tax revenues because it can run deficits, forcing legislators to increase taxes in order to spend more will place an effective limit on spending. Fortunately, the reduction in inflation, combined with indexation of income tax brackets, will greatly reduce the tendency to hide the cost of increased spending with automatic revenue increases. A minor caveat is that real economic growth will still produce a growth of government revenues as a proportion of GNP, since rising real incomes increase average tax rates.

Balancing the budget will be extremely difficult since the budget planning cycle precedes the start of the fiscal year by about a year, during which Congress can pass a series of resolutions, appropriation bills, and sometimes, tax legislation. These resolutions affect the taxes, spending, and borrowing for the following fiscal year. The budgeting process thus begins two years before the *end* of the fiscal year to which it applies. Projecting tax revenues and budget outlays is an important part of the process, because each is affected by the course of the economy. Since it cannot be known whether the budget was balanced until an audit several years after the President's original budget message, we necessarily must discuss proposals for an *ex ante,* or planned balanced budget, rather than an *ex post* balanced budget. However, this obviously creates political incentives to shade forecasts of receipts and outlays.

This is why most economists, including myself, oppose an annually balanced budget, preferring that the budget be balanced over a longer period. A constitutional amendment requiring an annually balanced budget could impede the self-correcting tendency of the economy to deal with cyclical fluctuations. In fact, the amendment would tend to require changes in government taxes and spending in directions precisely opposite to those usually proposed, for example, in cyclical downturns. A preferable scheme would be a budget balanced over the business cycle, running deficits in recessions and surpluses in expansionary periods, but measured on a *conceptually proper* basis. This would require a separate capital account and comprehensive definitions of revenues and outlays. This is becoming painfully clear in the implementation of the Gramm-Rudman-Hollings Balanced Budget Act, which requires a balanced budget by 1991. Major items are excluded from automatic cuts, and though the accounting for spending and revenues may pass political muster, it would flunk an introductory accounting class.

The proposals to limit spending provide more short-term flexibility for fiscal policy discretion, but much less long-run flexibility. For example, as the baby boom generation approaches retirement shortly after the turn of the century, it may be desirable to have total Social Security benefits rise somewhat as a fraction of GNP. In addition, these spending limit proposals generally fail to deal adequately with off-budget items, problems of timing, unpredictability, *ex ante* and *ex post* forecasts and realizations, how to include quasi-government spending in terms of mandated private activity or special tax advantages, and so on. Thus, ambiguity concerning the definition of spending in limitation proposals may be a severe drawback. On the other hand, recent changes in the balanced budget and spending proposals have been addressing this issue with some success.

A number of structural reforms in the current system are possible and should be tried to improve the decision-making process. These include extension of the authority of the congressional budget committees to establish separate spending limits on each appropriations bill, rather than just on their total; requirement of a multi-year budget growth forecast for all items in the budget; and establishment of more specific veto power for the President (such as a line-item veto). If these reforms fail, the country may turn to some sort of constitutional amendment forcing Congress to limit spending or balance the budget.

While I am sympathetic to those who are dismayed by the current congressional budget process and want to restrict discretionary increases in government spending, there is no doubt that any spending or balanced budget proposal enacted would spend many years in the courts, with the definition of many important items in litigation. Moreover, the passage of any amendment — however cast and defined — is certain to bring forth further creative attempts to enlarge quasi-government spending via various special loan guarantees, tax advantages, and so on. One idea is to require more than a simple majority (perhaps 60 percent or even two-thirds) of Congress to pass appropriation bills, thereby making logrolling more difficult.

Another interesting proposal, worthy of consideration, is the requirement of a marginal — not necessarily total — balanced budget policy, which would require that if the *sum* of spending decisions (and expected taxes) exceeded a deficit figure to be agreed to, an *automatic* tax surcharge would result. Thus, all marginal finance would be from taxes, not borrowing, making the cost of spending decisions harder to hide.

Conclusion

It is clear from the discussion of the Reagan budget program in this chapter, as well as in Chapters 4 and 5, that Reaganomics has a substantial unfinished agenda. This will be discussed more fully in Chapter 13, but the basic goals of the Reagan program — and a very substantial fraction of its specific proposals — are worthy of implementation. It may seem obvious, but any program which is not desirable, even if the budget were balanced, should be eliminated; they certainly cannot be afforded in the current fiscal climate. Many programs should be reduced in scale, and the benefits targeted more directly to those who need them. Many services could be transferred to the private sector or to state and local governments. User fees can be charged for those services where the direct beneficiary can be identified. Better management in the federal government — the world's largest business — is desperately needed, and this could start with an improved budgetary process. In short, an important start has been made, but a huge unfinished agenda remains to be implemented.

◆ *Chapter 8* ◆

Structural Tax Policy

By 1980, the U.S. tax system had reached a crisis, creating pressure for fundamental tax reform. Several factors were at issue: net business investment in plant and equipment slumped in the 1970s, partly due to historic cost depreciation in a rapid inflation; bracket creep — the increasing number of people pushed into higher marginal tax brackets due to inflation rather than real income gains — was accelerating; the fraction of the population subject to very high marginal tax rates had quadrupled between 1965 and 1980, during a major productivity growth slowdown (see Figure 1); and the top marginal tax rate on investment was much higher (70 percent) than it was on earnings (50 percent). Our tax system was widely perceived to be pro-consumption and anti-saving, in a society that had an extremely low saving rate.

Traditional conservatives troubled by growing government spending were also concerned by the automatic extra revenue generated by inflation and an unindexed tax system. Mainline economists such as Martin Feldstein and myself, traditionally concerned with incentives in the economy, were worried about high and rising marginal tax rates, and even more worried about the rising effective marginal tax rates on corporate investment (see Figure 2). Liberals were concerned that the tax base was eroding. Despite the fact that the overall ratio of taxes to GNP was lower than in most advanced economies (see Figure 3), numerous special tax features were giving marked advantages to certain sources and uses of income, enabling some to escape taxes completely.

Against this backdrop, President Reagan proposed dramatic reforms

FIGURE 8-1   **Growth in Taxes, 1960–1980**

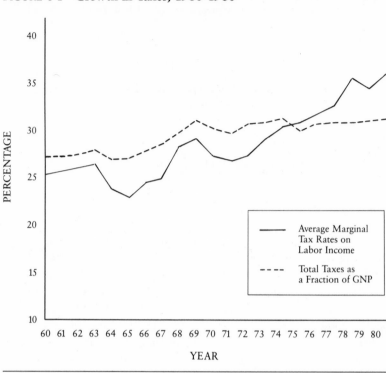

Source: Barro, Robert J. and Chaisat Sahaskul, "Measuring the Average Marginal Tax Rate from the Individual Income Tax," *Journal of Business*, Vol. 56, No. 4, October, 1983.

of the tax system. Many of these were enacted in 1981, though some were later gradually reversed. Marginal personal income-tax rates were reduced rapidly, depreciation was accelerated, and saving incentives were made universal. The good news about these changes was that they focused on marginal tax rates and capital formation incentives in the structural tax reform. The bad news was that Congress added substantial additional tax cuts, and with the very limited success in controlling domestic spending, we could not afford all of them. The large real tax cut (the sharp reduction in inflation accounted for about one-third of reduced revenues), combined with an actual increase in the share of GNP devoted to federal government spending, created large and potentially pernicious budget deficits.

FIGURE 8-2   Effective Tax Rates on Capital Income of the
Nonfinancial Corporate Sector, 1964–1980

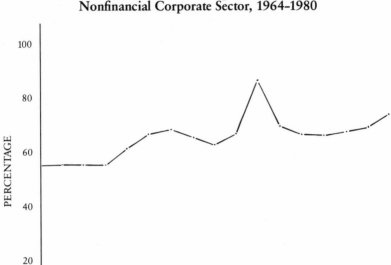

Source: Feldstein, Martin S. and Lawrence H. Summers, "Inflation and the Taxation of
Capital Income in the Corporate Sector," *National Tax Journal* 32 (December 1979).

In the course of President Reagan's first term, exaggerated claims were
made both for and against the tax program. The supply-side tax cuts did
have some supply-side effects; they are discussed and documented more
fully below. Once the recession ended, investment was stimulated. There
was a substantial reflow of revenue from the lower tax rates, but not nearly
enough to offset the budget deficits. The structural tax reforms were neither as inequitable nor as impotent in their incentives as critics predicted.
The jury is still out both because of major changes in these structural tax
reforms in the 1982, 1983, and 1984 tax increases, and because of the
fundamental 1986 tax reform, which takes effect in 1987 and 1988. In
some dimensions the 1986 tax reform greatly expands the supply-side
nature of the original Reagan proposals by further reducing marginal rates;

FIGURE 8-3   Total Government Receipts as a Percent of GNP

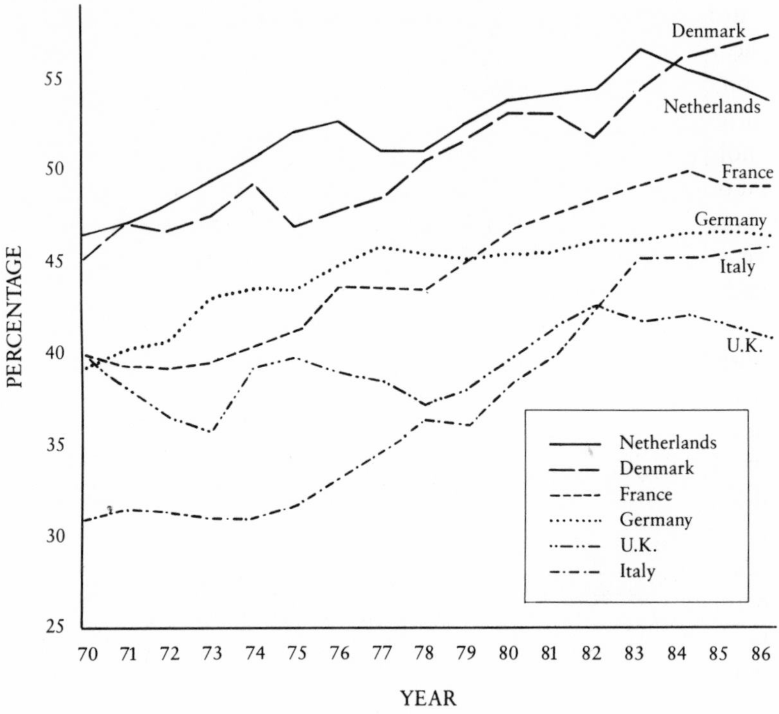

Source: Annual Economic Report, 1986–1987, Commission of European Communities

in other ways it reverses the original tax changes, such as the curtailment of capital formation incentives.

This chapter will discuss criteria for evaluating the structural tax policies enacted at a rapid pace in recent years. It presents evidence on the economic impact of the various features of the tax reform, and provides a preliminary evaluation of the likely impact of the 1986 Tax Reform Act, the most fundamental in decades. It also concludes that there is yet an unfinished agenda, and that the tax laws are likely to change yet again. I suggest how they ought to change in order to cement the best features of the structural tax reforms, while limiting the deleterious effects of the bad features.

Evaluating Structural Tax Policies

Colbert, Louis XIV's finance minister, claimed "the art of taxation consists in so plucking the goose as to achieve a maximum of feathers with the minimum of hissing." This might still pass as the politician's definition of tax policy, though the economists' principal concern is to minimize distortions in major economic decisions. Such distortions can affect choices involving consumption and saving, investment and risk-taking, labor supply and human investment, and the like. Taxes can distort the choice between consumption and saving. For example, with a comprehensive income tax, saving is taxed twice: first as a part of earned income and again when it earns a return.

Taxes produce two kinds of economic effects. First, and most obviously, they transfer resources from the private sector to the government, reducing after-tax income available for the private sector to spend or save, and increasing revenues for the government. Second, and often more important, taxes change the *relative prices* of different commodities and different factors of production. For example, income or payroll taxes drive a wedge between the gross wage rate paid to workers and the worker's take-home pay. Reducing the net wage has two effects on employment decisions: it makes work in the marketplace (as opposed to the home or underground economy) less remunerative, reducing the incentive to work; but by reducing after-tax income, it may also make work more necessary, creating an incentive to work more. Since there is now considerable evidence that taxes *ultimately* affect these choices,[1] a major objective in designing a tax system is to find the most desirable combination of distortions, thus minimizing the damage they do. While an income tax distorts both the work/leisure and consumption/saving choice, excise taxes on different commodities distort consumption patterns. And so on.

Economists use the concept of "deadweight loss" to measure the economic waste caused by the tax system. Deadweight loss occurs when taxes distort decisions, e.g. reduce consumption of a product that is heavily taxed. The size of the loss is the difference between the value to consumers and the cost of production. For example, suppose a product that costs one dollar to produce is taxed one dollar per unit, thus raising the price to consumers to two dollars. Consumers value their last unit of consumption at two dollars, whereas it costs society only one dollar less of other goods to produce it. If the tax causes consumers to buy one less unit, the loss is only one dollar, but if consumers buy far fewer units as a result of the tax, the loss can be very large. In short, the size of these losses

depends on both the size of the tax wedges and the responses to them—
that is, to the elasticities of supply and demand for different commodities. This analysis suggests it is desirable to tax more heavily goods and
factors that respond only slightly, if at all, to those taxes, thus minimizing distortions; and to avoid high tax rates where demand or supply is
highly responsive to changes in price caused by the tax.

Besides the economist's commitment to minimize distortions caused
by taxes, another objective should be to minimize administrative and compliance burdens in paying taxes. The ideal is a tax system that is simple
and easy to administer and thus not excessively costly for taxpayers to
comply with, so that huge amounts of resources are not consumed in order
to collect the revenue. Another important value is stability. If major tax
changes occur frequently, added uncertainty about future tax policy will
impose extra costs to the economy, for instance by reducing long-term
investment. In the 1970s, the combination of high and fluctuating inflation made effective tax rates on corporate investment very uncertain. The
higher the inflation, the lower the real value of depreciation allowances,
which were based on the historic cost of assets. Annual changes in inflation thus changed tax rates even in the absence of changes in the tax laws.
The experience of 1981–86 highlights the difficulty in making major tax
policy changes and sticking to them. Although we obviously want to continue our efforts to improve tax laws, we should avoid the temptation to
enact changes too frequently.

Equity is also important in designing a tax system. However, equity
means different things to different people. Some argue quite forcefully for
what might be called "horizontal equity," the equal treatment of equals.
In general, this has been taken to mean that people with the same income
(measured as command over resources) should be taxed at the same rates.
But the criteria used to measure ability to pay—whether income or
consumption—represent outcomes after the fact; they say nothing about
possibilities before the fact. Enforcing horizontal equity may thus be
difficult and even undesirable. Nevertheless, gross departures from apparent horizontal equity do stir concerns that tax burdens are unequal and
thus unjust.

A second and more controversial concept of equity is "vertical equity."
Almost everyone believes that the rich should pay more in *total* taxes than
the poor; many also believe they should pay a higher *proportion* of their
income or consumption in taxes than the poor. But there is little agreement on the desirable degree of progressivity. Some even consider progressivity unethical. The personal income tax in the pre-1987 tax system

features a nominally progressive tax structure; however, the combination of exemptions, deductions, and exclusions make effective tax rates very different from nominal ones. Further, the more progressive the tax system, the higher the marginal tax rate at the top becomes, and the greater are the disincentives to work, save, and invest. Thus, progressivity may to a large extent conflict with efficiency.

The important point in analyzing vertical equity is to think of government's *entire* impact on income distribution and income security. My own belief is that clamors for progressive taxation are historically dated. The great bulk of public income redistribution and insurance is provided on the spending side of the budget and has little to do with the tax code. As shown in Chapter 7, we now spend much more on transfer payments to households than at any other time in our history, and such payments have exceeded federal spending on goods and services for many years. This redistribution dwarfs the redistribution that occurs—or could occur—under the tax system. My belief is that it is much more sensible to have an efficient tax system that raises revenue in the most effective way possible, minimizing its interference in the general performance of the economy. This revenue can then be used on the spending side to provide income security and redistribution. In the days when most government spending involved purchases of goods and services, the case for redistribution through progressive taxes was much stronger than it is today. Moreover, the overall fiscal structure is still enormously redistributive, even after the budget and tax changes enacted in the first Reagan term.

The President's Original Tax Policy: An Overview

The inflationary environment of the 1970s, the rising effective marginal tax rates on capital income, the decline in the real net rate of investment, and the abysmal growth performance all provided ample cause for substantial structural changes in tax policy.

The 1981 and 1982 Tax Acts:

1. Phased in reduction of marginal personal rates;
2. Reduced immediately the top-bracket rate on investment income from 70 percent to 50 percent;
3. Accelerated depreciation further, through the Accelerated Cost Recovery System (ACRS), and extended the Investment Tax Credit (ITC);

TABLE 8-1   Effective Tax Rates By Asset Type
(selected major categories)

Asset	pre-1981	ERTA	ERTA/TEFRA
EQUIPMENT			
Autos	17.0	-32.8	9.6
Office, Computing, and Accounting Equipment	2.3	-49.4	11.9
Trucks, Buses, and Trailers	10.1	-45.2	11.3
Service Industry Machinery	20.3	-28.5	8.3
Electric Transmission and Distribution Equipment	29.2	3.2	24.2
Enginges, Turbines	31.8	16.3	30.2
All Equipment	17.2	-18.8	11.4
STRUCTURES			
Industrial Structures	49.6	38.4	38.4
Commercial Structures	46.8	35.6	35.6
Farm Structures	41.1	35.8	35.8
All Structures	40.8	30.0	36.1

Source: Jane Gravelle, "Capital Income Taxation and Efficiency in the Allocation of Investment," *National Tax Journal,* 1983.

4. Amended ACRS in the "out years" in the 1982 Act;

5. Adopted universal IRA accounts;

6. Implemented the Research and Development Tax Credit; and

7. Indexed tax brackets beginning in 1985.

Economists agreed that the rate of accelerated depreciation was decelerating because of the interaction of inflation and the corporate tax prior to 1981, as discussed in Chapter 2. Higher inflation decreased the real value of depreciation based on the historic rather than the replacement cost of assets. There was also general concern about the large number of asset classes and the complicated structure of depreciation guidelines. Many economists, myself included, believed that even if a separate corporate tax was retained for a while, the case for moving to immediate expensing was overwhelming. While this could have been done in various ways to prevent an abrupt short-term revenue loss, expensing would have greatly simplified the tax system and created a much more neutral system of tax incentives than previously existed. With ACRS, the set of asset classes was simplified and effective tax rates on new investment generally reduced. Unfortunately, ACRS still generated effective marginal tax rates under alternative hypothetical inflation scenarios and adjustment of gross interest rates to inflation, which varied markedly from asset type to asset type. On balance, as one can see from Table 1, the before-tax return required to yield any given after-tax return was lower than that after-tax return, implying negative tax rates, i.e., subsidies.[2] To redress this, as well as reduce the staggering projected deficits, the 1982 Tax Act (TEFRA) lopped off the phase-in of the last parts of ACRS — thus greatly reducing the effective cut in marginal tax rates on investment income (see Table 1). On balance, however, ACRS was a well-founded attempt to simplify the tax system and accommodate the reality of inflation.

My view is that a properly indexed corporate tax is impossible to design because it is too difficult to measure such things as capital gains and losses, inventory profits, and inflation premiums in interest payments and deductions — consider, for example, the clever but enormously complex procedures the Treasury Department recommended in its 1984 proposal. For this and equity considerations, I favor scraping the separate corporate tax, integrating it with the personal tax, and expensing all investment. Such a system would produce far greater neutrality — and thus fewer distortions — than current law. Although TEFRA was designed to limit the combination of investment credits and depreciation so that they are no more generous than expensing, TEFRA still left us with large variations in effective marginal rates by asset type. Moreover, given the different production processes and possibilities in different sectors of the economy, TEFRA also produced widely varying effective marginal tax rates by industry and sector of the economy (see Table 2). In any event, it is clear that the combination of the 1981 and 1982 tax laws lowered tax rates and thus increased the demand for new capital. Unfortunately, without a corresponding increase in the supply of capital, the result could only be an increase in interest rates. While higher real rates eventually would produce some additional saving, the enormous government deficits would more than compensate for the extra personal and business saving that could be expected from these tax incentives.

TABLE 8-2   Effective Tax Rates on New Investments, by Industry
(selected major industries)

Asset	pre-1981	ERTA	ERTA/TEFRA
Agriculture	29.5	16.7	25.6
Oil Production	14.1	9.8	11.3
Manufacturing	36.8	19.1	27.6
Services (non-residential)	38.9	22.5	29.5

Source: Jane Gravelle, "Capital Income Taxation and Efficiency in the Allocation of Investment," *National Tax Journal,* 1983.

The general rate reductions, though partially offset by bracket-creep, should have some modest effect on saving in three ways. First, lower marginal taxes increase the after-tax return to taxable assets and therefore slightly increase saving over time.[3] The reduction in the top rate from 70 percent to 50 percent produces the greatest response in saving. Despite objections on equity grounds, taxpayers in this highest group have the highest propensity to save, and the large reduction in this high rate should generate additional saving. It would be absurd, however, to think that increased saving by these high-income individuals could substantially increase the national saving rate. There just aren't enough of them. Making Individual Retirement Accounts (IRAs) available to all taxpayers produced some increase in saving, but part of the apparent increase was due to tax arbitrage, as people shift assets either from taxable forms or borrowing into IRA accounts rather than generate additional saving.[4]

Congress also raised additional revenue in the 1982–84 period by increasing excise taxes, including the highway tax and taxes on alcohol and tobacco. Excise taxes accounted for 5 percent of all taxes collected. The most notable change was in the composition of taxes, where corporate tax receipts declined and Social Security taxes increased as a fraction of the total (see Figure 4). Since the latter taxes are earmarked for Social Security benefit payments, their propriety depends more on assessment of the spending side (see Chapter 7). Further, the Social Security tax is levied at a flat tax rate with no exemptions or deductions up to a maximum earning level; thereafter, the marginal rate is zero. Thus, the tax has a very broad base and does well by efficiency criteria. Also, since

FIGURE 8-4   **Sources of Government Finance, United States, selected years**

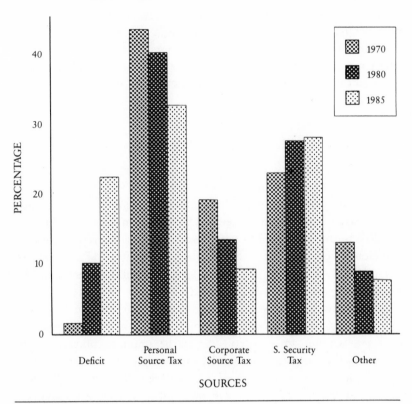

Sources: Economic Report of the President

we finance Social Security benefits with a separate payroll tax, the decline of corporate receipts as a fraction of receipts net of social insurance taxes is much less pronounced than when Social Security is included in the total along with income taxes, as it is in many other countries. However, everyone pays the corporate tax, whether as shareholders, consumers, or workers. Those concerned about the decline in corporate taxes should place their emphasis on the taxes ultimately paid on corporate-source income, not on whether the tax is paid on the corporate or personal level. Thus in Figure 4, the personal taxes paid on corporate dividends and interest paid is added to compute corporate source revenues, and these amounts are subtracted from personal taxes. This produces a markedly different picture. While the corporate source tax share fell from 1970–85, it fell only about half as much as the commonly quoted figures suggest, and because this issue was not carefully considered, it led to the worst parts of the 1986 tax reforms—a partially disguised shift of a large part of the tax burden from the personal tax to the corporate tax. In summary, while ERTA and TEFRA were big improvements over what they replaced, a more consistent and neutral tax policy was possible.

Economic Effects of Tax Policy—1981–84

The tax cuts embodied in ERTA were projected to reduce revenues by some $787 billion over the period between FY82 and FY88. More than $500 billion of this total was a reduction in individual income taxes, $200 billion was in corporate income taxes, and $40 billion in other taxes. In 1982 TEFRA, pushed by Senate moderates such as Bob Dole, Pete Domenici, and Howard Baker, reduced this total by $244 billion—$72 billion less in individual reductions, $131 billion less in corporate reductions, and $41 billion less in other taxes. We shall focus here on the structure of tax policy—that is, on changes in the tax structure that attempted to lower rates for individuals, accelerate depreciation, and other structural changes—without, for now, considering the amounts collected or the impact on the economy from this lack of revenue.

The first thing to note is that ERTA/TEFRA left us with both lower effective marginal rates on capital income and a smaller but still substantial variation in tax rates (see Tables 1-3). As for distortions caused by taxes, several interesting analyses have studied the changes in the deadweight loss resulting from misallocation of the capital stock and assessed distortions in such decisions concerning whether to spend or to save, which types of investment to make, which goods to consume, and other choices discussed above. There has been particular interest in calculating the misallocations of capital among different uses resulting from variations in tax rates across asset types and industries. It is interesting to note that these studies generally conclude that ERTA/TEFRA substantially *reduced* distortions, relative to the pre-1981 law. For example, Jane Gravelle estimates that the deadweight loss from non-neutral taxation of capital assets was less than one-half under TEFRA what it had been in pre-1981 law. However, she examines exclusively the misallocation of capital stock among different uses and does not deal at all with the distor-

TABLE 8-3   Effective Tax Rates for All Assets, 1965–1982, Selected Years

	Auerbach[a]	Hulten-Robertson,[b]
1965	35.7	26.3
1970	49.7	52.3
1975	37.0	32.1
1980	31.9	33.1
1981	17.7	4.7
1982	24.6	15.8

[a]Alan Auerbach, "Corporate Taxation in the United States," *Brookings Papers on Economic Activity*, 2:1983. Auerbach assumes a 4% real after-tax rate of return and forecasts inflation based on past values.
[b]C. Hulten and J. Robertson, "Corporate Tax Policy and Economic Growth," Urban Institute Discussion Paper, December, 1982. These estimates assume a 4% real after-tax rate of return and, for 1981 and 1982, a 6% rate of inflation.

tions over time, that is, in decisions to spend versus save — which, after all, were the primary motivation for acceleration of depreciation and the expansion of the investment tax credit. In an extremely careful and exhaustive study, Alan Auerbach estimates that under ERTA/TEFRA the welfare cost of the distortions within and between industries was approximately half of the average over the previous decade. Auerbach concludes, like Gravelle, that ERTA/TEFRA was a substantial improvement over pre-1981 law in its effects on the allocation of capital. In fact, their estimates suggest that ERTA/TEFRA allowed us to save billions of dollars a year by increased efficiency in the allocation of the *existing* capital stock.

One further distortion, documented in Chapters 2 and 6, relates to the decision to spend or invest. Various attempts to measure intertemporal distortions (i.e., in choices between consumption and saving) generally conclude that the intertemporal distortions are much larger than distortions among sectors.[5] Since ERTA/TEFRA substantially reduced the cost of capital and the average effective marginal tax rate on new investment (see the estimates in Table 3), ERTA/TEFRA was *pro-investment.* It substantially redressed the misallocation caused by the tax system toward consumption and away from saving and investment. It did so imperfectly, and improvements could have been made, but compared to pre-1981 law, the worst distortions were reduced considerably.

In addition to reducing the cost of capital and average effective marginal tax rates on investment income, ERTA/TEFRA addressed the double concern that in the 1970s we were both investing too little overall and investing too much in housing compared to plant and equipment. This was caused in part by high rates of inflation acting in combination with particular tax advantages enjoyed by real estate. Thus, ERTA/TEFRA was designed to deal with all of these issues at once: too low a rate of overall investment, a misallocation of existing capital stock among different industries, and excessive investment in housing away from business plant and equipment. The 1981–82 tax laws redressed each of these problems to some extent, though not completely. Their success also depended on overall monetary and fiscal policies.

A few extremists argued that the tax cuts would produce such a frenzy of economic activity that we would quickly see large increases in saving, investment, and new work effort. These increases, they argued, might even increase tax revenues, rather than reduce them. But as I have mentioned, there were several reasons to believe this would not happen, at least in the short run. The tax cuts were implemented at the beginning of a substantial disinflation. Since it was clear a substantial recession would then follow, it was unreasonable to expect an investment boom as demand for products fell off, businesses started accumulating inventories, orders were reduced, and capacity utilization rates plummeted. Indeed, gross private domestic investment fell substantially during the recession, from about 16 percent of GNP in 1981 to around 12 percent by late 1982. Some people concluded from this that the supply-side tax cuts had failed; this conclusion is no more justified than the assertion that the investment boomlet of 1983–84 was due entirely to the tax changes. Nevertheless, one might conclude that the tax changes did play a substantial role because the investment boom occurred even in the face of inordinately high real interest rates over the period.

Similarly, private saving, which had declined in the late 1970s (see Chapter 2), was quite disappointing in 1982 and 1983. It rose substantially in 1984; much of this was business-retained earnings to finance replacement, not new investment. Net private saving is still at the relatively low level of 5 to 6 percent. Why didn't the tax cuts generate a huge, instant gush of private saving? To answer this question in relation to IRAs, it is clear that some of the movement of funds into IRAs at the *outset* was from currently taxed assets rather than from new saving. As less assets remain to be switched the IRAs should gradually have a greater impact. Further, the very high interest rates accrued disproportionately to older people in the population, who because of their savings pattern, own a disproportionate share of assets. Many of these people have reached the point in their lives where they have stopped saving and are even drawing down their assets. Therefore, an increase in real interest rates could not be expected to increase their saving, and it might even accelerate their dissaving. As they planned on greater returns from their investments to finance their retirement, they could afford to consume more, thus offsetting the increased saving by the still-working population. Finally, the high real interest rates led to a sharp decline in contributions to defined benefit pension plans, since at higher interest rates decreased the actuarial amount necessary to fund given benefits.

There are also many problems with the traditional manner of gathering saving statistics. They ignore, for example, capital gains and losses. Just as the saving rate was probably understated in the 1970s when there were substantial unreported capital gains on housing, so too the several hundred point increase in the stock market has left people with substantial capital gains relative to two or three years ago. This implies an amount of saving in the increased value of stock which completely overshadows the small measured changes in personal and corporate saving rates. The big news in saving, of course, is government borrowing, which we will address in the next chapter. Clearly, however, the increase in federal borrowing is far greater than any conceivable increase in private domestic saving, and the difference is being met by borrowing from abroad.

In conclusion, the verdict is still out on the *long-term* effects of supply-side cuts.[6] Certainly we should have known in advance, and have now learned the lesson, that they are not revenue neutral. Those who look at the recession and argue that the supply-side tax cuts were a failure ignore their basic long-run purpose. Since the recovery was more robust in 1983–84 than normal, and business investment grew more rapidly than in the typical post-war recovery, should it be concluded that the supply-side program was then working? The problem is that many of the basic indicators are simply swamped by their cyclical pattern. The rates of investment and productivity growth usually decline substantially in a downturn and grow robustly during the first part of a recovery. Given the magnitude and length of the recession, the decline in investment was not out of line with previous experience. The most strikingly atypical patterns were those of business and personal saving. The latter reached a long-term low in the middle of the 1983, whereas the former was substantially buoyant during the recession.

With respect to the supply of labor, Robert Haveman estimates that a modest increase in the amount of labor supplied by the labor force during the 1980s, from one to 2.5 percent, is primarily the result of the impact of personal tax rate cuts, and to a lesser extent, the impact of tightening eligibility standards in various transfer payment programs. In an interesting study for the Urban Institute, Alan Blinder examines whether various measures such as saving, investment, and labor force participation are running higher or lower than three of the major macroeconometric models would have predicted. Since these models largely ignore supply-side effects and changes in relative prices, Blinder reasons that if their calculations have underpredicted these variables, one possible explanation is that supply-side influences were beginning to play a role. He finds that saving was lower than the models predict, but investment higher through 1983. By 1984, a year after Blinder's study, both undoubtedly would be higher than predicted by these "supply-sideless" models.

The single most important feature of the structural tax changes was that the extended investment tax credit and ACRS were available only on *domestic* investment. This is a crucial but subtle point that is often overlooked in the discussion of the effects of deficits and tax cuts. About half of the fiscal deficit is being made up by an increase in *net* imports of foreign capital: we are importing *more* foreign capital, and exporting *less* capital from the United States. A major reason for this is because the ITC and ACRS were available *only* on investment in this country. Thus, while the tax cuts would certainly not be self-financing in the aggregate, some of the tax changes do have features that offset the potential deleterious impacts of deficits. The limitation of the ITC and the ACRS to investment in this country thus had an offsetting effect, as less direct investment is made abroad and therefore more of it is available for domestic investment.

It should be clear from this discussion that supply-side economics is basically a long-run concern.[7] It deals with the attempt to increase the economy's capacity to produce; for example, it attempts to analyze the important interactions between rates of capital formation, technological progress, and the long-term growth rate. It also represents an attempt to free incentives to work, save, invest, and innovate as much as possible from government interference — given the fact that revenue must be raised to finance public services. While some advocates of supply-side economics may have overestimated what it could deliver, the long-run promise remains. But rapid changes in the rate of investment, the growth rate, saving rates, and long-term productivity should not have been expected in response to tax changes.

These changes are bound to be slow for at least three reasons. First, throughout the Reagan Administration it has been unclear which taxes would remain permanently and which would be abandoned or altered by Congress. For example, TEFRA eliminated much of the business tax reduction of 1981, Social Security taxes were raised in 1983, the Deficit Reduction Act of 1984 changed various other provisions, and the 1986 bill revised many features adopted in 1981. This continuing change cannot help but produce great uncertainty, which will lead to lower investment — even though temporary advantages may lead some to bargain shopping. Second, major impacts on investment, the capital stock, and productivity can only occur over a prolonged period. Leaving out cyclical influences, it would take years for us to increase the capital stock substantially, and therefore, to realize major productivity gains. Each year, net investment is a small fraction of GNP and a smaller fraction of the existing capital stock. Even if the new investment embodies more up-to-date technology, it will take a decade or more for the standard of living to change noticeably because of it. Third, there are all sorts of offsetting influences. I have already discussed that these policies were adopted in the midst of an even more urgently needed disinflation program. The impact of the saving incentives will vary substantially depending upon the age of a household and the opportunity to arbitrage currently taxed assets, among other factors. Asking these policies to perform miracles is unreasonable. In combination, a number of important factors were almost certain to produce an increase in saving and investment in the years ahead. These included the reduction in inflation, the reduction in effective marginal tax rates on capital income, and the universality of IRAs. But this must be understood as an average outcome still subject to cyclical fluctuation and other shocks. There was no guarantee of an immense increase immediately and forever.

What can one conclude about the supply-side nature of the tax cuts? Although the program was certainly oversold, a strong case nevertheless existed to redress the disincentives to save and invest. For this purpose the disinflation and 1981–82 structural changes in tax policy represented a sound beginning. The tax cuts were not the only reason for the recovery (the defense buildup and monetary policy played a role, among other factors). However, the tax reforms were certainly in part responsible for the investment boomlet in the United States in 1983–84, and also for the increased share of domestic investment in GNP thus offsetting some potentially harmful effects of the deficits.

My conclusion is that the so-called supply-side tax cuts, which were heavily focused on investment and saving incentives and reductions in marginal tax rates, were, given estimates of the amount of revenue to be raised, far preferable to the pre-1981 laws and were partially responsible for the robustness of the recovery and the surprising strength of the investment sector despite massive government deficits.[8] Those who wrote off the supply-side completely were certainly mistaken. In fact, my NBER colleague Larry Lindsay estimates that a substantial reflow of revenue — though far too little to offset the deficit — did indeed occur. He estimates 47 percent of the cost of the 1981–83 rate reductions was recouped from higher-than-expected reporting of taxable income. The largest cuts, the immediate top rate reduction from 70 percent to 50 percent, may actually have increased tax revenue from these very wealthiest households because so much more income was reported.[9] However, as documented above, the tax laws circa 1986 still left us with numerous problems. The laws were complex, and featured far too many special exclusions, deductions, and exemptions. In addition, they contained tax rates that still provided a disincentive to producing income and wealth. Partly because of heightened awareness of the impact of tax policy on the economy, the 1986 Tax Reform Act was viewed as an opportunity to do even better.

Fundamental Tax Reform

Various factors led to proposals for a virtually complete overhaul of the tax system. First, it was widely believed — to some degree correctly — that the tax system was needlessly complex and cumbersome. The average taxpayer apparently spent a substantial amount of time and effort in both filing tax forms and figuring out ways to reduce his or her taxes. The Internal Revenue Service, in a field survey, discovered to its amazement that the proportion of taxpayers who hired professional tax preparation services greatly exceeded the fraction who itemized deductions! In other words, a substantial number of households apparently felt it necessary to hire tax preparers even to fill out the short form with a standard deduction. Second, it is clear that while the 1981–84 changes improved the *intertemporal* misallocation of resources the tax system had created, the *intersectoral* misallocations were still a problem. Recall that taxes can distort investment decisions in two fundamental ways: they can distort the decision whether to save or invest a dollar or to spend it; and, for dollars to be invested, they can distort the choice of investments. A major goal of tax policy should be to minimize these distortions so that investment decisions are based on true economic returns, not on special tax considerations.

Third, there was continued widespread belief that tax rates were too high, and that the personal income tax system was too progressive, at least in its nominal rate structure. If rates are lower, the incentive to underreport income, or to reallocate it for tax reasons, is reduced. But the only way, in the short-run, to lower tax *rates* without losing revenue is to broaden the tax *base*. The tax system was riddled with special exemptions, deductions, and exclusions. Undoubtedly, each was originally proposed and defended for serving an apparently noble social purpose. Many of them, such as the charitable deduction, in fact did. Taken together, however, the tax base had been so eroded that tax rates had to be much higher to collect the same revenue than they would have if there had been a broader tax base. One estimate put taxable income at less than half of the total income in the United States. Transfer payments, fringe benefits, and a host of other features were excluded from the tax base, as were a variety of other deductible items. Consider for instance, that net partnership income filed for tax purposes across all partnerships in recent years has been negative.

There were several major income tax reforms under consideration in the reform debate: the "FAIR" tax plan of Senator Bill Bradley and Representative Richard Gephardt; the Fair and Simple Tax plan (FAST) of Representative Jack Kemp (who was a primary proponent of the 1981 tax cuts, sometimes called the Kemp-Roth tax cuts), and Senator Robert Kasten; a proposal put forward by the Treasury Department (Treasury I); and a plan partly based on Treasury I proposed by the President. Three basic expenditure tax reforms were also proposed. One was the personal cash flow tax, which I have elsewhere supported, and which was detailed in a landmark document prepared by the Treasury staff under the direction of David Bradford and released by Secretary William Simon as *Blueprints for Basic Tax Reform* in 1977. A close approximation was introduced by Representative Cecil Heftel as a substitute for current income taxes. One of the most important and intriguing tax reform proposals was the so-called flat-tax of Robert Hall and Alvin Rabushka, of the Hoover Institution at Stanford University.[10] A consumption tax, it allows immediate write-off, expensing, of all investment. A similar proposal was introduced as a bill by Senator Dennis DeConcini. These plans are examined in detail in the Appendix.

The New Tax Laws

With a background of competing proposals and clamor for reform, Congress moved in 1985–86 to pass the most sweeping tax reform in decades. Ways and Means Committee Chairman Dan Rostenkowski and Senate

Finance Chairman Bob Packwood agreed to a last-minute compromise that "saved" tax reform. It contained some elements of each of the proposals, but the end product is not very similar to any of them. Appendix Table 1 compares the old law and its transition through the political process to the new law. Reading across a row, one may see the evolution of the treatment of any major tax law feature, e.g., rates, depreciation, or the treatment of capital gains.

The most important feature of the new tax law is very sharp reductions in tax rates in the personal income tax: two rates of 15 percent and 28 percent, with a complicated surtax that will put some in a 33 percent bracket. Thus, the top marginal tax rate in the personal income tax will have gone from 70 percent in 1980 to 28 percent by 1988, an astounding reduction, making the *top* marginal tax rate in the United States lower than the *bottom* marginal tax rate in many countries. The tax base in the personal income tax was broadened *slightly* with elimination of the deductibility of state sales taxes and substantial limitation of miscellaneous deductions. A very large increase in the personal exemption will remove approximately six million poor from the tax rolls, and while their tax burden under the current personal income tax does not amount to much, this is sensible social policy and will reduce the burden on them and the IRS. Further, the earned income credit for the payroll tax was extended substantially, giving further tax relief to the poor. A substantial fraction of additional taxpayers will no longer itemize deductions, thereby simplifying their taxes. But for most of the population, the difficulty of the reporting requirements, tax forms, record keeping requirements, and so on, will be reduced only slightly. The reduction in the number of tax rates did not really simplify the tax system, though the reduction in the level of rates did: at much lower rates, the incentive to try to shelter or reallocate income in order to reduce taxes is greatly reduced.

The next most important feature of the tax reform is a substantial shift of the tax burden from the individual to the corporate tax, amounting to about $120 billion over the next five years. This occurs despite the fact that the basic corporate tax rate is being reduced from 46 percent to 34 percent because of a very substantial increase in the corporate tax base, achieved through the elimination of the investment tax credit (common to all the reform proposals), much slower depreciation, and a stiff alternative minimum tax for corporations (to insure that no corporation that reports current profits to its shareholders will avoid paying taxes). A large fraction of the tax increases is industry-specific, especially those with respect to defense contractors, real estate, and financial institutions.

For example, banks will no longer be able to tax arbitrage tax exempt bonds, passive loss rules for real estate tax shelters will be tightened substantially, and defense contractors will see changes in the completed contract method of accounting. It is worth noting that much of this $120 billion is not an increase in corporate taxes, but a shift in their timing closer to the present. In subsequent years, revenue problems will re-emerge.

Other important features of the personal and corporate tax reforms are incentives to save and invest. The tax incentives to defer compensation are curtailed substantially. The tax deductibility of IRAs will be income-tested; well-off individuals will no longer be able to use them. By 1984–85, $30 to $40 billion a year was flowing into IRAs, and the best estimate is that about half of it was new net saving. Other tax deferred retirement accounts, such as 401(k) plans, will be sharply limited by the amounts that individuals can contribute (reduced from $30,000 to $7,000 per year, with an offset for any contribution to an IRA); and, incredibly, capital gains will be taxed in full as ordinary income, with no inflation adjustment for the basis of the asset.

These specific changes in capital income taxation, such as removal of the investment credit, slowing depreciation, full taxation of capital gains, and limits on tax deferred saving accounts, are a complete reversal of a historical trend that began about a decade ago. The easiest way to understand this is to recall the distinction between an income tax, which taxes saving and investment twice (first when it is earned as part of income and then when it earns its own return), and a consumption tax, which taxes saving and investment only once (when it is ultimately consumed). Our personal and corporate income taxes have always been something of a hybrid of the two. Some types of saving and investment are taxed only once, whereas others are taxed twice. Housing and the universal IRAs, are examples of types of saving taxed only once. Saving in ordinary money market instruments, such as bank accounts or saving and loan deposits, are examples of saving taxed twice.

On the corporate income-source side, the changes are a little more complex. Equity income is taxed first at the corporate level and again at the personal level when dividends are paid or capital gains received from the retained earnings. But the tax on the capital gains tax is deferred, debt financed investment is favored, and a variety of investment incentives reduce the burden on new investment. It is fair to say that the tax system had been moving, until this latest tax reform, closer toward the consumption tax norm than the income tax norm, i.e., toward taxing a weighted average of all saving and investment in the economy closer to once than twice. Examples are the reduction in capital gains tax rates in 1978, the investment tax credit extension, the acceleration of depreciation in 1981 (truncated in 1982), and universal Individual Retirement Accounts. But *this resulted in very uneven taxation of types of saving and across types of assets.* Examples are given in Tables 2 and 3 of the variation of tax rates by industry and asset for a new investment in each. Substantial variation remains, despite the fact that the variability was less than in the pre-1981 tax law.

Impact of the New Tax Laws

The tax reform is so complex that its net impact on the economy in the short- and long-run will reflect the interaction of numerous factors, as well as the interaction of the tax rules with monetary policy and general economic conditions. Indeed, this uncertainty over the economic effects led some senators and congressmen, such as John Danforth and Bill Archer, to question the wisdom of agreeing to major changes in conference committee before they could be fully evaluated. A few basic features deserve considerable attention, especially in light of the evidence accruing concerning the efficacy of the supply-side structural tax cuts of 1981 on investment, and to a lesser extent the effect of IRAs on saving noted above.

This tax reform has been viewed as pro-consumption and anti-saving and investment. But it is easy to overstate this fact by focusing only on the removal of specific incentives, such as the removal of the investment tax credit, slower depreciation, the full taxation of nominal capital gains as ordinary income, or the sharp limits on tax deferred saving. *Offsetting* these are lower marginal tax rates which should increase saving slightly, and more importantly, sharply reduce the incentive to borrow at both the corporate and personal level. With interest payments tax deductible, there is a tax advantage for debt-financed (as opposed to equity-financed) corporate investment, and also a substantial advantage for debt-financing of many consumer purchases, such as automobiles. Interest payments will be deductible at a much lower marginal tax rate for both corporations and individuals. In addition, consumer interest payments will no longer be deductible. At first glance, it might seem that it would be easy for a homeowner to circumvent this by increasing his or her mortgage and using the extra equity to finance desired purchases, such as an automobile, while deducting the extra interest. At least nominally, however, the new tax law confines the use of tax-deductible interest payments on mortgages to housing, educational financing, and medical expenditures. Undoubtedly, this will be difficult to enforce, but combined with the lower marginal tax rates, there should be less borrowing on average over the business cycle in the years ahead.

Thus, while saving may be less because of the structural tax changes, we also will probably borrow less. The net impact on saving will reflect the mix of the two sets of incentives. It is likely that the tax bill will be somewhat anti-investment and saving, but the impact predicted by people who look only at the removal of specific items will be partly offset by lower tax rates and other features. At any rate, it seems clear that the investment tax credit and depreciation schedules are very powerful determinants of investment. Two reasons for the sharp reduction in investment spending in 1986 were the uncertainty about which tax rules would ultimately prevail, and the fact that all the major reform plans proposed removing the investment tax credit were retroactive to January 1, 1986. My NBER colleague Larry Summers estimates that investment tax credits and depreciation allowances are very important because corporations use extremely high rates of discount for future cash flows.[11] Thus, cash flows in the near future, such as those that occur instantly with the investment tax credit and very quickly with accelerated depreciation, are given disproportional weight in investment decisions. I believe that there is something to this argument and that, *other things being equal*, the net impact of the tax bill will be to retard capital formation. But other things may not be equal. The investment rate will also reflect general economic conditions, the level of real interest rates (heavily affected by monetary policy), and other factors.

I have shown throughout this volume that a major problem confronting the United States is its very low national saving rate and low domestic investment rate. Capital formation is necessary to increase productivity, disseminate new technologies, raise the long-term growth rate, and allocate resources efficiently; it is clear that as a society, we are consuming too much of our income and not saving enough. This creates all sorts of problems beyond the trouble of financing the future retirement for today's workers or financing enough investment to equip the growing labor force with an adequate amount of new capital. The shortfall of national saving from domestic investment, caused for the most part by federal government deficits and also by the low private saving rate, tends to make the United States a substantial importer of capital. In the short run this prevents interest rates from rising still further and helps to finance domestic investment. But in the long run, the returns to this extra saving will accrue to foreigners, not to Americans. Therefore, these assets and their returns will not be available to finance the retirement of the baby-boom generation, for example. Put another way, it makes little sense to have an anti-investment and saving structural tax reform, which if continued indefinitely, would generate fewer *private assets* in the hands of American citizens. The national debt is growing rapidly relative to income, and hence, we are leaving our children and grandchildren greater *public liabilities*. We should be contemplating methods either to reduce the growing public liabilities or at least prevent ourselves from reducing private assets simultaneously.

Many economists, myself included, favored cleaning up the tax system by moving us toward the consumed-income tax, as outlined in the Treasury's *Blueprints For Basic Tax Reform* or the Hall-Rabushka proposal. Debates occur about which, if any, deductions — such as those for charity — ought to be allowed, and about the ideal rate structure, whether perfectly flat or somewhat progressive (through lower rates on a much broader base). A consensus was emerging, however, among professional economists and tax lawyers that the consumption tax norm was more desirable than the income tax norm on both equity and especially efficiency considerations. The consumed income tax would be *neutral* with respect *both* to the choice between consumption and saving and among types of investment. Rather than special incentives to certain types of investment such as the investment tax credit for equipment or accelerated depreciation of some assets, by immediate write-off of all investment net of borrowing, the tax would level the playing field in both dimensions: across assets and industries, and between saving and spending. The specific investment incentives would be replaced by a *general* one, which just offsets the double taxation of saving. A clean, comprehensive consumed income tax would be far better than the pre- or post-tax law. After a complex transition, a consumed-income tax would be much easier to administer since most of the items that cause enormous administrative complexity revolve around capital income, such as keeping separate depreciation schedules, adjusting for inflation, and capital gains.

As I mentioned earlier, there is some evidence that there is a supply-side response to investment incentives. Capital gains revenues actually went up subsequent to the reduction in capital gains taxes in 1978. While other factors are part of the explanation, it appears that the reduction increased the incentive to realize capital gains. Capital gains are taxed only at realization (not as accrued) and are entirely forgiven at death. The new law runs the risk of a reduction in realizations, including a greater proclivity to hold the asset until death, when no taxation will occur.

Why, then, are the anti-savings and anti-capital-formation qualities of the new tax law tolerated? Apparently, in the search for a political compromise that would allow for lowering the top marginal rates without the accusation of a giveaway to the rich, and in the mistaken belief that corporations were not paying their fair share, as discussed above, it was easiest to shift large amounts of the tax burden to the corporate tax. In short, a very substantial additional personal tax cut (above and beyond the three-year, 25 percent Kemp-Roth tax cut enacted in 1981–83, followed by tax-bracket indexing) was financed by a very substantial corporate tax increase. I believe this is a mistake. Some of the items are quite sensible, e.g., the attempt to equalize tax rates across different types of investment so that the allocation of capital stock will be more efficient. But the gains to the economy from doing so will be modest and will take some time to accrue.

Since no one is absolutely sure who ultimately pays the corporate income tax, it was easy for politicians to say almost all Americans were going to get a tax cut. But $120 billion of additional corporate tax collections was conveniently ignored, and not attributed back to the people who would ultimately pay it: the shareholders, workers, and customers of the corporations. It really is remarkable that so little attention was paid to the ludicrous claim that almost every American will get a tax cut from a bill that claimed to be revenue-neutral. The truth is, a large portion of the population will have a tax increase, although it will come in a round-about way via lower dividends, higher prices, or slower wage growth, and perhaps even through short-run disruption in employment.

The impact of tax reform on the short-term macroeconomic performance of the economy can be partly mitigated by Federal Reserve policy setting an activity or GNP target, which, as noted in Chapter 6, it appears to be doing. While it is not fully offsetting the deleterious short-run consequences of tax reform and previous tax uncertainty on investment, it is clear that the full impact on GNP can be offset. The composition of GNP, unfortunately, may shift still further toward consumption and away from saving and investment. If so, this will gradually result in worsening long-term economic performance. Unfortunately, our political process does not deal with insidious creeping problems, and tends to respond only to obvious crises.

Further Reform

Additional rounds of tax reform will undoubtedly succeed this round, for several reasons. First, in the next year or so many technical corrections will be necessary. Second, it will become apparent that some specific features of the new law are either unworkable, inequitable, or inefficient,

as various anomalies unfold. Third, the potential deleterious consequences on investment and saving eventually will have to be dealt with.
This may happen in the short run, but it may also take a crisis of the sort
that might be precipitated in the 1990s, when the retirement part of Social
Security runs a surplus, creating pressure to use it to fill the Medicare
deficit. If this occurs, there will be increased clamor for private saving
incentives in the tax laws to provide for the baby-boomers' retirement,
as the future of Social Security becomes more obviously uncertain. Or
it may come much sooner as it becomes more difficult to import foreign
capital to finance domestic investment.[12]

The large budget deficits also create concern about the possible instability of the structural tax reforms. If budget deficits cannot be dealt with
exclusively via spending reductions, there will be growing pressure to raise
tax revenues as a last resort. If tax rates are raised, a large portion of the
potential benefits of the lower rates will be lost, including those which
will decrease the incentives to finance through debt, thereby offsetting
some of the decreased saving incentives. The lower rates also reduce the
distinction between investment in housing and investment in plant and
equipment.

We also need to move toward a tax system which can remain in
place — and can be counted on to do so — for many years, rather than just
a year or two. There have been five major tax bills in less than a decade.
Tax instability is becoming as much of a problem as monetary instability. The present tax reform may be a step in that direction, since the lower
marginal tax rates mean that the value of remaining deductions is
decreased. This may gradually erode political opposition to broadening
the tax base on consumption-type items in the personal tax, and the resulting additional revenue can be used to restore saving and investment
incentives — or really, to remove disincentives to save and invest that occur
with double taxation. These should be general, not specific, incentives,
or they will distort the allocation of capital among assets and industries,
and create the foundation for tax shelters.

At the very least, if additional revenue must be raised, the marginal
revenue ought to come from a tax which is neutral with respect to the
choice between consumption and saving. In the short run, this may lead
to a broader-based personal income tax, e.g., including some fringe
benefits in the tax base. In the future, it may lead toward the consumption tax I prefer, or toward a very broad-based, consumption-type, value-
added tax. If so, it will be necessary to accompany this broad-based, value-
added tax with additional structural restraints on spending to prevent the

tax from financing unnecessary government spending. It will also be important to prevent erosion of the tax base in a value-added tax (if that is the last resort for revenue) rather than riddle it with exemptions for specific items. Concern about effects on the poor should be dealt with through refundable credits, not by exempting items such as food for everyone, rich and poor alike. Creating exemptions for everyone would result in either reduced revenue or higher tax rates. What is needed is a targeted assistance program for low-income taxpayers.

The current reform has many laudable features besides lower marginal tax rates, a broader personal tax base, and equalization of tax rates across types of investment (this latter only partially achieved). These positive features include elimination of 6 million poor people from the tax rolls, some tax simplification for other low- and middle-income taxpayers who will no longer have to itemize their deductions, and perhaps the most important effect, if indeed it does occurs: making taxpayers feel the system is fairer. The tax system was badly in need of a restoration of citizen confidence. While many persons and corporations who paid little or no taxes in a given year under the previous tax laws will continue to do so under the new tax law, there will be fewer complaints that the typical individual paid more in taxes than certain corporations, which managed to pay none. Though before, personal taxes were probably paid on dividends from these corporations, and in addition, these corporations may have paid no taxes because they carried forward substantial losses from previous years, we still will benefit from a less strident attack on our tax system. Perhaps the Internal Revenue Service was overly concerned that tax cheating and evasion were becoming so pervasive that it would have a difficult time collecting the revenue, but some of that concern was valid. However, I believe that in attempting to ameliorate these problems, we have gone too far with the alternative minimum tax, the full taxation of nominal capital gains at ordinary rates, and a variety of other features. I think these will cost the economy much more than they are worth, and I hope some balance can be restored in the not-too-distant future.

The capital gains tax differential may have been a very effective device to generate funds for risk-taking in the economy, but it also was part of the archetypical structure of abusive tax shelters set up to depreciate an asset more rapidly than its value really declined; the asset was then sold, and capital gains taxes were paid only on the difference. Often, these tax advantages were leveraged with various multiples. As these became blatantly advertised in the media, it is clear that some action had to be taken. Confidence in the tax system was eroding on the one hand, and scarce investment resources were being misallocated on the other. In the long-run the economy will benefit from a more efficient allocation of capital stock based on fundamental economic returns, rather than tax consider-ations. But we need to avoid major damage to the economy in the course of doing so, and this will require us to consider saving and investment incentives in the near future.

Finally, the research and development tax credit appears to be one item that survived the axe. Generally, neutrality ought to be the standard in tax policy: one investment ought not to be subsidized at the expense of another, such as equipment at the expense of structures, or industry X at the expense of industry Y, as has been the case under previous tax laws. But a substantial amount of statistical study by economists suggests that the returns to society from research and development may dramati-cally exceed the return appropriable by the individual entrepreneur or firm. In fact, estimates suggest that the value *returned* to society may be many times whatever personal or corporate fortune is obtained. Under the tax reform plan, the R&D tax credit is to be continued only through December 31, 1988, rather than made permanent, and eligibility has been tightened to insure it is targeted at activities likely to generate public returns. The research and development tax credit should be kept: it is one of the few activities for which a strict taxation neutrality standard would not be in society's best interests.

Summary

The new tax rules contain both desirable and undesirable features. Taken as a whole, I think the new law, *plus the possibility of improving it,* is probably preferable to the old tax law. The new tax law and the consid-erable uncertainty it has generated already have caused some damage to the economy, and there may be some deleterious consequences to invest-ment and saving in the future. These will be partly offset by other desira-ble features, such as lower marginal tax rates. The final impact of the 1986 tax reforms will depend on subsequent tax reforms, how the deficit is han-dled so as to avoid pressure to raise rates substantially, and whether tax rules can be stabilized for a span of years. Each of these factors is uncer-tain at this time, but I am cautiously optimistic that common sense and good economics will eventually move us toward a more stable tax system that keeps most of the benefits of lower marginal tax rates while broaden-ing the tax base on personal consumption items and restoring some saving and investment incentives that were removed in this round of reform. These things will not happen all at once, but will unfold over a span of years, as directed by the vicissitudes of the economy's performance and by our political capabilities. Recall, despite the myth that President Reagan has refused to allow any tax increases since his original tax cuts, that we had tax increases in 1982, 1983, and 1984. The mix of deficit reduction between spending cuts and revenue increases may differ pre- and post-Reagan, but it is important to recognize, in evaluating the pressure deficits will place on revenue versus spending changes for the next two years, that President Reagan went along with three tax increases in his first term.

◆ *Chapter 9* ◆

Do Deficits Matter?

When Ronald Reagan assumed office in January 1981, the national debt was under $1 trillion. Today it exceeds $2 trillion, and even if the 1985 balanced budget act succeeds in producing a balanced budget by 1991, more than one-half trillion dollars will be added to this total. Such numbers are often cited by critics of the President. Indeed, taken at face value, they are staggering. Who would have imagined when Ronald Reagan assumed office that the national debt would almost triple and budget deficits would run $200 billion a year—5 percent of GNP—for many years in a row?

Supporters of the President find another way to look at these same numbers. The increase in the national debt is partly a product of inflation, and must also be understood relative to the size of the economy. With respect to GNP, the national debt has increased from about 33 percent of GNP to a little over 40 percent. If the balanced budget act is successful, the ratio of national debt to GNP will first stabilize and eventually decrease. To place these numbers in perspective, the national debt was more than 100 percent of GNP at the end of World War II, and declined steadily to a postwar low of 23 percent in 1974 before it started to climb again. Those who believe that deficits and debt, at least at this level of magnitude, are much less pernicious than is commonly argued, feel that an increase of 7 or 8 percentage points in the ratio of debt to GNP for a few years is really not an issue at all.

The truth is that a long stream of large deficits and the buildup of the national debt relative to GNP do cause some substantial problems, but both are blamed for far too much. Their impact often is more subtle and less severe than the press hysteria would suggest. No doubt it took a popular conservative Republican president with a strong sense of budgetary and tax priorities to get away with such large deficits and buildup of the national debt. It also took some remarkable changes in the economy, including substantial inflows of capital from abroad, to offset, at least in the short-term, the potentially severe impacts of the fiscal deficits.

The relationship between the federal budget deficit and other economic variables has sparked a tremendous debate. Depending on the school of thought, it was argued that deficits (1) are inflationary, (2) helped the recovery from recession, (3) shift the composition of output away from investment and net exports, (4) raise interest rates, or (5) do not matter. Obviously, all of these arguments cannot be true simultaneously. Since it is clear that the federal government has run very large deficits recently and, despite Gramm-Rudman-Hollings, may do so for the foreseeable future, it is important to understand the true impact of large deficits. All of the above arguments may have some truth to them, depending on the circumstances. Are deficits so serious that something needs to be done about them *soon*? Is the Gramm-Rudman-Hollings Balanced Budget Act a sensible solution to large deficits? The question of whether deficits matter is really several questions rolled into one: first, which economic variables do deficits affect? Interest rates? The inflation rate? Real GNP? Or the composition of output? Second, under what economic conditions do deficits have these effects? Third, what is the mechanism by which deficits affect the economy? Is it through an impact on interest rates? Exchange rates? Disposable income? Inflation expectations? Or the behavior of the Federal Reserve? Fourth, does the *source* of the deficit (increased spending or decreased revenues) make any difference? Fifth, what are the likely magnitudes of these effects? And finally, does it matter whether they are dealt with on the spending or the tax side? An exhaustive review of the role of budget deficits in the economy is beyond the scope of this book, but these questions provide a framework for analyzing several key aspects of the relationship between deficits and the economy.

When Do Deficits Matter?

When the economy is at substantially less than full employment, a tax cut or spending increase can produce *some* stimulus in aggregate demand and income, as indicated in Chapter 3. However, this effect is much less than traditional textbook Keynesian models predict, for several reasons. The most important of these is that the economy is much more open to both trade and capital flows than the textbook models describe. This severely limits the possibility of substantial fiscal stimulus. A deficit may produce a slight rise in interest rates, attract foreign capital, appreciate the dollar, curtail exports, and stimulate imports. An example of the importance of this effect the 1981–82 recession, when 47 percent of the decline in real GNP was in net exports. The potential effect of deficits on interest rates may also be slightly offset by increased private saving. The rise in interest rates, if sustained over a long period of time, should increase saving. Statistical results indicate that this effect will be important, but neither large enough nor rapid enough to offset the direct dissaving induced by the deficit.[1]

At full employment, a continuing substantial deficit *eventually* leads to monetization of the debt by the Federal Reserve and to acceleration of inflation. This occurs because there is a limit to the amount of government bonds the private sector and the rest of the world are willing to hold. Eventually, even the dollar holdings of foreigners will reach a saturation point: deficits cannot be financed abroad forever. There are only two alternatives: (1) the Fed buys the bonds, re-igniting inflation, or (2) we change our fiscal policy. However, to guarantee an inflationary outcome would require substantial deficits run over *many* years. There is no necessary short-term relationship between deficits and inflation whether through monetization by the Federal Reserve or otherwise (in the high inflation of the late 1970s, the Fed monetized very little of the deficit). Moreover, there is not much evidence at this time that deficits will inevitably lead to inflation in the next year or two.

While the empirical evidence is hardly overwhelming, it is very likely that large deficits do contribute to high interest rates, both directly through government borrowing in credit markets, and indirectly through uncertainty over their likely economic effects. Since economists cannot agree about deficits, one cannot expect private investors to think the outcomes are certain. Some economists claim business investment is crowded out dollar for dollar with the deficit. This is overstating the case dramatically. First, as shown by the recent foreign capital inflow, interest rate increases attract foreign capital, which both limits further interest rate increases and supplies additional capital for investment. Second, it is not only business investment which is competing for capital, but also state and local governments and residential construction. A more plausible estimate is that crowding out is roughly two-thirds or three-quarters of a dollar for each dollar of the deficit, and no more than fifty cents per dollar comes at the expense of business investment.[2] Finally, we should distinguish the effect of the U.S. federal deficit on interest rates from the *combined* fiscal deficits of *all* government units in the United States and the fiscal deficits of the other advanced countries. The combined U.S. fiscal deficit, including the state and local government *surplus*, is *matched* by a corresponding aggregate fiscal deficit in the United Kingdom, Italy, France, Japan, and Germany combined. Thus, the economic effects of a change in the U.S. fiscal deficit, say, by one percentage point of GNP, is substantially less than if all these governments simultaneously reduced or increased their deficit by one percentage point of their respective GNP.

Thus, deficits *do* matter, but the economic background is an important consideration in determining how *much* they matter. They can have a modest stimulative impact on the economy, and will twist somewhat the composition of output. At full employment, large deficits eventually will be inflationary. However, the commonly accepted "wisdom" on the debt *overstates* either the magnitude or timing of all these effects. The effects can be, and often are, important, but the hysteria of recent years was perhaps uncalled for, except for a brief period, discussed below. A careful sorting of the evidence is mandatory to solve the current deficit dilemma in a manner that will promote relatively stable prices, full employment, and rising productivity.

Measurement and Forecast of Deficits and the National Debt

It is important to realize that measuring, let alone forecasting, deficits and debt is no easy task. Large numbers of items are excluded by law from the federal budget, and various federal government accounting procedures are not consistent with the general notion of accrual accounting, separate capital and current services accounting, nor adjusting from par to market valuations.[3] For example, when we had a large defense build-down under President Carter, it was partially disguised by the fact that new investment in military hardware was falling far short of the depreciation and obsolescence of the existing capital stock. Also, in 1980 the $59 billion nominal federal deficit was offset by a still larger decline in the inflation-adjusted value of the previously issued national debt held by the public. Further, the combined state and local government sector of the United States often runs a substantial surplus. It is not my intention to

TABLE 9-1a   **CBO Budget Projections-Baseline**[a]
(by fiscal year), 8/84

	1983 actual	1984 base	1985	1986	1987	1988	1989
Total Deficit[b], $billions	208	183	191	209	231	254	278
Deficit as % of GNP	6.4	5.1	4.9	4.9	5.0	5.1	5.2
Debt Held by Public as % of GNP	35.4	36.4	38.1	40.2	42.1	44.1	46.0

[a]Assumes no change in laws governing taxes or entitlement spending.
[b]Includes off budget deficit of $15 billion or 0.3% of GNP per year.

Source: U.S. Congressional Budget Office, *The Economic and Budget Outlook*, 8/84.

TABLE 9-1b   **CBO Baseline Projections** (by fiscal year), as of 1/87

	1986 Actual	1987 Base	1988	1989	1990	1991	1992
			Projections				
Deficit in $billions	221	174	169	162	134	109	85
Deficit as % of GNP	5.3	4.0	3.6	3.2	2.5	1.9	1.4
Debt Held by the Public as % of GNP	41.9	43.4	44.2	44.4	43.8	42.7	41.3

Source: U.S. Congressional Budget Office, *The Economic and Budget Outlook*, 1/87.

go through a complete reworking of federal accounting concepts here. Suffice it to say that care must be taken in interpreting even historical deficit figures, let alone in forecasting future ones.

With this in mind, let us consider the Congressional Budget Office's estimates, made in 1984, of deficits for the succeeding few years, shown in Table 1. When presenting its budget to Congress and the CBO, the Administration is also required to present budget forecasts for the following five years. While budget forecasts are both difficult to make with precision and subject to political manipulation,[4] it is clear from these estimates that for the first time in post-World War II history, the United States entered a period of substantial budget deficits as compared to a fraction of Gross National Product. These deficits are now projected to decline, but as I show below, *they were large enough under the circumstances to lead to potentially severe economic problems.*

Previously, whenever substantial budget deficits occurred, circumstances had usually changed and eliminated them. Large deficits were usually associated with wars or recessions, and vanished quickly thereafter. However, in the 1980s for the first time we faced sustained large deficits that were not automatically vanishing with an economic recovery. Unless there is a sustained period of much more rapid economic growth than is prudent to forecast at this time, or unless fiscal policy is changed either to reduce spending or to raise revenue, large deficits will persist. The Gramm-Rudman-Hollings Balanced Budget Act creates pressure to reduce deficits gradually until the budget is balanced in 1991, but either major programmatic cuts, which Congress has thus far been loathe to make (other than in defense), or tax increases, which the President resists, will be required to reduce deficits any further.

The 1983–84 CBO estimates showed deficits rising both in terms of dollars and as a percentage of GNP through 1989. The Administration estimates showed a downward trend to one-half the 1989 CBO estimate, but most of the difference rested on an Administration forecast of interest rates falling to 5 percent, which was much lower than the CBO forecast. Deficits were forecasted to run about 5 percent of GNP, which is also about the same size as the net private saving pool (to be discussed below). Deficits of this magnitude are not uncommon. As noted above, the federal government of the United States has run deficits of this size in the depths of recessions (for example, the one in 1975), and of much larger size in wartime. Many other countries have run deficits of this magnitude or larger, relative to the size of their economy, and some important economies are running larger deficits today, relative to their economy.

What is unique about the current large U.S. deficits is that they were expected to continue, despite a strong recovery, and that the ratio of the national debt to GNP was expected to rise substantially. The CBO estimated that this ratio would increase by more than one-third over the succeeding few years, under the policies in place in 1984. The most important characteristic of these deficits is undoubtedly their huge absolute size, because even if relatively precise estimates of the economic impact of smaller deficits could be made, it would not necessarily be wise to extrapo-

TABLE 9-2   Decomposing the Projected Deficit Into Policy Changes

	1985	1989
Budget deficit 1981 Policy continued % of GNP	2.1	-0.2
Tax cuts (net)	3.0	3.8
Defense Buildup	0.9	1.4
Nondefense spnd. cuts	-1.4	-1.5
Interest rate	0.5	1.7
Current Projection	4.9	5.2

Source: Estimated from CBO, August, 1984, op. cit.

late from these estimates the effects of much larger deficits.

Will large deficits continue indefinitely, or will Gramm-Rudman-Hollings alleviate the problems? Will the debt leave a tremendous burden for our children and grandchildren? The answers to these questions depend in part upon fiscal policies yet to be undertaken, and upon the performance of the economy over the years ahead. My own opinion is that the deficits and the ratio of debt to GNP are likely to remain a potential problem for some time, but the effects won't be as bad as some short-term predictions suggest. My colleague Robert Hall has extrapolated revenues, outlays, and deficits beyond the standard 1989 time horizon.[5] He found that, given predicted spending and taxes, the deficits and the ratio of the debt to GNP will eventually shrink. However, deficits of this size cannot continue *indefinitely* without rekindling inflation.

Causes of the Deficits

How did we get deficits of this size? The proximate "causes" are portrayed in Table 2. Simply put, spending has gone up somewhat and taxes have gone down substantially under President Reagan. Very high real interest rates and the cumulative effect of continuing large deficits mean larger interest costs on the debt. Thus, if one considers the deficits projected for 1989 as of 1984, the pre-Reagan policies with 3 percent real defense growth and no tax cut would have led to a balanced budget by about 1989 under the usual economic assumptions. The defense spending increase was almost offset by the non-defense, non-interest spending decrease, but interest payments on the national debt and the tax cuts combined to raise the budget deficit to about 5 percent of GNP for several years, which was predicted to continue. The recent two-year halt of the defense buildup plus the decline in interest rates reverse this trend if extrapolated, as by the CBO (see the second panel of Table 1). Thus, under these assumptions the deficits and debt/GNP ratio will fall rather than rise for the next few years. While still a problem, outright runaway budget deficits and public debt growth now appear to have been forestalled.

Two further points deserve mention. First, it is alleged by some that President Reagan is to blame for the deficits because of the large tax cuts and his subsequent refusal to raise taxes. This is inaccurate. We had tax increases in 1982, 1983, and 1984; we almost certainly will have one — probably in excise taxes — in 1987. Others blame Congress for refusing to cut spending growth. They have done so — modestly in domestic programs and substantially (the last two years) in defense. Second, there was nothing magical about the 1980 level or composition of government spending. Explaining the deficits as the difference between what spending and taxes would have been if previous policies had been maintained begs the question of whether they should have been maintained. Further, about 40 percent of the reduction in income tax revenues in the early 1980s was due to the successful reduction in inflation. Prior to 1985, the tax system was not indexed for inflation, so much lower inflation meant much lower tax revenues. The Administration *and* Congress might be faulted for not having a contingency plan (except the short-lived contingency tax plan of Martin Feldstein and the *original* budget and tax *plans* of Congressman James Jones that tied the third year of the tax cut to achieving spending cuts) in the event the disinflation's success was achieved rapidly, but should not be faulted for the disinflation itself.

Throughout the debate over the deficits, numerous government officials have done something about them — the Senate Republicans, led by Majority Leader Howard H. Baker, Jr., Finance Committee Chairman Bob Dole, and Budget Committee Chairman Pete Domenici, pushed several deficit reduction packages, including spending cuts and revenue raisers. This indicates that deficit reduction was not a partisan battle between President Reagan and Congressional Democrats. Many government officials, in both parties in both houses of Congress and the Administration, compromised in order to make even small reductions in projected deficits. As the deficit problems emerged, a bipartisan budget appeal led by eminent former cabinet officials such as former Treasury Secretary William Simon and Commerce Secretary Peter Peterson called for a three way compromise: one-third consumption tax increase, one-third cuts in defense, and one-third cuts in entitlement programs. In practice, a partial, but incomplete, echo of these suggestions emerged: various excise tax increases (with probably more to come), a halt to the defense buildup, and minor domestic spending changes.

Can we conclude that we were overspending? Or were we undertaxing? If the tax cuts had not occurred, would spending have grown even more rapidly? The answers to such questions depend on one's political beliefs. The deficit is projected to continue for the foreseeable future, and it may ultimately cause substantial harm to the economy, though how much harm is difficult to estimate. Chapter 6 showed that the deficit aided, but unbalanced, the recovery. The sharp decline in our trade balance is certainly due in part to these deficits (see Figure 1). To decide whether we should spend less or tax more requires us to evaluate all of the government spending programs in relation to what we would have to forego in order to finance them: namely, private consumption and investment. In Chapter 7, I show that there was substantial room for decoupling of middle class entitlements from transfer payments to the poor, and eliminating a myriad of government programs that do not serve any particular general social purpose. It follows that substantial saving could and should be made on the spending side, and while the need to cut spending may be made more acute by the specter of such large deficits, we should do so whether or not deficits are a problem.

A deficit is the difference between spending and taxes; thus, a deficit could be created either by keeping the level of government spending constant and cutting taxes, or by raising government spending and not increasing taxes. These two policies could lead to the same deficits, but to very different economic outcomes. Furthermore, the economic impact of deficits is greatly affected by the *kind* of taxing or spending. For example, one concern is that deficits eventually may crowd out private investment. If this happens, it would be silly to have an anti-investment, structural tax increase in order to reduce the deficit and eliminate the potential problem with investment. Likewise, if the federal government is investing enormous sums with borrowed funds, this liability cannot be considered unfair to future generations if they will be the ones enjoying the proceeds from this investment. The potential economic effects of large

FIGURE 9-1   Comparison of CBO Projected Budget Deficit and
              Multilateral Trade-Weighted Value of the U.S. Dollar

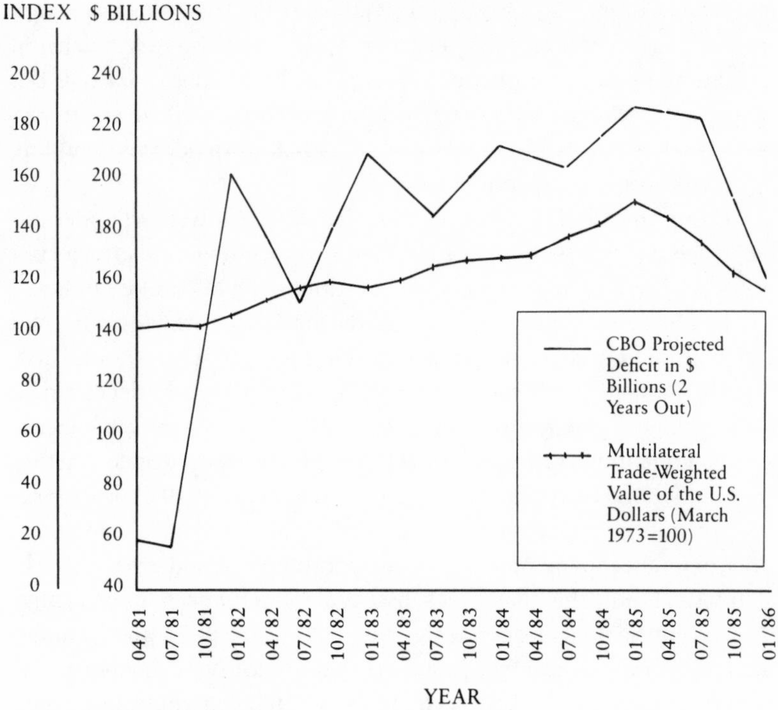

Source: Congressional Budget Office, Economic Outlook, various issues

deficits must be examined very carefully to decide whether to cut spending, raise taxes, do both or neither, or rely on Gramm-Rudman-Hollings
as a contingency plan, in the event that fiscal policy changes and economic
growth do not slow down the deficits.

Deficits, Recessions, and Recovery

Previously, the standard textbook model in macroeconomics held that
a tax cut or a government spending increase would lead to a still-larger
increase in national income via the so-called multiplier effect. Either the
extra government spending or the extra private spending from a tax cut

would work its way through the economy with a large fraction being continually respent, until the ultimate impact was much larger than the original change in government spending or taxes. It was even supposed that a balanced budget fiscal operation of equal spending increases and tax increases would still expand GNP, because the multiplier for spending would exceed the multiplier for taxes by one. Those trained in the neo-Keynesian orthodoxy tend to give substantial credit for the recovery to the stimulation of aggregate *demand* by the Reagan tax cuts and the defense buildup.

It is important to distinguish between the potential impact on aggregate demand of an unexpected increase in government spending, and of the impact of tax cuts for constant levels of government spending. If the deficit is increased because of an increase in government spending above its expected levels, it will cause GNP to expand. The extent to which GNP will expand depends upon a variety of factors, but if the increase in the deficit causes a slight rise in interest rates, interest-sensitive activities such as private investment and especially net exports may be curtailed, partly offsetting the expansionary effects of the government spending increase.

The effects of a tax cut for a *given* level of government spending are less likely to be expansionary. Besides the offsetting interest rate effects just mentioned, it is also possible that private saving will increase *pari passu* with increased government borrowing, as proposed by Barro.[6] As discussed in Chapter 3, the increased deficit financing implies future taxes of the same present value as the tax cuts. Thus, the private sector may save more in anticipation of having to pay these higher taxes later, and undo the government's attempt to reallocate spending over time. I believe that there is some truth to the Barro offset effect, but the evidence in support of it is quite mixed. Has a $200 billion annual increase in saving offset the deficit? The answer to that question in the usual measure of saving is definitely no. However, there have been substantial increases in asset values in the stock market, and this may explain why there has not been a greater increase in private saving. I believe a judicious interpretation of the Barro effect is that it probably does exist, but it is nowhere near dollar for dollar, and therefore, tax cuts for a given level of government spending are expansionary, though not as much as commonly believed.

So far I have focused on the income effects of the tax cuts. As discussed in Chapters 3 and 8, the relative price effects of the tax cuts can also be important when they alter the incentives to work or consume lei-

sure, or to invest or consume. I attribute some part of the recovery to the
Reagan tax cuts and the structural change in tax policy that led to greater
incentives to work, save, and invest,[7] and some to the defense buildup,
but I believe the primary cause of the expansion was the looser monetary
policy pursued by the Federal Reserve following a very tight monetary
policy in the period of disinflation, as shown in Chapter 6. Thus, a pro-
deficit policy is somewhat expansionary, but this is likely to be muted by
both increased private saving and a slight increase in interest rates, which
cause an offset in interest-sensitive spending such as net exports and investment. It seems that fiscal policy is likely to be less effective than monetary policy in causing swings in nominal GNP, and certainly does not offer
much hope for fine-tuning the economy and dampening the amplitude
of economic fluctuations.

In addition, it should be noted that there is another direction of
causality: not only can the economy go from deficits to recessions, but
also from recessions to deficits. In an economic slowdown, revenues fall
and social spending increases, thereby increasing the deficit. While this
cyclical component of the deficit is likely to disappear when the economy recovers, the additional deficits that occur when real interest rates
are high will leave us with a larger interest burden in the future. This point
is important to remember when discussing the course of likely economic
policy and the budget deficits over the next few years. The forecast assumes
a modest real average growth rate and no recession. While I do not believe
that a severe recession is in the offing, a substantial slowdown could easily add $50 billion or more to the deficit in any year.

Finally, it must be repeated that fiscal and monetary policy interact
with one another. Large deficits may reduce the capacity of the Fed to
be expansionary without accelerating inflation. As discussed in Chapter
6, some economists argued that a looser monetary policy could have been
combined with smaller deficits to reduce the severity of the recession. But
as already indicated, I doubt these analyses correctly model inflationary
expectations, and therefore I believe that inflation would *not* have been
reduced any more with the combinations of fiscal and monetary policy
proposed in the Urban Institute simulations, for example.[8]

Deficits and Inflation

The notion that fiscal deficits lead to inflation has a long and interesting
history. The common belief that it is wise for an individual not to spend

more money than he or she earns has engendered the idea that if the federal government spends more than it takes in, prices will inevitably rise.
As the economy expands close to full employment of capital and labor,
the argument goes, the deficits threaten to re-ignite inflationary pressure.
The Keynesian argument outlined in Chapter 3 posits that an excess
aggregate demand will increase nominal GNP, and with no room for output of goods and services to expand, the full rise in nominal GNP (or
close to it) will occur in prices. An alternative scenario, which is not necessarily mutually exclusive with the first, is that the federal government's
large borrowing demand (well over half of private saving and one dollar
in every five of government spending), when added to growing private
demand during recovery (recall that investment demand was depressed
in the 1981–82 recession due to idle capacity and meager prospects for
selling increased output), will drive up interest rates that equilibrate the
supply and demand for new capital. This in turn will put pressure on the
Federal Reserve to abandon its disinflationary monetary policy in an effort
to bring interest rates down. Further, large fiscal deficits are associated
with massive imports of foreign capital that contribute to the overvalued
dollar. The return of the dollar to purchasing power parity would signal
a sharp rise in prices in about a year.

How much truth is there in these arguments? At *full employment*,
massive deficits *ultimately* lead to inflation, because there is an *upper limit*
to the amount of government debt that private citizens and foreigners are
willing to hold. Consider a simple calculation: with the 1984 CBO projections of real growth and interest rates, a deficit (*net* of its interest component) of 3.0 percent of GNP, continued indefinitely, would ultimately give
rise to a ratio of the national debt to GNP of about 6 to 8.[9] This would
occur over a span of many decades. But such an inexorable rise must take
into account that the current ratio of the value of all capital in the United
States to GNP is only 3. Therefore, either the U.S. private sector must
accumulate two to three times as much wealth relative to its income as
it currently does, or a corresponding additional amount of Treasury bills
would have to be sold abroad. The Treasury can certainly sell a substantial amount of its bonds to foreigners, but ultimately even they will limit
the amount of their investment in dollar-denominated securities, because
ultimately the risk of having a progressively higher fraction of their assets
denominated in dollars becomes too large compared to the potential
return. When a foreign firm or individual contemplates moving from 10
to 15 percent of its assets in dollar-denominated securities, there is not
much incremental risk. But 50 or 70 percent implies a massive depen-

dence on events in the United States. At that point, only two things are
likely to occur: either the Federal Reserve will buy up the bonds and mone-
tize the debt, unleashing a growth of money supply which will accelerate
inflation, or the fiscal policies that produced such large deficits will be
abandoned. Perhaps Gramm-Rudman presages this.

None of this, however, suggests that the debt necessarily has a short-
term impact on inflation, or that the threat of continuing deficits over a
few years should radically affect current behavior. Indeed, I believe that
there is still time to get the deficits under control without re-igniting inflation, since the combination of state and local government surplus and
net foreign capital imports is likely to continue for some time. Thomas
Sargent has developed a telling argument pinning the blame for hyper-
inflations in Europe and their subsequent rapid elimination, on fiscal
imbalances.[10] In effect, inflation eventually became the primary vehicle
for transferring resources from the private sector to the government, and
once unleashed, the spiral continued to worsen progressively until it came
to an abrupt halt when a fiscal harness was imposed.

Most economists would lay the blame for the original acceleration
of inflation in the late 1960s to President Johnson's attempt to finance
the war on poverty and the Vietnam war simultaneously without a tax
increase. The resulting deficits pushed aggregate demand still further
beyond productive capacity and drove up prices. An accommodating
monetary policy helped as well. But it is much less obvious that the episodes of inflationary acceleration experienced in the 1970s were due to
contemporaneous fiscal events or monetization by the Federal Reserve.
For example, I have already noted that the Federal Reserve monetized only
a small fraction of the government debt in the 1970s (less than 10 percent). Thus, the simple and appealing explanation is not factually correct. The proximate cause of the acceleration of inflation appears to be
episodes of rapid expansion of the supply of money by the Federal Reserve
shortly before the inflationary episode. This led to a cycle of inflationary
expectations, with the Fed pressured to pump up the economy at any sign
of a slowdown. No brake was put on inflationary expectations until the
1981–82 recession and the Reagan support of disinflation.

Thus, my interpretation is that while various factors—such as the
energy price shocks, the ill-fated attempt at wage and price controls, the
undervalued dollar of the late 1970s, and the fiscal deficits—all contributed to the burst of inflation, but the predominant cause was the rapid
and fluctuating expansion of the money supply by the Federal Reserve.
It was not merely because the Fed became the buyer of last resort of gov-

ernment bonds, as the small amount of monetized debt indicates but because as shown in Chapters 2 and 3, the tax rules in an inflationary environment caused the Fed to underestimate how expansionary its monetary policy had become.

If large deficits are run over a long span of time in a relatively full-employment economy, they ultimately lead to inflation, and may have some modest feedback to inflationary expectations if they are anticipated to continue for the foreseeable future. Therefore, are the current or projected deficits likely to lead to a sharp resurgence of inflation? As indicated in Chapter 6, inflation is certainly not under control at this point. It has been cut to one-third of its previous double-digit levels, but it is still running at close to the level that caused President Nixon to impose wage and price controls. There remains the danger of a temporary acceleration, due to the recent rapid depreciation of the dollar. It is too easy to forget how much inflation can disrupt the economy.

The important point is that there is time before the economy reaches full employment. The funds from the state and local government sector and net foreign capital imports give us a respite, and this may enable us to get the deficits back within an economic safety zone. In Chapter 7, I give reasons why I think this should be done mostly on the spending side of the budget, both for macro- and micro-economic reasons. There are many programs that could be cut or eliminated, and if we show the courage to control the deficit by cutting spending, rather than passively raising taxes, it would send a better signal to financial markets about how future fiscal imbalances would be dealt with, such as the impending fiscal crisis in Medicare.

Thus, I believe that something should be done about the deficits, but not because we face a sharp acceleration of inflation in the near future. There is simply no evidence to support panic claims to this effect. However, we *cannot* rely indefinitely either on state and local governments to run large surpluses,[11] or on large net imports of foreign capital to finance the federal fiscal deficits. No one can predict exactly when the latter will slow, but as the investment incentives from the 1981 tax act wane, and real U.S. interest rates slowly fall relative to the rest of the world, it is clear that the incentive to move capital into the United States, or keep it here, will gradually decrease. We need to gradually reduce our fiscal imbalance by a prudent long-term policy that will stabilize the potential explosive growth of interest payments on the debt and thus of the debt itself. Such a policy will avoid long-term inflationary pressures and other harmful effects of chronic deficits, without risking short-term problems.

Deficits and the Composition of Output

While a pro-deficit policy may be slightly expansionary during a recession, and ultimately may rekindle inflation, as the economy gets close to full employment the most likely impact of deficit finance—as opposed to tax finance—is a rise in interest rates, which will crowd out interest-sensitive activities such as investment and net exports. The traditional argument is shown in panel A of Figure 2, where the additional demand for capital made by government borrowing drives up the total demand for capital to D_T, which in turn drives up interest rates from i_0 to i_1. This picture is true for a closed economy, but ignores foreign capital imports, and has a supply of capital curve that responds slightly to increases in interest rates, allowing for some additional private saving but not enough to finance the deficit itself. In this framework, the question is to what extent interest-sensitive activities would be curtailed.

One must consider the interest elasticities of the demand for investment, residential construction, state and local government capital expenditures, and the interest sensitivity of export and imports. Each of these categories appears to be quite sensitive to interest rates, other things being constant (such as inflationary expectations and the level of real economic activity). Thus, a substantial tax cut and shift to deficit finance could lead to an increase in consumer spending, and in the traditional analysis, would shift the composition of output to less investment and net exports. This simple analysis in a closed economy setting has led many economists and policymakers to conclude that the recovery must be unbalanced, and the deficits responsible for the very high real interest rates. While these have been falling recently, they are still quite high, averaging 3 to 4 percent, double the historic average. Longer-term securities are yielding several percentage points more, but the difference is due to extra risk and the expectations of higher inflation in the future.

Certainly, high real interest rates in the United States contributed to the sharp overvaluation of the dollar prior to 1985 (about 25 to 30 percent on a trade-weighted basis) and caused a substantial increase in the foreign trade deficit, which ran over $100 billion per year and ballooned still further in 1986. While this partly reflected the stronger and more rapid recovery of the U.S. economy and thus the proclivity to purchase imports, it also heavily reflected the price disadvantage of the overvalued dollar, making our exports more expensive and our imports less expensive than their competitors. Private domestic investment, however, rebounded more rapidly than in typical postwar recoveries, as documented in Chapter 8. This is largely because the investment incentives in ERTA offset the effects

FIGURE 9-2   Government Borrowing and Interest Rates in Closed
and Open Economies

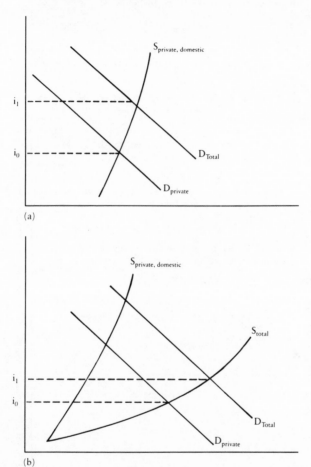

(a)

(b)

of high real interest rates. Thus, for a while, the effective cost of acquir-
ing new capital—while driven up by higher real interest rates—was actually slightly lower than several years ago.

However, what is more important is that real interest rates have not
risen, they have actually fallen, although much less than nominal interest rates. Nominal interest rates dropped from over 20 percent to the 5.5
to 10 percent range, whereas real interest rates fell from 10 percent to 3

TABLE 9-3 U.S. Net Saving and Investment, 1951–86

	1951–60	1961–70	1971–80	1981	1982	1983	1984	1985	1986
Total Net Saving	6.9%	7.5%	6.1%	5.2%	1.6%	1.8%	4.0%	3.1%	1.9%
Net Private Saving	7.2	8.0	7.1	6.1	5.4	5.9	7.4	6.5	5.4
Personal Saving	4.7	4.7	4.9	4.6	4.4	3.6	4.3	3.2	2.8
Corporate Saving	2.5	3.3	2.2	1.4	1.0	2.3	3.2	3.3	2.6
State-Local Govt. Surplus	-0.2	0.1	0.9	1.3	1.1	1.3	1.4	1.5	1.4
Federal Govt. Surplus	-0.2	-0.5	-1.9	-2.2	-4.8	-5.4	-4.8	-4.9	-4.9
Total Net Investment	7.0%	7.5%	6.3%	5.4%	1.6%	1.8%	3.8%	3.0%	2.1%
Net Foreign Investment	0.3	0.5	0.1	0.2	-0.2	-1.0	-2.6	-2.8	-3.4
Private Domestic Investment	6.7	7.0	6.2	5.2	1.8	2.9	6.4	5.8	5.5
Plant and Equipment	2.7	3.5	3.0	3.1	2.0	1.5	2.4	2.9	5.2
Residential Construction	3.2	2.5	2.5	1.3	0.6	1.8	2.4	2.4	
Inventory Accumulation	0.8	1.1	0.7	0.9	-0.9	-0.4	1.6	0.2	0.3
Memoranda: Capital Consumption	8.9%	8.5%	9.9%	11.2%	11.7%	11.4%	11.0%	11.0%	10.8%
Gross Private Saving	16.1	16.4	17.0	17.2	17.1	17.3	18.4	17.5	16.2

Notes: Data are averages (except for 1981–86) of annual flows, as percentages of gross national product.
Total net saving and total net investment differ by statistical discrepancy.
Detail may not add to totals because of rounding. 1986 figures are preliminary.
Source: U.S. Department of Commerce.

or 4 percent. Part of the reason why real interest rates have crept down and not reaccelerated, despite the very large and growing deficits, was the substantial inflow of foreign capital. Panel B of Figure 2 depicts an economy with international capital inflows and outflows. Just as the federal government demand for funds is added to the private sector demand for funds (D_p), so the potential flow of capital from abroad is added to the available net private saving. The flow of capital from abroad is very sensitive to interest rates, and therefore, the aggregate available short- to medium-term supply of saving is much more "elastic," i.e., the amount available is much more sensitive to interest rates. Following the above line of reasoning, the extra demand for funds from federal government borrowing drives up interest rates much less due to this elastic supply of funds from abroad. Were these funds to be quickly withdrawn, interest rates would rise rapidly, but there is no reason to believe that the flow of such funds will abate instantly. The net capital inflow is likely to continue for some time, but ultimately at a slower rate. When supply-side economics came on the scene, few were predicting that much of the supply would come from abroad.

Table 3 shows how the fiscal deficit of the federal government has largely been offset by state and local surplus and capital inflow from abroad. In the 1950s through the 1970s, net private saving averaged between 7 and 8 percent of GNP. This has fallen to 5 or 6 percent in the last few years. State and local governments that had run roughly balanced budgets in the 1950s and 1960s moved into surplus, beginning in the 1970s, and have more or less remained so ever since. The federal government, which more or less ran balanced budgets in the 1950s and 1960s, and averaged slightly under 2 percent of GNP for its deficit in the profligate 1970s, ran deficits for 1985 and 1986 of about 5 percent. This leaves us with net national saving—the sum of what the private sector saves, state and local governments save or borrow, and the federal government saves or borrows—at about half the levels of the 1950s through the 1970s.

If this were the end of the story, U.S. net investment would have fallen still further. While gross investment has rebounded, net investment still remains at historically low levels. Fortunately, one-third to more than one-half of it was being financed by a net capital inflow from abroad. The United States has changed from being a net exporter of capital in the 1950s and 1960s to a large net importer of capital in the last couple of years. This large *net* import of foreign capital has two salutary effects: it prevents interest rates from rising still further, and provides funds for badly needed domestic investment. Ultimately, of course, the returns to the investment by foreigners will be enjoyed abroad, and ultimately we will have to export more than we import by an amount sufficient to cover these (net) payments to foreign owners of our capital stock. Each year this huge flow of foreign capital continues increases the ultimate size of the adjustment. It would be better if the United States were generating its own private saving to finance this investment. Further, the fiscal deficit causes a fundamental imbalance between national saving and investment. Even as the dollar falls, we cannot expect the trade deficit—and foreign capital inflow—to abate totally until national saving is balanced with domestic investment.

It is instructive to trace through the numbers for 1986, as presented in Table 3. Net private saving was 5.4 percent of GNP. The state and local government surplus was 1.4 percent of GNP (although much of this is in state and local pension funds which are also accruing future liabilities). Thus, 6.8 percent of GNP would have been available for investment had the federal government run a balanced budget. But as the last column of Table 3 reveals, the federal government ran a deficit of 4.9 percent of GNP.[12] Thus, as a nation, we saved only 1.9 percent of GNP! Such low saving rates are not untypical at troughs of recessions, but are highly unusual in relatively prosperous times. While private saving is running about one percentage point or so below its norm, the big news in national saving is federal government borrowing. The federal government was borrowing almost as much as the private sector was saving!

Turning back to the figures for investment in 1986, we see that private domestic investment was 5.5 percent of GNP, 2.1 percent of which was financed by Americans and 3.4 percent of which was financed by borrowing from abroad.[13] For the first time, in 1986, more of our net investment was financed by foreigners than by Americans! Comparing the 5.5 percent private domestic investment to the 1.9 percent total net national saving, it is clear that the difference must be financed by investment from abroad. So long as we run such an imbalance between our national saving—the sum of what households, businesses, and federal and state and local governments save (net of their borrowing) and our domestic investment—we must finance the difference by importing foreign capital. In a society with a very low private saving rate and very modest rate of private domestic investment, it is clear that the federal government is seriously imbalancing our national saving and investment, thereby causing massive inflows of foreign capital and resulting in severe strains in the world's capital markets. Interestingly, the world's second largest economy, Japan, has the reverse phenomenon. Its saving rate substantially exceeds its investment rate, and even though its federal government is running a deficit, that is only decreasing its lending to the rest of the world. Further, the Japanese government is a large net investor because government investment including the Social Security surplus exceeds the budget deficit. That is, the Japanese are using their tax and borrowing revenue for different purposes than are we.

Finally, note that as long as we run deficits of this size, unless either our private saving rate increases substantially—which is unlikely in a short period—or our private domestic investment plummets—a national disaster—federal government borrowing will lead to massive inflows of foreign capital such as we have experienced for the last three years. This in turn creates further pressure on our economy. While in the short-run it helps keep interest rates down and finances our domestic investment, it is also generating inexorable pressure for a restructuring of our economy in the future. Each year that we import approximately $150 billion of capital increases the claims of foreigners on the returns to such an investment by the rate of the return times the $150 billion. Suppose, for example, that interest and dividend rates are about 10 percent. That means that in the future foreigners will receive a flow of $15 billion *annually* on each year's investment. If such inflows of foreign capital continue for another five years, cumulating to $750 billion, this would require, at the 10 percent rate of return, $75 billion per year thereafter of additional repatriation, immediately or eventually, of these earnings to foreigners. This will *require* that our exports exceed our imports by this amount each year! Adjusting our economy from a massive trade deficit to a trade balance will be a remarkable structural change, but each year that we import such large amounts of foreign capital will force us to become a larger and larger net exporter in the future, requiring the pendulum of large trade deficits to large trade surpluses to swing still further.

Thus, it is likely that in the short-run deficits pose only a small threat of increased interest rates, or of accelerating inflation, but in the long run continued net capital inflows and large state and local surpluses cannot be relied on to bail us out. We must get our fiscal house in order prior to a sharp slowdown of capital imports or loss of the state and local government surplus to avoid a sharp rise in interest rates. This in turn would put enormous pressure on the Federal Reserve to reaccelerate money growth and abandon its anti-inflation fight, and therefore, would not augur well for future inflation, investment, net exports, or productivity and growth. The potential for reacceleration of inflation is worsened because of the growing external debt—the net debtor status of the United

States. Inflation would reduce the real value of outstanding debt—including that held by foreigners. The larger our external debt, the greater the temptation to reinflate. The more apparent this incentive becomes, the greater the risk to foreign investors. Hence, upward pressure will be placed on interest rates.

Finally, I must reiterate that the effect of a deficit on the composition of output depends heavily on the nature of the spending and taxes whose difference comprises the deficit. The impact, for example, on productivity might differ substantially if the spending were on government investment, e.g. on roads or airports, than if it were on government consumption. Likewise, the *net* impact on private saving will be different if much of the deficit is financing interest payments to U.S. citizens who are likely to reinvest the interest than if it is on transfer payments to individuals with a low propensity to save. Thus, the "impact of the deficit" depends on the nature of the taxes and spending.

The Effects of Deficits on Interest Rates: Statistical Evidence

From the discussion above, it is clear that the potential effects of deficits on interest rates depend upon many factors. The effect of a change in *our* deficit on interest rates depends in part upon such things as the reaction of monetary and fiscal policy in the rest of the world and the time horizon being considered. It is not surprising, therefore, that statistical studies of the effect of deficits on interest rates come to a wide range of conclusions, depending upon such things as the sample period covered and the inclusion of other variables assumed to affect interest rates. It is worth noting, however, that a substantial number of recent studies update and improve the earlier work done by Martin Feldstein and Otto Eckstein, and conclude that increases in deficits do indeed lead to an increase in interest rates. A careful reworking of some of these studies by James Barth, et. al., concludes that a more careful specification of the deficit variable into its structural and cyclical components, and a variety of other adjustments, tend to reinforce these findings. It should be clear that such studies can only give us a rough idea of the average historical impacts, holding various measures of other impacts on interest rates constant, such as expected inflation.

Two somewhat less-direct avenues for examining the potential impact of deficits on interest rates are to examine their impact on the demand for money and on aggregate demand. Again, recent evidence suggests that increases in the federal debt do have a positive impact on the demand for money, and therefore are likely to lead to higher interest rates. Finally, the results of Robert Eisner and Paul Pieper, Feldstein, and myself suggest that deficits, particularly when adjusted for measurement problems such as those due to inflation, lead to an increase in aggregate demand and real GNP.[14] As I have mentioned earlier, there could be exceptions to this—for example, limits on the impact of a pro-deficit tax cut on real GNP—but nevertheless some fiscal stimulus still remains even after one has made all these adjustments. Further, it should be realized that the debt neutrality hypothesis assumes a given level of government spending. An increase in government expenditures is likely to raise total aggregate demand to a certain extent (to what extent depends upon the nature of monetary policy) and therefore also can affect interest rates. There are many ways by which deficits, government spending, and various forms of taxes can affect interest rates and the composition of GNP, as well as the level and growth rate of nominal GNP and its division into real and inflation components. However, Keynesian finetuners who dominated economic policymaking in the 1960s and 1970s undoubtedly overestimated the "bang-for-the-buck" that fiscal stimulus could achieve.

The likely effects of federal government deficits on the composition of GNP can be understood by examining the actual correlation between changes in the deficit and various components of GNP. Since the federal government deficit is simply the difference between federal government spending and taxes, it must equal the sum of private saving, net foreign capital inflows, and the state and local surplus or deficit, less domestic investment. Simply put, if the level of GNP is held constant, increases in the deficits must crowd out something. Will they lead to an increased private saving, increased foreign investment in the United States, changes in state and local surpluses, or decreases in domestic investment?

A provocative, but very rough study by Lawrence Summers suggests that budget deficits call forth increased private savings of about 30 cents per dollar of deficit.[15] This results from a combination of extra savings for future tax liabilities resulting from the deficits, the sensitivity of savings to higher real interest rates caused by deficits, and the crowding out of consumer durable expenditures due to higher interest rates. In addition, he estimates that deficits crowd out net exports by attracting foreign capital—in this case, about twenty-five cents on the dollar. He also estimates approximately a five-cent increase per dollar of deficit in state and local surpluses, and a forty-cent per dollar decrease in net investment.

Of course, the business net investment must be separated from residential investment, which is crowded out at about twenty cents on the dollar. I have obtained similar results, with slightly larger foreign capital effects.[16] These estimates are highly preliminary and subject to many statistical problems. They are discussed here merely to point out the fact that the deficit almost certainly does not crowd out business investment in plant and equipment dollar for dollar. The total crowding out of investment is likely to be much less, and business investment in plant and equipment will only be part of this. As noted above, the exact mix of what gets changed by the federal government deficit will depend not only on the size of the change in the deficit, but on the nature of the spending and taxes proposed.

Who Bears the Burden of the National Debt?

When the federal government increases its national debt, either directly by issuing traditional bonds or implicitly with large increases in promised Social Security benefits, who pays for it? One view is that since current resources are used for spending, deficits and taxes have an identical burden. Another, more plausible view is that the burden of the debt can be shifted onto future generations. The modern restatement of the first proposition by Barro is an important contribution, and lends some credence to the notion that the private sector will at least partially undo the intergenerational shifting of the burden of financing government spending implied by a shift from tax finance to debt finance. However, as noted above, my conclusion is that this effect is only very partially operative, that deficits eventually do matter, and that debt is not completely neutral.[17] Therefore, I believe there are two mechanisms by which the debt may be shifted to future generations: first, with constant interest rates, a larger debt will imply a larger interest cost, and therefore, a greater burden in financing that interest cost for the government in the future, which must be paid for by future taxes and/or new debt. Second, as mentioned above, deficits eventually crowd out some investment, and if this is the case, future generations will inherit a somewhat smaller capital stock and be somewhat less productive than they otherwise would have been. Thus, they will be doubly burdened: higher interest payments on a larger debt, and lower incomes with which to pay them.

However, it is important to examine the *nature* of the government spending and taxes, as well as the deficit. If the anti-investment qualities of the deficit are offset by direct government investment or by special tax incentives to encourage private investment, the deficit may come almost exclusively at the expense of current consumption, and hence, not be a burden for future generations. In addition, one must take into account that real incomes generally grow over time. Recall that from 1948 to 1973, real per capita income grew at about 2.5 percent per year, a rate sufficient to make each generation almost twice as wealthy as the one that preceded it. Further, recall that the growth slowdown in 1973–82 left a decade of almost no gains in productivity per worker. If the economy returns to anything like its historical rate of growth, successive generations will be much wealthier than we, and the ethics of leaving them some burden — such as the debt following the large defense buildup to counter the Soviet threat — seems to me much more defensible.

Quantitative estimates of these burdens are hard to come by. As noted, they are likely to be *much* smaller than figures based on the assumption that deficits crowd out private investment dollar for dollar. The crowding out is perhaps no more than half of this. If that is the case, it would take a very long time before this slightly lower rate of investment led to a much smaller capital stock and much lower productivity growth; it amounts to 10 or 20 percent over an entire generation. It is important that we understand these relative quantitative magnitudes when discussing the emotional issue of the burden of the debt, as their effects are important, both ethically and economically.

Summary of the Effects of the Deficits

The economic effects of deficits are important and complicated. Economists' inability to define precisely what happens to the economy for a given change in the amount of the deficit has led to a certain amount of nihilism by politicians and the public, which I believe is misplaced. While one cannot say precisely what the impact of the deficit is likely to be, I do believe a fair reading of the evidence suggests the following conclusions:

1. The stimulus to aggregate demand from a pro-deficit increase in government spending is more modest than is commonly believed, both because of the potential impact of interest rates on interest-sensitive activities and the induced effects on private saving and capital flows. However, the impact of increases in government spending is likely to be larger than those of tax cuts. Deficits of the magnitude we have seen in the 1980s — 5 percent of GNP —

substantially reduce the flexibility of fiscal policy during a recession, as raising the deficit from these levels is considered politically unacceptable. But fine tuning is not very desirable anyway, and monetary policy is likely to influence GNP more quickly and to be quicker to implement, if desired.

2. The fiscal stimulus must be understood in light of the components of spending and the nature of the incentives created in the taxes used to raise the bulk of the revenue, as well as in the light of U.S. domestic monetary policy and the monetary and fiscal policies being followed in the rest of the world.

3. Thus, an expansionary fiscal policy can help somewhat in eliminating a recessionary gap between potential and actual GNP, but the fiscal stimulus is also likely to be smaller and less effective than traditional Keynesian analyses suggest.

4. If continued indefinitely, large deficits might ultimately cause inflation if they were to require an eventual holding of debt much larger than the private sector is willing to hold, relative to its income. This could be the case if the deficit stays as large as it is now for decades to come. Of course, fiscal policy will be altered before that occurs; but if it did not, the result must eventually be a re-ignition of inflation. There is no reason why this should occur in the near future, and there should be no surprise that it has not occurred already.

5. The federal government's fiscal deficit is being offset largely by net imports of foreign capital (both foreign capital flowing into the United States and less U.S. capital flowing abroad) and the state and local governments surplus. These cannot be expected to continue to finance the deficit and take pressure off interest rates forever. But it is uncertain how rapidly such capital inflows are likely to slow. Because our private saving rate is so low, the federal borrowing drives national saving far below private domestic investment, thereby requiring imports of foreign capital. If our private saving rate were much larger, and exceeded our private investment rate, as is true, for example, in Japan, the large deficits would merely decrease our lending to foreigners.

6. Deficit finance, as opposed to tax finance, probably affects the composition of GNP substantially. It probably shifts the composition away from investment and net exports toward less interest-sensitive activities, such as consumption. Again, the exact effect on the composition of GNP depends on the nature of the spending and taxes,

as well as on the corresponding monetary policy and worldwide fiscal and monetary policies. As a very rough general guide, the amount of investment which is crowded out is about forty or fifty cents per dollar of deficit, at close to full employment, with the bulk of this—but certainly not all—coming at the expense of business investment in plant and equipment. The remainder is made up by increased private saving and foreign capital inflows.

While much work remains to be done to develop more precise estimates of the likely impacts of deficit finance, given the nature of taxes and spending and of monetary policy, the idea that deficits never matter and we need not ever worry about them is simple-minded. Those who saw the deficit as the cause of all the nation's economic ills, and the likely cause of any future economic malaise, are also overstating the problems. Deficits do matter sometimes under certain conditions. They can affect inflation, real GNP, and the composition of various components of real GNP. But these effects are subtle and depend on a variety of other factors. This should not provide an excuse for inaction, but should help us to place the deficit into some perspective. The current deficit dilemma is a cause for concern, not panic. President Reagan was right not to launch a major tax increase during the recession, despite calls to do so, and to combine it with a major monetary expansion before inflation had been reduced substantially. Over the next few years, a prudent and stable fiscal policy must be developed, a policy that can be maintained consistently. Gramm-Rudman-Hollings is a blunt instrument for doing so, but it is a start. Whether we shall have the political will to make real programmatic cuts—other than in defense—or to raise taxes remains to be seen.

Conclusion

The nation is at a fiscal impasse, but not a permanent one. The attempts of the last two years to reduce spending have focused exclusively on defense. Indeed, as noted in Chapter 7, real defense spending has not grown at all during this period. The projection of no real growth in defense spending is part of the reason why the Congressional Budget Office now believes the deficit is on a downward course, although a balanced budget will not be achieved soon unless a serious spending cut or tax increase—or both—are enacted. The fiscal dilemma revolves around three basic issues. First, should the budget be balanced? If not, what is the appropriate fiscal norm? The idea of balancing the budget, whether annually or over a longer period of time, e.g., running deficits during bad times and accruing surpluses in goods ones, is simple and easily understood. A more complicated fiscal policy rule, such as a cyclically adjusted, inflation-adjusted, balanced budget on current services account, with a separate capital account, makes an enormous amount of economic sense, but may be too complicated to understand, too difficult to implement, and too prone to manipulation. In any event, an improved budgetary process must take into account inflation adjustment, separate capital accounting, off-budget nondirect spending such as loan guarantees, and accruing liabilities in pension and insurance programs. Thus, in a world where these concepts were broadly understood by the general public, as well as by politicians, I would argue that we could live with a deficit-to-GNP ratio of about 2 percent, given current levels of government investment, inflation, and very modest economic growth.

Second, what should be done when there is a need for a temporary substantial increase in government spending? Traditionally, these increases have been deficit financed. The recent military buildup is essentially such an instance, and in many ways, deficits can be thought of as desirable, both in terms of equity and efficiency: equitable, because they spread the burden across more than just the current taxpayers; efficient, because they smooth out the tax rate over time.

Third, the deficit dilemma is more than just an economic dilemma; it is very much a political one. It is not surprising that it has evoked very strong reactions on all sides, and not simply based on political ideology. President Reagan believes that the level of government spending is what matters, and whether you take it from the private sector by taxing or borrowing is either irrelevant or of secondary importance. Of course, if one wants to balance the budget on moral grounds, it is also a way to force reductions in the size of government.

On the other hand, the former Chairman of the CEA, Martin Feldstein, was properly alarmed by the size of the deficits and the prospect that they would seriously unbalance the recovery, put a tremendous pressure on net exports and net investment, and possibly explode in a rapid buildup of public debt and pressure to re-inflate. The first few of these predictions have been borne out, at least in part. The last has not, but at the time such an outcome was possible. Many in the Administration during Feldstein's tenure at the CEA were upset at his calling attention to these important issues, apparently because they thought it gave greater credence to those who wished to raise taxes, rather than reduce spending. While I am strongly sympathetic to the idea that the deficit should be reduced on the spending side of the budget, rather than the tax side, it is clear that *for a while there was the potential for an explosive long-run episode.* The worst scenario now appears to be extremely unlikely, compared to the 1982–84 period. But it should not be forgotten that such a scenario can re-emerge. The economy didn't fall off the edge, and it now appears to be unlikely to do so. But there is no guarantee that without action, it won't.

◆ Chapter 10 ◆

The Fairness Issue

Many people think that President Reagan's economic program benefits the rich at the expense of the poor. This judgment is at best only partially true; at worst it is seriously misleading.

Between 1979 and the depths of the 1982 recession the poverty rate rose from 11.7 to 15 percent. In 1983 it peaked at 15.2 percent, before falling to 14 percent in 1985. In considering the significance of these numbers, it is important to understand that by the time President Reagan took office in January 1981, the poverty rate had already risen to between 13 and 14 percent. Therefore, most of the increase took place *before* President Reagan took office. The severe recession certainly worsened the incidence of poverty, but the prolonged recovery has sharply reduced its incidence, to about the level President Reagan inherited. While much higher than the average, the poverty rate for blacks has actually fallen slightly. The trend in poverty is shown in Figure 1.

Likewise, other traditional measures of general well being (adjusted for inflation), such as per capita disposable income, consumption expenditures, or median family income, indicate substantial gains have occurred in the period since Ronald Reagan assumed office: about 10 percent for per capita income, 13.5 percent for per capita consumption, and 5 percent for median family income between 1981 and 1986 (see Figures 2 and 3). From 1978 to 1980, however, median family income had fallen about 5 percent while per capita income and consumption remained about constant. Thus, the poverty statistics and the median family income versus per capita income numbers reveal an untold story: the major deteriora-

FIGURE 10-1   **Overall Poverty Rate**

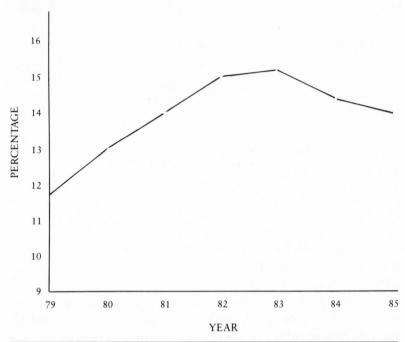

YEAR

Source: Money Income and Poverty Status of Families and Persons, various issues

tion was in 1978–80. On average, then, Americans were better off by the end of 1986 than the beginning of 1981, and those at the bottom of the income distribution were about as well off.

But there is a hidden element in this story. The federal government was borrowing almost $2,000 per year per family, and the gains in disposable income (income after taxes) and still larger gains in consumption came at the expense of future taxpayers—today's workers later in their lives and future generations. This issue of intergenerational equity is at least as important as that of fairness within a generation, and we shall return to it in detail below. At any rate, substantial real income gains did continue during the Reagan years, interrupted only briefly by the severe recession of 1981–82. Other measures of economic opportunities speak well for the Reagan program; for example, the enormous gains in employment made during the 1980s, over and above the larger gains made in the 1970s. By December 1986, employment was over 110 million, compared to just under 100 million in January 1981. Likewise, the unemployment

FIGURE 10-2   Median Family Income (1982 $)

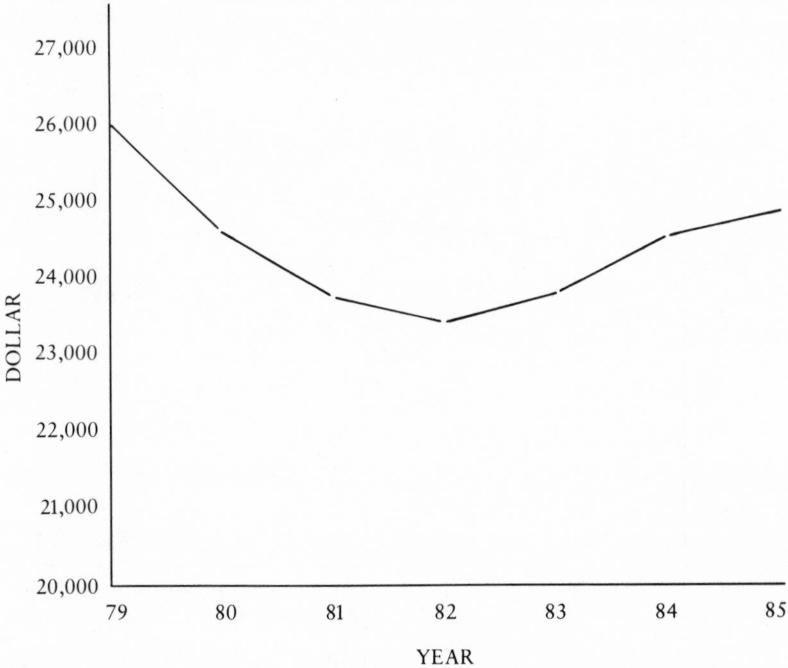

Source: Money Income and Poverty Status of Families and Persons, various issues

rate was 6.7 percent, the lowest since 1979, and below the 1976–80 average. The fraction of the population working stood at a peacetime high of 60.9 percent.

The Social Safety Net

The centerpiece of the Administration's economic program was the desire to limit the redistribution of income to a social safety net. In general, the Administration has explicitly rejected using the tax system to redistribute income in favor of policies designed to restore incentives to produce income and wealth in order to raise living standards, in an attempt to create an environment that will maximize long-run economic mobility for minorities and the disadvantaged. When economic growth is sluggish, those who are lowest on the economic ladder face the greatest difficulty in improving their lot, and those who cannot succeed at all face deteri-

FIGURE 10-3   Per Capita Disposable Income (1982 $)

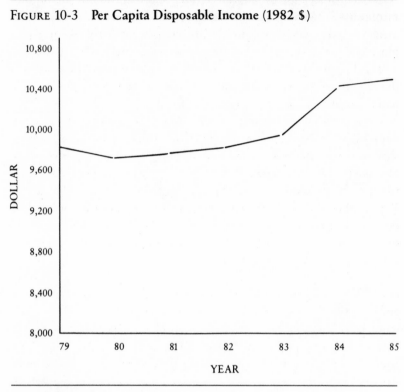

Source: U.S. Census bureau, Money Income and Poverty Status of Families and
Persons, various issues

orating political support for social spending. In a stagnant economic environment, the poorest are therefore doomed to suffer the most. The Reagan
approach, often called trickle-down economics, has been proven to work:
innumerable historical episodes demonstrate the high and positive correlation between rapid economic growth and the improvement of earnings
for low-income individuals and the growth of assistance programs for the
poor. In the United States, for example, the rapid economic growth in
the two decades after World War II laid the foundation for the provision
of more generous assistance programs from the rise in real wages. While
the causality works in both directions, real per capita disposable income
grew 218 percent from 1949–69, and the poverty rate reached its minimum shortly thereafter. Despite the decline in poverty among the elderly
since then, overall poverty has risen as growth has slowed, even prior to
the Reagan years.

The primary forces that affected the short-run well-being of low-income individuals under the Reagan Administration were reductions in means-tested benefit programs, the disinflation, the sharp rise in unemployment during the recession, and to a lesser extent, tax changes. Each will be discussed in turn. I then turn to long-run considerations, such as the substantial increase in the national debt, the deficits, trade, the dollar, and other policies that can affect growth.

It was extremely unfortunate that the sharp cuts in eligibility standards in means-tested benefit programs occurred simultaneously with a sharp recession. Normally, some fraction of those who are no longer eligible for such benefit programs are gradually able to obtain market work to supplement their incomes. This was much more difficult during the 1981–82 recession and, therefore, the incidence of poverty for the general population increased during the recession (although, as we indicated in the discussion on Social Security, the incidence of poverty among the elderly actually fell during this period).

There is now substantial evidence that some fraction of the federal government cuts were replaced by assistance programs from state and local governments, and from private sources. How large this substitution was is not easy to determine. Clearly, there were holes in the social safety net. One would hardly call it fair that well-off elderly individuals had their Social Security benefits increased while non-elderly poor households struggled. However, at the worst, the short-run reduction in benefits had a substantial impact on less than a quarter of the low-income population, and this impact was partially mitigated through the subsequent efforts of state and local governments; in the long run some of these poor replaced the reduction in income with their own earnings. The proportional tax rate cuts in the personal income tax obviously did very little for low-income households since they were already paying little or no personal income taxes. In fact, the increases in payroll taxes were more important for this group, and those who were actually working saw slight increases in their taxes because of previously scheduled increases.[1] However, the 1986 Tax Reform Act does eliminate income taxes for the poorest workers.

The Victims of Inflation

During the inflation of the late 1970s, it was commonly asserted that inflation hurt the poor the most. However, there is little documentation of this effect. Obviously, the poor would suffer more or less depending on which prices increased more rapidly than average, and which less. Energy and food prices increased more rapidly than the average rate of inflation, whereas rent increased less rapidly. On balance, there is no strong evidence that inflation per se disproportionately lowered the real income of the poor, compared to the middle class or the wealthy, and therefore that it hurt them more. One important exception is that some benefits — such as AFDC — are fixed in nominal terms, not indexed for inflation. While inflation in the 1970s eroded the real value of benefits, the 1980s disinflation actually slowed the decline in the purchasing power of these benefits.

Who then was hurt the worst by the recession? Clearly, those who lost their jobs suffered immensely, although the majority had their incomes substantially replaced by unemployment benefits, at least temporarily. The recession also caused a major decline in the value of real estate and shares in certain companies, which are owned for the greater part by the wealthy. The recession hastened a process of smaller levels of employment in certain industries in which wage rates had been artificially elevated due to unionization. In such cases, many of the workers who have lost their jobs will not be able to replace them with jobs of equal pay, and will suffer a decline in their standard of living.[2] This process was inevitable due to increased international competition and deregulation of industries. In many cases, it was the regulation that allowed the wages of workers to be elevated above competitive levels. Bankruptcies and farm foreclosures increased public awareness of the disruption borne by certain sectors of the economy.

Tax Policy and Fairness

Another common allegation is that the original Reagan tax cuts of 1981–83 favored the wealthy, at the expense of the poor and the middle class. Actually, a huge fraction of the total tax cuts accrued to the middle class, and the tax cuts most beneficial to the wealthy were not originally proposed by President Reagan, but rather by the Democrats on the House Ways and Means Committee.[3] If one looks at proportional reductions in tax rates, the tax cuts clearly were neutral with respect to the income distribution. However, they did nothing for those who were not already paying taxes, and therefore, did not help the lowest income individuals directly. Also, the reduction in the maximum tax rate from 70 to 50 percent on investment income benefited the rich. Since the ratio of taxes to income goes up as one moves up the income scale, a proportionate reduction in tax rates would mean that more *dollars* would be saved in taxes by the wealthy. To some, this was an abomination. Why should the rich have a larger dollar tax cut than the middle- and low-income groups? To others, this was a ludicrous question, since everyone was getting the same proportionate reduction. Attempts to limit the tax cut to those with incomes below upper-middle-class levels failed repeatedly. I believe the reason they failed had less to do with the influence of the wealthy in Congress than with the widely shared perception that it was the reduction in *marginal* tax rates that was important, not the shifting of minor amounts in the tax burden among different deciles of the income distribution.

The Tax Reform Act of 1986, discussed in detail in Chapter 8, certainly will cause both substantial capital gains and losses for various industries, persons, and regions in the United States, by raising the taxes on some types of investments and lowering it on others. To the extent that this is an inevitable product of unexpected tax changes, any tax reform will carry such windfall gains and losses; therefore, as proposed in Chapter 8, tax reform should be undertaken infrequently. Nevertheless, important components of the 1986 tax reform aid the average citizen, and especially the poor. Over 6 million poor will be completely removed from the income tax rolls, undoubtedly the fairest part of the tax reform. While most of these persons paid only modest amounts of taxes, they will be relieved not only of taxes but in some cases of the need for filing.

A variety of other features of the Tax Reform Act of 1986 deserve mention. Income will be much more evenly taxed regardless of the source from which it comes and the use to which it is put — a concept that economists call horizontal equity, i.e., equal treatment of "equals" by the tax system, if current income is the yardstick for ascertaining equality. Figuring the *vertical* equity of the tax system — how progressively tax payments should rise as income increases — is more complicated. First, the nominal rate structure will be much less progressive, comprising only two rates above the much larger exemption level. This means it is more progressive at the bottom and less progressive at the top, with *respect to the statutory rates*. However, a large number of exclusions, deductions, and preferences in the old tax law made it possible for many well-off people to pay taxes substantially lower than the statutory rates at their level of income. Thus, a direct comparison must take into account the sources and uses of income, as well as its tax level, in determining whether the new taxes will be raised or lowered.

More complicated still is determining who will ultimately pay the $120 billion corporate tax increase over the next five years (and much more beyond that). The thorny problem of the corporation income tax was discussed in Chapter 8. Suffice it to say that most economists, myself included, believe that a substantial fraction is borne by shareholders or the owners of capital in general, who tend to be relatively wealthy, and thereby the new corporate tax law will disproportionately hurt the wealthy rather than the poor and middle-income classes, at least wealthy owners of new investment. The corporate rate reduction conferred capital gains on owners of investment already made. However, it is possible that some of the tax may be shifted in the long-run to labor, through slower wage growth than would otherwise have occurred because of decreased capital formation, and some of it may be shifted forward to consumers. If either occurs, that component will be regressive, but it is likely to be dominated by the share of the tax borne by shareholders or capital in general.

It is difficult to conclude that Reagan tax policies were really a giveaway to the rich at the expense of the poor and middle class. In fact, an analysis of the 1981–83 tax reforms, as well as the 1986 tax reform, reveals a much more complicated set of actions and interactions that must be evaluated before one can come to a conclusion. But the original impact appears to be much more proportional and even populist than most people would believe, aiding low-income individuals and the working class at the expense of holders of corporate securities.

Perhaps the least-fair element of the Reagan program was its inability to do anything about substantial welfare for the rich: it failed to decouple the well-off elderly from the indigent and middle-income elderly in Social Security and Medicare transfers, and to halt the explosion of agricultural subsidies, for instance. These and a myriad of other programs not only resisted reduction, but actually rose in real dollars and as a fraction of the budget. Old myths die hard. Despite the fact that the incidence of poverty among the elderly is quite low, and actually fell during the recession, the typical discussion of Social Security revolves around indigent elderly individuals. Therefore, the most unfair part of the Reagan economic package largely escapes notice in popular discussions, while attention focuses on more subtle interpretations of other issues. It is addressed in depth in Chapter 7.

The Budget Cuts and the Poor

A common criticism of the Reagan program was that it decreased short-run disposable income for the poor. If one focuses exclusively on the distribution of short-run disposable income, it is clear that many of the nonpoor receiving benefits in the late 1970s suffered. The attempt to preserve the safety net for the truly needy was largely, but not totally, successful. The intent of the Administration's program was to reduce the fraction of Americans receiving transfer payment income, i.e., dependent on the dole. The *hope* was that combined with a variety of other actions this would eventually lead to a higher level of income for these people and their children.

The taxing and spending changes made by the Administration moves us toward a society with a smaller fraction of its population dependent on transfer payment programs. They encourage increased productivity for workers of the future and hence stimulate earnings growth. It is true that the Reagan economic program will lead to a more unequal distribution of income than would have resulted from a continuation of previous programs. But to criticize it on this basis would be misleading. There has been substantial, if incomplete, progress in eliminating poverty and providing social insurance against serious income losses, to the point where returns from further redistribution would diminish rapidly while costs would disproportionately accelerate.

In addition to the short-run fall in disposable income for some poor households, the part of the Reagan program which engenders the most debate is its philosophical approach, which explicitly rejects a government role in attempting a *general redistribution or equalization of income* in favor of a more limited government role of alleviating poverty and mitigating the harm of temporary economic distress. This change was long overdue. Only those who believe that the relative, rather than the absolute, standard of living best measures economic well-being should take much umbrage at the Reagan program.

The rapid real growth of means-tested benefit programs in the 1960s and 1970s was brought to an abrupt halt, but the actual level of benefits remained about the same. Some grant programs were cut sharply, but state and local governments seem to have achieved flexibility in the remaining grant programs to offset the cuts in social services. If one examines the relationship of the Reagan cuts and proposals to those proposed by President Carter, some interesting comparisons can be made. A close look at spending for safety net programs reveals that by 1984, actual outlays for safety net programs were $68.8 billion. In April, 1981, President Reagan proposed $56.7 billion, while President Carter's program earlier that year had proposed $75.1 billion (all in constant 1980 dollars). About one-quarter of the actual savings occurred because Congress made permanent previously enacted temporary changes. Human capital expenditures for education, employment, and social services had grown rapidly, and reached $23 billion by 1980. President Carter himself proposed cuts of 10 to 15 percent, whereas President Reagan's original budget, as documented in Chapter 7, proposed cuts of about 50 percent. Congress agreed to cuts of about 18 percent.

The hallmark of the Reagan proposals was the targeting of benefits much more precisely to low-income families—the real poor—not to near-poor, low-, or middle-income families. As John Weicher notes, "In nearly every program area eligibility has been lowered to reduce aid to those who were relatively well-off. Thus, in housing, the income limit was reduced from 80 percent of the local median income, to 50 percent, which is roughly the poverty line. For food stamps, the cutoff was reduced from 160 percent to 130 percent of the poverty line."[4]

A careful analysis of the data is also quite interesting when broken down program by program. The primary cuts projected for 1984 were approved in the 1981 omnibus budget reconciliation. These included $1.9 billion of cuts in cash benefits ($1.4 billion in AFDC and $0.5 billion in the earned income credit), and $5.6 billion in in-kind transfers (of which $4.1 billion was in food and nutrition, $1.1 billion in Medicaid, and $0.5 billion in housing). One way of judging the target effectiveness of the program is to examine the share of the benefits going directly to reduce poverty, rather than to enhance the incomes of those above the poverty line—even if the total is slightly lower than what President Carter projected and somewhat higher than what President Reagan proposed. For cash benefits, this figure rose from 44 percent in 1979 to 57.2 percent in 1984, and the corresponding figure for in-kind benefits paid to the non-elderly poor rose from 26 percent in 1979 to 35 percent by 1984.[5] If the entire poverty income deficit is examined—the amount of income transfer needed to lift every poor person out of poverty—it rose from a low of $22.2 billion 1980 dollars in 1973–74 to $29.7 billion by 1980. It peaked at $38 billion in 1983 and has since fallen to between $35 and $36 billion. If income in-kind is included in the disbursements, such as subsidized housing, food, and medical care, the deficit figure is then reduced to about two-thirds of this amount. How much of this increased deficit was due to program cuts and how much to other factors? Most analysts agree that the bulk of the increase in poverty in the early 1980s was due to the recession and the sharp rise in unemployment.[6] Sheldon Danziger and Peter Gottschalk document a one-tenth of one percent increase in the poverty rate due to demographics, such as the increasing share of households headed by single women. Thus, on purely demographic grounds, there has been a gradual rise in the incidence of poverty in the United States as traditionally measured.

What can be said in summary about the Reagan budget cuts and their impact on the poor? Clearly, a much larger share of the slightly smaller amount of benefits is now going to the poorest part of the population, due to changes in eligibility rules and other features. For example, a major welfare reform increased the rate at which welfare benefits were reduced if welfare recipients earned income in the labor market: after the first four months, they were to be reduced dollar for dollar, rather than the approximately two-thirds of a dollar of lost benefits for each dollar of earnings that occurred previously. This targeted the funds to those at the bottom of the scale, but also decreased the incentive for part-time work. The choice to leave welfare and work or leave work for welfare becomes much more clear-cut.

The dilemma facing all attempts at welfare reform has been balancing the level of basic payments, this implicit tax (or benefit reduction per dollar of earnings) and the break-even level of income at which welfare is no longer received. For a given break-even level confined to a modest fraction of the population, the higher the benefit level, the higher must be the tax rate, and conversely. But higher tax rates—the poor face the highest (implicit) tax rates of anyone—may decrease work incentives, expand the welfare rolls and lead to permanent dependency. To lower the rate so as to increase incentives to work requires *lower* benefit levels for those who do not work and/or benefit payments too far up the income scale. The Reagan Administration bit the bullet despite its ideological predilection towards the negative income tax and decided to opt for very high tax rates in order to keep benefit levels as high as possible without sharply increasing the break-even income level.

While hardly definitive, Weicher's study notes that the first year of the revised welfare program also seems to indicate that in general the working poor have continued to work and have left the welfare rolls rather than drop out of the labor force.[7] Further, Weicher documents a substantial offsetting of federal cuts that occurred at the state level via increased eligibility standards and substitution among various federal grant programs for social services.

Manpower Programs

Manpower programs have shrunk substantially, from $14 billion in the 1970s to only $4 billion per year recently. As I noted earlier, these programs were never too successful. One important exception is classroom training, which appears to have provided some help for women and for new entrants and re-entrants in the labor force with little recent job experience, primarily by increasing their amount of work, rather than their wage rates. A CBO study suggests that this increased the average annual earnings of females by $800 to $1,400, but only by $300 for males. Manpower programs have helped somewhat for some particular subgroup of participants. They were not a total waste, but only a small subset of them have provided benefits exceeding their costs. Other manpower programs were enormously inefficient. The Job Corps, for instance, cost about $1,400 for one-person year of experience, three times the cost of other types of programs. Thus, manpower programs have not been very successful and were not a major factor in reducing poverty. The reduction in poverty through the mid- to late 1970s came about primarily because of the increased cash assistance programs of the federal government, together with a fairly robust economy.

Reagan Policies and the Middle Class

Some critics charged that the middle class is in the process of shrinking, and that society is increasingly composed of two classes, the wealthy and the poor. This appears to be a generalization from the perception that fairly well-paying jobs have been lost, particularly in heavy manufacturing such as the steel and auto industries, and in some deregulated industries, such as airlines, where wage cuts for highly paid workers have been substantial. Certainly, the long-term job security in highly paid jobs which some workers had taken for granted proved to be illusory. While this was accelerated by the pace of deregulation and intense international competition, due in part to the overvalued dollar, it was inevitable. This vision of a doomed middle class makes good headlines in the press: the fear that the move to high-tech and service jobs will continue until all are working at unskilled jobs in the electronics industry or at McDonald's, while jobs in the auto, steel, and other heavy manufacturing industries evaporate totally. Actually, the data reveal that such predictions are somewhat fanciful, and a more careful analysis suggests that the proportion of middle-income jobs still varies only modestly from durable goods to services. Even if all jobs became high-tech and service related (ignoring, for the moment, adjustment in relative wages), a huge shift out of the middle class is not likely to occur. The belief that it will seems to be due to data uncorrected for important demographic changes. The Department of Labor projects that the broad sectoral and occupational composition in the United States will be about the same at the end of this century as it is now. In short, the major changes have already occurred.

Clearly, some specific industries have suffered a decline in the number of well-paid middle- to upper-middle-class jobs. As noted above, such losses are most likely to happen in industries that are facing increased foreign competition, deregulation, or both. It will take some time before these displaced workers get back on their normal job trajectory and are able to bring their incomes back to previous levels. By fostering deregulation, and by inadvertently overvaluing the dollar, which stiffened foreign competition, the Reagan administration hastened the inevitable transformation of the economy.[8] In general, the middle class was helped substantially by tax acts and reforms, which increased their short-run disposable income.

Long-Term Fairness

Fairness has many dimensions. It can be measured as the distribution of well-being among current persons, such as middle class versus rich. It can be measured across regions, occupations, industries, or between men and women, persons of different ages, or of different races. There is also a substantial international dimension to fairness, considering both the impact that the U.S. economy has on the rest of the world and the immense income gap between the advanced industrial economies and the Third World. Indeed, perhaps the greatest unfairness of disinflation in advanced economies during the early 1980s and the concomitant recession was the tremendous strain it placed on the income growth of poor countries. Other considerations of fairness are also possible, such as by sources or uses of income. For example, unanticipated inflation helps debtors and harms creditors; conversely, the sharp disinflation—which was more rapid than anticipated—hurt debtors and benefited creditors, since payments were made in dollars whose value had declined less rapidly than anticipated.

A tremendously important dimension of fairness is the relationship between the present generation and future generations, including the relationship between present persons of all income classes and future low-income individuals. It does not take much analysis to conclude that issues of fairness concerning future and present generations depend heavily upon several factors, of which the most important is the economic growth rate. In a rapidly growing economy, such as that of the United States in the quarter century after World War II, each generation will be much more wealthy than the generation that preceded it; in a slowly growing economy, it will be hardly better off at all. It also appears that in a rapidly growing economy, those individuals within the same generation group who are better off are more willing and able to pay taxes to assist those left behind. Thus, one important dimension of fairness between generations revolves around the rate of economic growth. The next chapter discusses issues concerning actual growth performance and the possible impacts of alternative policies on growth, especially those policies enacted under the rubric of Reaganomics. Suffice it to say that despite the 1981–82 recession, real output per worker has grown somewhat more rapidly in the 1980s than it did in the period 1973–80, a period of terrible productivity growth. Whether this higher real output per worker growth path remains stable, accelerates, or decelerates is an issue closely related to the amount of resources society devotes to research and development for advanced technology and to saving and investment—and correspondingly, closely related to the level of deficit and debt.

The ethical and political issues of this dimension of fairness deserve mention. Some defense buildup was necessary, and a reduction of nondefense government spending was necessary to free up resources to generate increased investment necessary for growth, for the only alternative would have been reduced private consumption. But the bulk of middle-class voters had experienced little gain in their standard of living in the 1970s, as shown in Chapter 2, and simply would not have stood for reduced consumption. Because of this climate of opinion, the tightening of eligibility for transfer payment programs (which targeted them more effectively to the poorest) and the 1981 investment incentives in the tax law were combined with large personal tax cuts. This made the program popular with middle-class, taxpaying workers. The Administration hoped that more rapid long-term growth would not only improve the lot of the general population in the future, but also of the future poor.

One major part of the Reagan program has received enormous attention with respect to fairness between generations: the very large deficits. I am among those who argue that the deficit and rapidly rising national debt are unfair to our children and grandchildren. But we must go beyond simple analyses and look at matters in somewhat more detail. We have seen that the ratio of the national debt to GNP has increased somewhat. During a brief period the confluence of deficits, interest rates, and growth rates created a potentially explosive situation, but it appears we will probably avoid the worst scenario, that of a rapidly growing debt-to-GNP ratio, which would have left immense burdens to future generations. It now seems likely that the ratio of national debt to GNP will stabilize and then eventually shrink. Indeed, this has been the historical experience in previous episodes of substantial increases in the national debt, such as that of World War II and thereafter.

These larger deficits imply substantial increases in future interest payments in the budget to be paid out of future taxes, and it is not certain who will be paying them. If the debt/GNP ratio does decline, a substantial amount of those taxes will be paid back by current workers later in their lifetimes, rather than by their children. Further, as shown in Chapter 9, there is a case to be made for financing a temporary government spending increase by deficits rather than taxes, especially if it is for investment purposes. The efficiency argument claims that a smoother pattern of tax rates over time reduces the deadweight loss to tax distortions, while the equity argument claims that the burden of financing a long-lived stream of benefits from the investment should be borne by those who enjoy those benefits, not just by the people paying current taxes. Still, the large budget deficits and the large debt burden are among the most salient outcomes of Reaganomics. The extent to which it will be unfair to future taxpaying workers and future generations depends heavily upon the extent deficits can be reduced to a share of GNP smaller than the rate of growth of the economy, and thereby reduce the debt/GNP ratio and the pressure of future interest payments in the budget.

The next-most important question of long-term equity concerns Social Security and Medicare expenditures. With the exception of the 1983 amendments, described in detail in Chapters 4 and 7, the Reagan Administration has *protected* these middle-class entitlement programs, assiduously avoiding cuts in Social Security even while proposing and accepting cuts in programs benefiting the nonelderly poor. Large and growing Social Security benefits result in substantial shifts of wealth across lifetimes and between generations. My analysis suggests that Social Security results in the transfer of trillions of dollars between generations, amounts that are much larger than those more hotly contested in the income tax reform.[9] The distribution of economic well-being across generations will be greatly affected by the pressure of the baby-boom generation's retirement, and the subsequent imbalances in Social Security benefits and taxes. The point to note, however, is that the Reagan Administration continually adopted the policy of exempting Social Security from budget cuts, protecting this source of income for the elderly. But payments to the *well-off* elderly come at the expense of current taxpayers, including low-income ones.

To conclude, the issue of generational equity involves the possibility

that a larger public debt will leave greater public liabilities to future generations (to be financed by increased taxes), the difficulty of financing the
baby-boom generation's retirement, and uncertainty concerning the restoration of rapid economic growth over long periods of time. This long-
term dimension of equity or fairness is more subtle and has only recently
been debated publicly in the United States. Demographic, economic, and
fiscal forces will combine to bring it to the fore in the 1990s.

Reaganomics and Fairness: A Summary

Much less has happened in the realm of social policy than might be sus-
pected, given the tremendous amount of media publicity surrounding
every proposed budget cut affecting the poor. The strident rhetoric on
both sides is partly political posturing in preparation for a compromise.
There have been reductions in some key programs, documented above,
and undoubtedly distress in some quarters, though much less than is commonly supposed. Further, as John Palmer and Gregory Mills note,[10] many
of the proposed decreases and enacted program cuts had already been
proposed by previous administrations, including Democratic ones. Indeed,
the authors go on to say, " . . . some of the program changes proposed
by Reagan had long standing antecedents and were widely considered
meritorious . . . examples are reductions in the guaranteed student loan
subsidy . . . and scaling back public service employment." The greatest
philosophical conflict occurred when, after two decades of social engineering that resulted in the enormous expansion of social welfare spending,
the Reagan Administration sought to discredit social engineering as an
acceptable policy. It succeeded only in calling a halt to its growth, not
in dramatically reversing it. Even if the legacy is only fewer new programs
in the future, this is still a remarkable achievement.

The Reagan Administration came into office steadfastly opposed to
social engineering via the tax system and spending programs. It wanted
spending programs confined to a social safety net to protect the poorest.
This evoked a howl of protest, especially when *some* of the original budget cuts subsequently enacted were in programs benefiting low-income
individuals and families. But the rhetoric was far removed from reality.
The Administration proposed many cuts which had been proposed by
previous administrations; programs for which there was a consensus that
they were not delivering very much for their high cost. Further, the
Administration, which received only some of the proposed cuts, appar-

ently succeeded in targeting a much higher fraction of them to people below the poverty line. Simultaneously, actions by state and local governments offset some of the federal cuts in low-income assistance programs. As a result, it appears that the net effect of federal budget cuts on the incomes of those below the poverty line has been quite modest. Somewhat larger reductions have occurred for those above the poverty line who previously received benefits and are now relying exclusively on earnings for support.

The Reagan Administration's tax changes also focused on incentives at the margin, and specifically rejected the notion of using sharply progressive tax rates to redistribute after-tax income. In fact, the various tax reforms, especially the 1986 tax reform, have as their hallmark much more horizontal than vertical equity. The 1981–83 tax cuts were virtually proportional across the board. The 1986 reductions are much more complicated, since we must consider the sharp increase expected in corporate tax revenues and must probe deeply into the sources and uses of income, where dramatic changes have occurred, before distributional conclusions can be drawn. One unambiguous result is that six million poor will be removed from the tax rolls.

Disinflation, as documented in Chapter 6, was achieved at a much lower cost in terms of lost output and unemployment than many had predicted. This is the single-greatest achievement of the Reagan economic policy. Other things being equal, disinflation harmed debtors and aided creditors. The temporary rise in unemployment was the primary cause of the increase in the poverty rate from 1981 to 1983. But the poverty rate has now declined to about the level it was when President Reagan assumed office. Further, ten million additional jobs have been added to the workplace, above and beyond the twenty million added in the 1970s.

The budget deficits and the buildup of the national debt will leave larger liabilities to be paid in the future, since higher taxes will be necessary to pay the interest on the larger debt. If the debt-to-GNP ratio is stabilized or reduced, most of these taxes will be paid by the current generation of taxpaying workers, not by their children. But the large buildup of debt may continue and may result in greater public liabilities for our children and grandchildren. Simultaneously, with the low rate of saving and investment, we may leave future generations fewer private assets, thereby doubly reducing their future after-tax incomes. However, so long as the growth rate of the economy is reasonable, they are likely to be much richer anyway. While it cannot be blithely assumed that growth will continue and be unaffected by economic policies, it is also true that in general, succeeding generations grow increasingly richer. Only if growth rates remain depressed will the confluence of Social Security burdens and large public deficits prove to be dramatically unfair to succeeding generations. Finally, it seems that reports of the decline of the middle class are a bit premature. Indeed, the middle class will benefit the most from the various tax cuts enacted by the Reagan Administration.

All of these fairness issues are affected by continued major structural changes in the U.S. economy: shifts among industries and occupations, demographic changes in the labor force, deregulation of previously regulated industries reducing the income security of workers, and increased foreign competition doing likewise for workers in firms exporting and competing with imports. Certainly this was dramatically aggravated by the long-overvalued dollar and the tremendous pressure this put on sectors of the economy such as agriculture and automobiles. But the basic trends in the poverty rate and the overall distribution of income have had much more to do with underlying structural changes in the economy and pronounced demographic changes than with the policies of the Reagan Administration.

While the average American is better off now than six years ago, some have been left behind, and some are much worse off than they were in 1980. This varies by age, race, sex, occupation, industry, and region. Among the hardest hit are those in agriculture and those low-middle income persons who previously had managed to get publicly financed transfer payments despite being above the poverty line. As noted above, numerous subsidies for the rich continue — such as agricultural subsidies and Social Security for the well-off — woven into the complex structure of programs designed to help the less-fortunate.

No set of economic policies, let alone one as comprehensive and as complex as Reaganomics, can pretend to treat everyone equally. Nor should the status quo necessarily be considered as a desirable benchmark in the distribution of income, wealth, or other measures of economic well-being. The Reagan Administration was much less concerned with distributional issues in creating an economic environment which maximized the opportunity for more rapid economic growth. I believe it has been partially successful in doing so in some dimensions, and quite unsuccessful in others, although this is not the same thing as saying the growth rate will be higher as a result of these policies. Many other factors are involved. To regard the Reagan economic program as blatantly unfair drastically overstates its likely impact on those generally thought of as the poor: those below the poverty line. Certain groups were aided, and certain groups harmed, as a result of Reaganomics, especially because of the sharp disinflation and the overvalued dollar. But no policy, especially one designed to redress such major economic disruptions as rapid and wildly fluctuating inflation, will affect all groups equally. Demanding this of any economic policy is a recipe for economic disaster. Too stringent a notion of fairness would paralyze the economy, making us incapable of taking serious action against rampant inflation, sluggish growth, and severe unemployment.

I believe that the Reagan Administration's primary goals of reducing the amount of social engineering in budget and tax policies and making transfer payment programs more cost-conscious and target-effective do not violate any reasonable definition of fairness. The rhetoric was much more provocative in this regard than the reality. A close examination of the evidence reveals that the effects on aggregate measures of income distribution, poverty, and other dimensions of fairness were quite minor, despite the fact that some specific individuals and groups fared poorly or were hurt by the policies.

Chapter 11

Long-Term Growth

When Ronald Reagan became president in 1981, the American economy was in the midst of a frightening long-term growth slowdown. Real per capita income, a rough measure of the standard of living of the average person, had grown only about half as much per annum since the late 1960s as in the twenty preceding years. Real output per worker had grown even less rapidly. While other advanced economies also experienced the long-term slowdown (see Table 1), their reduction was from rapid to modest growth, while ours was from modest to virtually no growth. Combined with the rapid increase in marginal tax rates on the typical working taxpaying American family, as documented in Chapter 2, a large fraction of American families had witnessed virtually no gain in their standard of living (measured in real after-tax terms) for a decade or more.

During this period, the economy provided employment for 20 million additional workers, including the baby-boomers then entering the labor force and growing numbers of women as second-earners in the household. But a number of persistent troubles — the slowed increase of capital stock per worker, high and fluctuating inflation, an unindexed tax system, paltry real wage growth, and other factors — combined to make Americans ask, for the first time since World War II, whether their children would be better off than they were.

The compounded impact of even a modest increase in the growth rate is enormous. The United Kingdom, for instance, with an economic growth rate of only one percentage point per year less than the United States, France, and Germany, transformed itself from the wealthiest society

TABLE 11-1   Annual Growth Rate in GNP per Employed Worker

Country	1963 to 1973	1973 to 1979
United States	1.9	0.1
Japan	8.7	3.4
Germany	4.6	3.2
France	4.6	2.7

Source: Economic Report of the President, 1980.

on earth to a relatively poor member of the Common Market in less than three generations. In any given year, the difference between a 2 percent rate of growth and a 3 percent rate of growth may seem a low-priority issue, but compounded over a generation, such a difference will dictate whether succeeding generations are much wealthier, or only slightly wealthier, than the present one. In addition, with rapid, long-term economic growth, the poor benefit not only from the expansion of economic opportunity, but also from the willingness of taxpayers to share their gains via a more generous safety net program.

To highlight the importance of achieving a higher long-term growth rate in the years ahead, Table 2 presents data on demographic trends projected for the United States and abroad. During that period, all advanced economies will be aging rapidly. Early in the next century, the ratio of workers to retirees in each of these economies will shrink precipitously. Greater productivity from the workers will be necessary to support the retirees — to finance, for instance, the demand for public medical care spending to benefit the growing fraction of the extremely old (over eighty-five) among the elderly population. More rapid economic growth would increase the resource base, which would finance these increased demands. Slow growth would mean that social tension and economic disruption would heighten as workers and retirees fight over the distribution of slowly growing resources. Each of the world's economies therefore has a stake in rapid, or at least acceptable, growth rates. For the United States, more than just economic benefits are at stake, as our rate of economic growth will substantially affect our position in the world community of nations, both as the leader of the free democracies of the West and as an example to the masses hovering on the brink of subsistence in the Third World and desperately seeking a way to improve their standards of living.

TABLE 11-2a	Growth in Older Population, Actual & Projected, U.S.	
Year	Percent of Population Over Age 65	Percent of Population Over Age 65
1900	4.0%	0.2%
1920	4.7	0.2
1940	6.8	0.3
1960	9.2	0.5
1980	11.3	1.0
2000	13.1	1.9
2010	13.9	2.4
2020	17.3	2.5
2030	21.1	2.9
2040	21.6	4.2
2050	21.7	5.2

Source: U.S. Bureau of the Census, Current Population Reports, Series P-23, No. 128, Sept. 1983.

TABLE 11-2b	Ratio of the Number of Aged People (65 Years or More) to Total Population				
	1950	1970	1985	2000*	2020*
Japan	4.9	7.1	10.1	15.6	21.8
Germany	9.4	13.2	14.0	16.5	21.2
France	11.4	12.9	12.4	14.8	18.1
U.K.	10.7	12.9	14.7	14.9	17.4
U.S.	8.1	9.8	11.5	11.7	15.4

* Estimated

The Reagan Position

It is not surprising that Ronald Reagan made a growth-oriented economic policy his main objective. To achieve this, he focused on disinflating the economy, reducing government domestic spending, regulation, and taxes, and decentralizing government to the state and local level, hoping to free

TABLE 11-3   Comparative Real Economic Growth Rates, 1982–85

Country	Three Year Cumulative Real Growth Rates in GNP, 1982–85
United States	12.3
Canada	12.2
Japan	14.1
France	3.0
West Germany	6.0
Italy	4.4
United Kingdom	8.4

Source: OECD National Accounts

up resources for private enterprise. Indeed, as seen in Chapters 2 and 7, the primary role of the federal government had become redistributing income, rather than providing goods and services. President Reagan sought — and in substantial measure, achieved — a reorientation of budget priorities toward production of goods and services and a more target-effective and cost-conscious safety net.[1] But if there is one thing that he stood for, it was a reorientation of government from redistributing wealth to creating an environment conducive to producing it.

The change in the nature of government activity, the changing economic and political agenda toward growth-oriented policies rather than redistribution of existing wealth, disinflation, certain aspects of tax reduction and reform, and other changes in budget policy augur well for future economic growth. Other policies, such as the large budget deficits and some aspects of the recent tax reform, do not. In what follows, I shall examine the proximate determinants of economic growth, including the limits of what economists know concerning them, in more detail. I shall then compare the performance of the economy and Reaganomics' contribution to economic growth. If budget deficits are brought under control — and that is an uncertain proposition — and if some improvements are made in the tax reform act of 1986, the Reagan program should be beneficial to long-term economic growth. If not, the ultimate decline in our rate of investment (discussed in Chapters 8 and 9) will drain our capacity for rapid growth.

TABLE 11-4   **Output and Productivity Growth in the U.S. Economy**
(average annual percentage rates of growth)

Year	Real Gross Product	Real Product Per Employee Hour
1948–73	3.6	2.9
1973–81	2.0	0.6
1981–85	3.0	1.4

Source: U.S. Dept. of Labor

It is worth noting here that from the trough of the 1981–82 recession through 1985, cumulative real GNP growth in the United States was four times that of France, three times that of Italy, twice that of Germany, and half again as large as that in the United Kingdom. The "sluggish growth" of 2.5 percent in 1986 was about average for the advanced economies. Only the Canadians, whose economy is tied closely to the United States, and the Japanese fared as well in the 1980s (see Table 3). Real output per worker also did better in this period, as Table 4 demonstrates. This at least *begins to reverse* the depressing pattern of the late 1960s to 1980s. However, preliminary data for 1986 suggest an abysmal year for productivity growth. Whether the rebound in the first half of the 1980s is cause for cautious optimism remains to be seen. Also, one must interpret comparative productivity performance cautiously. While labor productivity growth has been more rapid in Western Europe than in the United States, this is partly because high wage rates and inflexible labor markets have led many European economies to invest heavily in labor-saving capital formation. Of course, European employment has been stagnant, whereas that in the United States has grown rapidly.

A Framework for Analyzing Long-Run Growth

The studies of economic growth generally attempt to decompose the rate of growth of real GNP—or some related measure—into the various factors thought to influence it. These include such categories as increased labor input, increased capital input, improved resource allocation, and a general residual category often labeled technical change. The ability of the economy to improve standards of living per capita depends heavily on the capital/labor ratio, the rate of technical change, and the rate of improvement in the quality of the labor force, among other factors.

The phrase "economic growth" is often used in political and press discussion to refer to growth over a few quarters, perhaps from the trough of a recession. An economist focusing on the long-term growth rate has a much longer time horizon, and attempts to net out cyclical fluctuations. In the best-performing advanced economies, increases in real per capita income over the last century have averaged a little under 2 percent per year. This number is substantially larger in rapid-growth episodes in less-developed countries, so let us consider a 1.5 to 2 percent increase as a reasonable long-run growth performance. By compounding real per capita income over two generations in two hypothetical economies, one at 1.5 percent and the other at 2 percent, one can see that the more rapidly growing economy is one-third again as wealthy as the less-rapidly growing economy. When evaluating growth performance, even differences of *fractions of a percent* are important in the long term growth rate. Increasing the growth rate (at minimal opportunity costs) by a couple of tenths of a percentage point may not sound like much, but it is nevertheless an enormous economic and social achievement.

Policies designed to alter the rate of economic growth directly tend to focus on enhancing technological advances, the quality of the labor force, and the level and growth rate of capital per worker. It is important to note, however, that the only way to raise the long-run growth rate *permanently* is to increase the rate of technical change or to increase the rate of improvement in the quality of the labor force. Loosely speaking, the rate of technical change is affected by R&D expenditures, while the rate of improvement in the quality of the labor force is increased by investment in human capital, such as education and training. A policy that increases the capital/labor ratio (for example, by increasing the rate of investment and net capital formation) can lead to permanently higher income levels but will only lead to a *temporarily* higher growth rate. This is not just semantics. The situation is described in Figure 1, which shows the economy's original growth path, given its presumed (for the moment exogenous) constant rate of technical change. Real per capita income grows at the rate of technical change and of labor quality improvement, given the capital labor ratio. Any policy—tax policy, for instance—that increases the desired capital stock of firms (or perhaps more accurately, the desired wealth of the population, relative to levels of income), leads

FIGURE 11-1   **Alternative Growth Paths: Technical Change and Capital Formation**

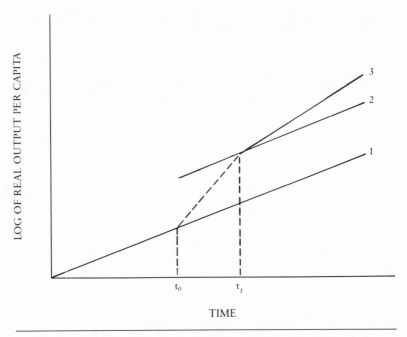

t_0: Pro-investment policy leads to higher capital formation and transition to higher level of income

t_1: Economy resumes long-run growth rate or through interaction of investment and technical change moves to more rapid growth path

to an investment boom for a span of years, causing a spurt in the short-run growth rate along the dotted path in Figure 1 until the new long-run growth path (labeled 2) is achieved. Note that the level of per capita income is permanently higher along growth path 2 than on 1, but once the transition to the new growth path is complete, the rate of economic growth (given by the slope of the output curve) returns to the original rate as a result of underlying factors of the rate of technical change and improvement in labor force quality.

What causes this rate of technical change? Clearly, it has not been constant; this is just a convenient abstraction for the sake of representation. But is it really exogenous? Are there economic policies that can per-

TABLE 11-5 Federal Outlays By Category, Selected Years (billions of constant 1972 dollars; percentages of GNP in parentheses)

Fiscal Year	Total Outlays	Physical Investment Defense	Physical Investment Non-Defense	Grants-in-Aid	R&D Defense	R&D Non-Defense	Payments to Individuals	Net Interest	All Others
1949	85.3 (17.3)	4.0 (0.8)	1.8 (0.4)	0.9 (0.2)	2.0 (0.4)	0.5 (0.1)	17.6 (3.6)	8.4 (1.7)	50.4 (10.2)
1958	135.3 (19.9)	25.2 (3.7)	1.9 (0.3)	2.8 (0.5)	4.7 (0.7)	1.4 (0.2)	30.1 (4.4)	8.4 (1.2)	60.8 (8.9)
1968	224.6 (21.2)	30.2 (2.9)	3.4 (0.3)	7.6 (0.7)	11.4 (1.1)	10.2 (1.0)	60.1 (5.7)	13.5 (1.3)	88.1 (8.3)
1978	300.4 (20.9)	15.8 (1.1)	4.4 (0.3)	11.0 (0.8)	7.6 (0.5)	7.9 (0.5)	144.7 (10.0)	23.6 (1.6)	85.4 (5.9)
1984	363.5 (22.2)	31.3 (1.9)	3.2 (0.2)	9.0 (0.5)	11.4 (0.7)	5.9 (0.4)	182.0 (11.1)	44.6 (2.7)	76.1 (4.6)
1985	363.8 (21.8)	31.1 (1.9)	5.0 (0.3)	9.8 (0.6)	11.6 (0.7)	6.5 (0.4)	163.2 (9.8)	49.6 (3.0)	86.9 (5.1)

Sources: Office of Management and Budget, Budget of the United States, selected years, and appendices.

manently affect it? Are these policies worth the cost of enacting them (for example, foregoing some current consumption in order to finance R&D expenditures)?

Factors primarily affecting any of the major components of gross national product — consumption, investment, government expenditures, and net exports — obviously will also affect the level of aggregate demand, and therefore the fluctuations in output, employment, and price level. It is likely that the policies which most directly affect the generation of new technology, and therefore long-term growth, occur here, one level down from aggregate GNP in the allocation of expenditures in the economy. For example, while some people still believe that the level of real government spending controls economic fluctuations, the rate of technical change can be affected by the composition of that spending: R&D expenditures and physical and human investment obviously may affect long-term growth differently than do payments to individuals for income support, net interest, and purchases of non-investment types of goods and services. The most important of these is probably direct government support of R&D. Table 5 presents some data on recent trends in federal government support of R&D, and physical investment expenditures, as well as other categories of government spending. As can be seen from the table, real government R&D spending and real government physical investment are now both substantially lower as a percentage of GNP than in the 1960s, although defense investment and R&D have made something of a comeback in the last few years.

Tax policies make up a second set of policies that, by affecting the way in which the private sector utilizes its resources, can affect the generation of new technology. The structure of the tax system can affect the rate of investment in the economy, and the rate of R&D spending, by changing the relative costs of such expenditures compared to other activities the firm might pursue in order to produce its current or prospective new product. These issues were discussed in detail in Chapter 8. To summarize, the original 1981 tax reform was quite clearly pro-investment and pro-research and development, with its research and development tax credit and accelerated depreciation. The 1986 tax reform extends the research and development tax credit for three years, but reduces it to 20 percent while, sensibly, tightening eligibility. Other investment incentives, however, are severely restricted, and the reduction in tax rates only partially compensates for this. The net effect is somewhat anti-investment.

Large deficits also ultimately crowd out private investment. As discussed in Chapter 9, the crowding out is about thirty cents on the dollar, in the short run, more in the long run. One may also question whether the increased borrowing is financing government investment and research and development, or consumption. Monetary policy also can affect the composition of output, as well as the level of aggregate demand in the economy. Monetary policy potentially affects the before-tax cost of capital, interest rates, as well as the differential between short-term and long-term loans and thus the real cost of R&D or investment projects.

Finally, it is important to note some potential interactions of the composition of spending and the rate of technical change. Either of two appealing but difficult-to-document conjectures would imply that a society with a higher investment rate might not only have a temporarily higher growth rate in its transition to a higher growth path (as in Figure 1), but actually might also increase its long-run rate of growth. These are the so-called "learning-by-doing" and "embodiment" hypotheses. The former reflects the anecdotal notion that in the process of investment, new ways of doing things are found, such as new production processes, and new potential products become known. Thus, the rate of investment compounds the rate of technical change. This process is displayed by the growth path labeled 3 in Figure 1. At the micro level, consider the options opening up in the course of a major project, e.g., oil exploration in the frozen tundra or the ocean depths. Just as new technologies sometimes arise to meet such challenges, the rate of technical advance may depend on the level of investment. The embodiment hypotheses entails the notions that it is much too expensive to embody new technology in old capital by converting it, and therefore, the rate at which new technology really does augment productivity depends upon the rate at which new capital is generated, i.e., the investment rate. As the United States has a very low investment rate relative to other countries, these anti-investment policies may potentially cause damage to long-term growth.

Sources of Income and Productivity Growth

There are several basic ways in which an economy can improve the standard of living of its population. First, the available labor force can be made more productive by providing them with more capital per worker. For a long period, the average annual increase in the capital/labor ratio in the U.S. economy remained at 2.5 percent; from 1973–80, however, there was no increase at all. This implies two things: first, that workers were not getting more capital with which to work, and second that the production methods were changing more slowly. Hence the second potential vehicle for promoting economic growth: technical change. Just as providing workers with more capital will make them more productive, so providing them with better-quality capital will do the same. High-speed computers, for example, make many workers much more productive than they were with old-style computational capabilities. This in turn reduces the cost of producing certain goods or services, enables existing workers to increase their production, and frees part of the work force to produce other goods and services. Many famous innovations, ranging from the reformation of crop rotation systems in agriculture several centuries ago, through a series of important transportation advances, to the recent explosion in electronics, played an important role in economic growth. Many minor improvements in product lines, production techniques, and in the quality of the capital stock are also important.[2]

The third major method to promote economic growth involves improving the knowledge and skills of the labor force itself, so-called human capital. Economists have long believed, and have attempted to document, that efforts by workers to improve their personal skills in order to increase their future earnings can be regarded as investment. While it is perhaps most common to think of formal higher education in this regard, there are many other important forms of such investment: health, nutrition, mobility, and experience and training on the job. There are substantial difficulties in measuring investment in human capital and its rate of return, yet many recent commentators have suggested that in the United States the investment in human capital is perhaps as large as the investment in ordinary capital.[3] Certainly our society spends a much higher fraction of its income on advanced education than do most other societies.

Other factors may also influence economic growth for short periods. For example, improvements in resource allocation toward more efficient uses can increase the level of income and hence accelerate the growth rate temporarily, perhaps over several years. But such advances cannot increase the rate of economic progress indefinitely, because opportunities to improve resource allocation will eventually be exhausted.

There is much debate among economists about the relative contribution of these different sources of economic growth. Perhaps the most widely quoted study is Denison's on the sources of growth of national income per person employed. In the postwar period through 1969, Denison attributes about half of an adjusted growth rate of 2.6 percent to advances in knowledge and the other half to a combination of changes in capital and land per person employed, improved resource allocation, and the economies of scale of larger markets. Denison's large "residual" of advances to knowledge has been subject to attack from a number of sources. The most important study is that of Dale Jorgenson, who attributes almost half of economic growth in the U.S. from 1948–79 to increased capital input and only slightly under one quarter to the residual beyond the growth of inputs, i.e., technical change. This study uses much more sophisticated measurement techniques than does Denison and, despite shortcomings of all such studies, is the best currently available. While the debate continues over precise contributions to growth, it is clear that technical change and capital formation are extremely important vehicles for promoting economic growth and rising standards of living.

Capital Formation and Its Determinants in the United States

There are many types of capital and many sectors in which capital formation may take place. On the most basic level, the capital stock consists of land, structures, inventories, and knowledge; and each may be invested in the household, business, or government sectors of the economy. As a rough generalization, we can decompose notions about capital formation into the determinants of each of its major types. Saving in society serves two purposes: it provides a source of funds for new capital investments, and it provides savers with claims to future consumption when they desire it — for example, during retirement. The national saving rate includes the rate of personal saving, corporate saving, and government saving. Business saving comprises a substantial fraction of the total, government saving or dissaving was rather minor until recently, and about a quarter of the national total comes from the household sector. Further, funds may be made available for U.S. investment by foreigners, and conversely, U.S. saving may go abroad to help finance investment overseas. In 1986, the personal saving rate, already low by international standards, declined precipitously and now is at a forty-year low, slightly under 3 percent of GNP. Business saving, net of depreciation, has remained similar to the long-run average (see Table 3 in Chapter 9 for details).

Of gross U.S. investment, a substantial fraction goes into residential construction, much more than in other economies. The overwhelming bulk of gross investment in recent years has been in replacement of the depreciating and obsolescing capital stock and in increased expenditures on pollution abatement and safety. Only about 3 percent of GNP was real net investment in additional plant and equipment. In addition to the decline in personal saving rate and very low rate of real net investment in business plant and equipment, our share of GNP devoted to R&D, while still higher than in most other economies, has also fallen from 2.8 percent to 2.1 percent of GNP in the last two decades. This may lead to slower advances in knowledge and technical change in the future.

Our human capital expenditures are substantial, as mentioned above. The real issue is how much of these expenditures should be treated as investment as opposed to consumption, and how to get reasonable estimates of rates of return on such expenditures. It was long argued that the return on educational investment was substantially higher than that accruing to regular capital, and therefore that society was underinvesting in education. But it is now clear from a number of studies that, as a much larger fraction of the potential labor force is educated to a higher level than ever before, the marginal return to such investment is not as great today as it once was.

Finally, it might be noted that while the government, especially the federal government, was doing a large amount of investing in everything from roads to automobiles, from typewriters to submarines in the 1950s and 1960s, the rate of government investment has fallen markedly since then, though private investment has not fallen very much. Moreover, in recent years the declining personal saving rate and growing federal deficits have required importing foreign capital to finance an increasing fraction of our private investment. While this is a useful short-term solution to the problem, other successful examples of using imported foreign capital to sustain investment and economic growth all involve economies that at the time were not well developed—for example, the United States and Canada in the nineteenth century, and many less-developed countries today. Some scholars, e.g., Martin Feldstein and Charles Horioka,[4] suggest that the flow of international capital is predominantly a short-term phenomenon, and that investment ultimately must be financed from domestic sources. While this issue continues to be disputed and international capital markets are changing rapidly, as discussed in Chapter 9, relying heavily on imported foreign capital to finance the economy's future investment and achieve economic progress would be unwise.

Causes of the Great Productivity Slowdown

Several studies examined the causes of productivity slowdown in the 1970s but, unfortunately, reached conflicting conclusions.[5] Denison, for example, attributes over one-third of the productivity slowdown to such factors as accelerated reduction in average hours of work, a more rapid shift in the age/sex composition of the labor force, a slower increase in capital per worker, changes in the legal environment, and a slowdown in the gains from scale economies. He leaves over two-thirds of the slowdown in the unexplained "residual" series for advances in knowledge. Robin Siegel claims the single-largest element in the productivity slowdown was the stagnation in the capital/labor ratio after 1973; his study also confirms the importance of the shifting demographic composition of the labor force. Lester Thurow stresses the importance of substantial sectoral shifts in the economy, especially toward services, which is traditionally a below-average sector for productivity. Finally, Dale Jorgenson, in the most comprehensive study of this issue, attributes much of the decline in the rate of growth to a slowdown in technical change, especially when disaggregated by sector.

While we cannot be certain of the precise mix of causes in the decline of productivity growth, a general consensus exists that the following were major contributors:

1. High and rising inflation and marginal tax rates on the returns to saving and investment, and hence a declining rate of private capital formation;

2. The displacement of private economic activity by government economic activity;

3. The changing age, experience, and occupational mix of the labor force;

4. The shift in output, away from manufacturing toward services;

5. The growth of government regulatory policies; and

6. A slowdown in the rate of research, development, and innovation.

The Recent Growth Turnaround

As Table 1 showed, real gross product and real product per hour worked in the United States have grown more rapidly in the period 1981–1985, relative to the period 1973–1981. However, the preliminary data suggest that 1986 was a poor year for growth in real product per hour worked. Perhaps the quarter century after World War II should be thought of as an aberration, a special time when the U.S. situation in the world economy enabled us to grow more rapidly than is likely in the future. What caused this growth turnaround? In 1981–85, the rate of productivity growth was more than double that of the preceding eight years. About half of the increase can be attributed to a rapid growth in output. The rest must be due to other factors. John Kendrick notes that "these included the effect of disinflation and declining energy prices; relative increases of investment in research and development and in new plant and equipment; regulatory reforms; changes in the labor force mix; and joint labor-management efforts to increase productivity to meet increased domestic and foreign competition."[6] Kendrick's work stresses the lag between the spending on R&D and its commercial applications, which he estimates as typically about six years. He therefore attributes part of the decline in productivity growth in the 1973–81 period to the slowdown in R&D spending since the 1960s; despite the more recent increases in R&D spending, the lag involved in commercialization contributed to a smaller increase in productivity between 1981 and 1985, than could have been expected. Kendrick is also optimistic that the stock of R&D will grow rapidly in the last half of this decade (1986–90), even if R&D spending stays flat. Hopefully, this growth in the stock of R&D will help reverse the poor 1986 performance.

Other analyses of innovation and productivity abound. A particularly interesting analysis is presented by Martin Baily,[7] who notes that the rest of the world is catching up in productivity and industrialization. In the 1973–84 period, output per labor hour in the manufacturing sector grew 2 percent in the United States, but three and one-half times more rapidly in Japan and about twice as rapidly in France and Germany. R&D spending in these countries has risen faster than in the United States. I personally put great weight on their much higher rates of investment. Baily notes that the fraction of U.S. patents granted to foreigners has risen from 16 percent in 1960 to 41 percent by 1982. While the rate of productivity growth is only starting to rebound, the level of productivity in the United States is still quite high. Baily stresses the importance of innovation and technical change to long-run growth, and with Denison, adopts a position somewhat counter to that of Ingerson and the one taken here, that only 20 percent of productivity growth in the 1973–84 period was due to an increase in the capital/labor ratio. Of course, the growth rate of the capital/labor ratio has slowed, and this was one of the reasons why productivity has slowed—but it is not the only one, nor by some estimates, the most important.

Trends in multi-factor productivity growth, as opposed to labor productivity growth (the latter including increases due to a higher capital/labor ratio), are quite similar. If one focuses only on what determines the rate of R&D expenditures and innovation, it is clear that there is some exogenous component. For instance, a demand for new technology reflects the obsolescence and cycles of old products and production processes. Technologies mature, then await major breakthroughs, but in the meantime, a productivity growth slowdown may occur in the sector involved. Nevertheless, no matter how the productivity turnaround in the 1980s occurred, its magnitude is impressive. The major question is whether it will continue, and what effect President Reagan's economic policies will have on long-term growth, innovation, and capital formation. The President's macroeconomic and tax policies get a mixed scorecard in this regard, although the R&D tax credit, *if* it is made permanent, may have important effects.

What about capital formation? As noted by Princeton economist Alan Blinder, even phenomenally successful investment incentives will only add a modest amount to the long-run growth rate. He notes that if the share of investment in GNP is raised by 3 percentage points for a full decade — and that would be a substantial achievement — this would lead to a one percentage point increase in the growth of capital stock, which, after ten years, would represent a 10.5 percent increase. "With a share of capital in output of 30 percent, the level of real GNP would wind up 3.15 percent higher. That would be a spectacular achievement. If we take a 25 year perspective, it amounts to adding only 0.12 percent to the GNP growth rate."[8]

Similar reasoning has been used by others, including myself, to indicate that an increase in the rate of investment, and therefore the capital/labor ratio, takes a long time to have much of a payoff. That payoff has to be measured in fractions of a percent of the growth rate. Still, increasing the growth rate by an eighth or a quarter of a percentage point, if compounded over a generation or two, will lead to substantial improvements. Not only do the questions of the sources and the determinants of economic growth generate major controversy, since our knowledge concerning them is so imprecise, but our understanding of the effects of different policies on the factors that are assumed to lead to higher growth is also limited. Chapter 8 indicated, for example, the range of opinions concerning the effectiveness of tax incentives in increasing the rate of corporate investment. There is no precise way of judging how a particular policy will affect a particular component which has a specific impact on economic growth. We cannot push a particular lever, for example, make a change in tax policy; predict precisely what the outcome will be on one particular determinant of growth, say the rate of R&D spending or the rate of capital formation; and then know precisely how that change in the determinants will affect the rate of growth itself: our knowledge is insufficient. This is not an excuse for nihilism. Sound judgment does suggest that tax, spending, deficit, monetary, and regulatory policies do matter, but it should not be presumed that modest changes in any one of these policies will lead to enormous changes in any of the determinants of growth, thereby raising false expectations that our growth rate — that is, the long-term underlying growth rate — will increase rapidly, or very much at all.

I conclude that *if, and only if*, large fiscal deficits are reduced in a way that does not impinge on investment incentives (as raising corporate taxes still further would do) and if we adopt some proposed reforms in tax and regulatory policy, we will be in an environment more conducive to growth as a result of President Reagan's economic policy. I believe that a variety of factors augur well for future economic growth. Among the most important are the change in tax structure (with the exception of the erosion of investment incentives) and the sharp reduction in inflation, along with the commitment to keep inflation under control. The gestation lag between heavy R&D spending and the ultimate generation of commercial application of new technology is so long that periods of high and wildly fluctuating inflation and monetary uncertainty add an even greater risk to the already risky R&D process. This is one of the major reasons why the rate of R&D expenditures fell in the 1970s. A long period of modest growth, at low inflation, is conducive to greater R&D expenditures and innovation, to risk-taking in general, as well as to long-lived capital formation. Against these must be balanced the deleterious effects of large budget deficits and the elimination of many investment incentives in the 1986 tax reform.

I am cautiously optimistic that we will control the budget deficit, by means other than large increases in taxes on investment or substantial cuts in federal R&D spending; that we will continue, at least for the foreseeable future, to pursue a noninflationary monetary policy; and that we will take some cautious steps toward restoring some of the capital formation and risk-taking incentives in subsequent tax reforms. I am optimistic on these matters because of the disinflation and because we are moving away from a European-style welfare state, indicating that a more conservative and manageable share of resources will be devoted to social programs. If such reforms are pursued, the resources and incentives for technological innovation will exist, and uncertainty over economic policy may well be reduced.

◆ *Chapter 12* ◆

Is Reaganomics Exportable?

Call it a revolution, an experiment, or merely an episode, the Reagan economic program, both as proposed and as implemented, represents a challenge and an opportunity to the rest of the world. Because economic, political, demographic, and social circumstances differ widely among the world's nations, some parts of the Reagan program that were sensible and successful in the United States may not be immediately applicable elsewhere. However, many others are not only applicable to other economies, but essential to their future well-being.

In most countries of the world, the share of GNP passing through government coffers exceeds that in the United States; although it may be more difficult politically to reduce the role of government, the effects of doing so will likely be greater in most other places. The reason why is suggested by the most basic principles of economics, such as diminishing marginal returns and rising marginal costs: whenever the share of government spending as a percentage of GNP rises—for example, with ever more generous and extensive transfer payments—the incremental benefit of those increases will decline. In the meantime, the cost of financing the increases will itself rise, and this illustrates another general economic principle: very high marginal tax rates, at either the corporate or personal level, are counterproductive. Many economies have very high marginal tax rates, which people avoid either through special exemptions in their tax codes or through participation in the underground economy. Even the much-ballyhooed value-added tax, necessary for tax harmonization in the European Common Market, has become riddled with special exemptions, which do not redress the regressivity of the tax but require much higher tax rates in order to raise the necessary amount of revenue.

The Reagan revolution in tax policy, with its dramatically lower marginal tax rates, has some applicability to the world's other advanced economies. They may not wish to go as far as we have in reducing tax rates, but with top marginal tax rates of 70 percent or 80 percent, and corporate tax rates exceeding 50 percent, it is clear that a strong case exists in many countries for broadening the base and lowering the rates, *especially at the top*. In addition to the efficiency gained by reducing distortions caused by these high tax rates, such rate reductions may even produce some revenue gains, especially at the upper end of the tax scale. Likewise, the tendency for governments to subsidize various industries, and to own and finance state-run monopolies in various sectors of the economy, leads to substantial inefficiency. The recent privatization of industries in countries such as the United Kingdom and France is a hopeful sign and demonstrates official recognition of the problem. Even Sweden has retreated from industry subsidies in favor of subsidies to relocate displaced workers. More insidious, however, are export subsidies and other short-term measures to protect jobs in specific industries. Not only do they cause long-term damage to the domestic economy, but collectively they cause tremendous damage to the entire world economy. Finally, the partial success in economic and social deregulation in the United States is likely to lead to new debates over such things as better safety and cleaner air, and how much we are willing to pay for them. Similar problems will also arise in other economies.

A major distinction between the United States and the economies of Western Europe is the much stronger entrenched power of European labor unions. These unions kept wages up, but as economic growth rates slowed in Western Europe, the combination of high wage rates and sluggish growth has led to extensive unemployment. In most of these economies government spending still represents a greater percentage of GNP than in the United States, which suggests that reducing that share of spending could bring about even greater benefits. But it also suggests that it would be much more difficult to do so because a larger fraction of the population is receiving benefits, whether direct or indirect. The political problem of unraveling this morass of interlocking subsidies is even more acute in Europe than in the United States. But pressure from international competition will render bad policies ever more costly, suggesting that the political process will have to deal with these problems eventually.

Monetary policy in other countries is considerably constrained by balance of payments problems and the relationship of assets denominated

TABLE 12-1 **Comparison of Unemployment, Inflation, and Growth, Various Countries**

Country	Unemployment Rate (1985)	Percentage Increase in Consumer Prices (1985)	Three Year Cumulative Real Growth Rates in GNP, 1982–85
U.S.	7.2	3.0	12.3
Canada	10.2	3.5	12.2
Japan	2.5	1.0	14.1
France	10.5	2.5	3.0
W. Germany	7.9	1.0	6.0
Italy	6.3	3.75	4.4
U.K.	13.5	2.0	8.4

Source: OECD National Accounts

in domestic currencies to those denominated in foreign currencies. Two economies, Japan and Germany, have substantial influence on the economic performance in the rest of the world. Thus, the Bundesbank's and the Bank of Japan's monetary policies, in conjunction with those of the Federal Reserve, are important to the functioning of the world's economy. In smaller economies, the necessity for monetary coordination forces governments to condition their policies to the monetary policy of the larger economies.

Some movement toward reducing the growth of government spending, tax rate reduction, and tax reform is already underway. For example, the French cut personal taxes 5 percent across-the-board, and Japan is reducing the top marginal tax rates to slightly over 50 percent and considering adopting a value-added tax. New Zealand has also adopted a value-added tax, and Australia is lowering marginal income tax rates. Thus, the same kinds of pressures that led to the Reagan revolution were also occurring in other economies, and have been given additional impetus by some of the successes of the Reagan program, such as the curtailment of inflation with minimal lost output and expansion of employment opportunities.

The necessity and opportunity for curtailing inflation in other economies varies widely. In most advanced economies, inflation is about what it is in the United States (see Table 1). The real horror stories with respect

TABLE 12-2   Ratio of Man-Year Benefit Payments to Man-Year
              Worked in Business Sector, and Public Sector Share
              of GDP, Sweden

Year	Man-Year	Public Sector
1970	0.75	0.44
1980	1.15	0.62

Source: A. Harberger, ed., World Economic Growth, ICS Press, 1985.

to inflation are in less-developed countries. Here the reform opportunities are more complex. While in many of them, government spending may be a small share of GNP, there are so many tariff, tax, and regulatory distortions that the incremental benefits of even modest gains in income can be immense. The shining examples of Taiwan, Korea, Singapore, and Hong Kong, who have run supply-side policies for some time, fostering enterprise with low tax rates, modest social spending, and little regulation, serve as a beacon to the other LDCs, as the U.S. economy does to the economies of Canada and Western Europe.

I shall now turn to specific examples, rather than exhaustive summaries, of the opportunities for reducing the role of government in regulating business, subsidizing alternative activities, and transferring income to persons (especially to those above the poverty line). In considering tax reform and reduction, deficit policy, and monetary policy, we shall see that differences among countries are important in assessing which parts of Reaganomics are exportable.

Fiscal Policy, Government Spending, and Taxes

The substantial achievements of the U.S. economy in the last several years have left a deep impression on Europeans. Since 1970, U.S. employment has risen by almost 30 million workers, whereas European employment has been stagnant. In much of Western Europe, unemployment remains at over 10 percent of the labor force, as Table 1 indicates, and real growth rates in the last several years have been only one-third to one-half as high as in the United States and Japan. Even our sluggish growth year of 1986 was about average for the advanced economies.

TABLE 12-3   Growth of Government, as Share of Potential GNP, W. Germany

Year	Public Expenditure	Taxes
1960	32.8	33.3
1965	35.7	34.7
1970	39.1	36.5
1975	45.7	40.9
1980	48.2	42.4

Source: A. Harberger, ed., World Economic Growth, ICS Press, 1985.

As in the United States, social welfare programs, which had expanded in the first two decades after World War II, accelerated their rates of increase around 1970 (see Tables 2 and 3 for examples). In the United States, these increases were heavily concentrated in two areas: old-age benefits such as Social Security and Medicare, and means-tested entitlement programs. In Western Europe, things went much further. Transfer payments, whether directly from the government or mandated privately, have gone on to include safety, vocational training, childcare, maternity care, extensive housing subsidies, and many other areas. The special benefits to various businesses and industries became even more pronounced than in the United States, including agricultural price supports, protection through tariffs and quotas, and subsidies or special tax breaks for business.

Figure 1 presents data on the important example of Sweden, where subsidies as a share of national income doubled to 10 percent before they were reduced and more person-years are now spent receiving benefits or in public employment than in private business employment. Sweden's recent history is instructive. In the 1960s and early 1970s, Sweden ran large budget surpluses, despite large and growing government spending. In the late 1970s and early 1980s, industry-specific subsidies peaked, jobs were temporarily protected, spending rose, and large budget and external deficits accompanied deteriorating economic performance. Spending has since been reduced as a share of GNP, many subsidies eliminated, and the budget deficit reduced from 13 percent of GNP in 1982 to 4 percent currently (and falling). This modest move toward freer markets and government budget balance has been associated with much-improved eco-

FIGURE 12-1   Growth of Public Subsidies to Business Sector, by
Industry and Total, 1970–1980, Sweden

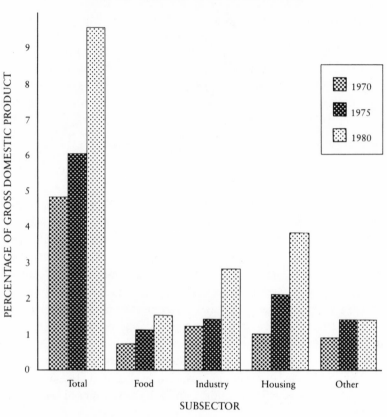

Source: Swedish Ministry of Economic Affairs, 1982
Government Medium-Term Survey

nomic performance. Simply put, a government, *especially* in an advanced
welfare state, must not run large budget deficits if it wants to finance the
investment necessary to raise productivity; and even modest freeing up
of markets can pay large dividends.

Not surprisingly, the share of government spending in GNP has
skyrocketed throughout Europe. For example, in Germany, government
spending grew from 33 percent of GNP in 1960 to almost 50 percent by
1980. The welfare programs in other Western European economies
exploded simultaneously. In Sweden, public sector outlays as a share of

GNP now exceed 60 percent. Apparently, the United States, at least temporarily, has been spared the deleterious long-run consequences of this extreme evolution of the welfare state. This means that some part of the population has less of a safety net than in Western Europe, but it also creates substantially greater flexibility and dynamism in the economy. When unemployment increased in the United States, for example in the 1981–82 recession, it was usually for a relatively short time, compared to what Western Europe experienced.

This substantial increase in government spending in Western Europe was financed by a substantial increase in taxes. While taxes as a share of GNP were relatively stable in the United States until the end of the 1970s, there were substantial increases in the fraction of the population subject to high marginal tax rates. This was redressed by the Reagan tax cuts and the indexing of the personal income tax. But the political climate in Europe led not only to higher taxes but to a disproportionate shifting toward the corporate income tax (taxes paid nominally by the corporate sector), employer contributions for social welfare programs, such as Social Security, and the value-added tax.

In addition to the tax disincentives caused by high marginal tax rates, including that on corporate-source income, the economies of Western Europe also went much further down the path of regulation. Not only were traditional economic activities regulated, but state monopolies became preponderant in the form of nationalized industrial enterprises encompassing transportation, communications, and public utilities. This not only caused the traditional kind of inefficiencies in government-run enterprises, but made it increasingly difficult to reallocate workers to more productive sectors of the economy. The economist and former Ambassador to West Germany Arthur Burns notes, ". . . establishing a new business may require up to 150 approvals in Germany, while moving a plant to a new location may entail obtaining several hundred permits."[1]

These economies therefore seem ripe for some reduction of social welfare spending. Can they have a Reagan-style across-the-board tax cut without some spending cuts to accompany them? Would substantial budget deficits do serious harm to these economies? It is much less likely that these economies will be bailed out by imports of foreign capital, as was the case for the United States. Therefore, tax cuts not matched by reduced spending will cause substantial budget deficits, which may do them serious long-run harm. Recall that in 1984–86, approximately half of the U.S. fiscal deficit was offset by inflows of foreign capital. There are undoubtedly many reasons for this. The dollar was the world's major trad-

ing currency, and assets denominated in dollars were relatively close substitutes for assets denominated in other currencies. The United States
offered a relatively safe investment whose returns looked quite attractive.
In addition, the United States was investing less in the Third World,
because of the sharp deterioration of conditions there.

A Reagan-style supply-side tax cut would probably result in large
budget deficits. This increase might be expansionary, which would harm
the trade balance and weaken the domestic currency, possibly accelerating inflation. It could also crowd out private investment. The U.S. experiment of cutting taxes without simultaneously cutting government
spending, thus generating a large budget deficit, neither increased inflation nor crowded out private investment; instead, a large inflow of foreign capital occurred. Former CEA Chairman Herbert Stein asks the
critical question: "Could France count on a similar result? If it cut taxes
and raised the budget deficit by x billion francs, could it expect a capital
inflow of approximately the same amount? The answer to that is almost
certainly negative."[2] The dilemma facing most Europeans, even in the
short-run, is that they probably could not get any major benefit from tax
reductions without simultaneously cutting government spending. And
cuts in spending are enormously difficult to achieve when programs have
become entrenched and especially when the fraction of the population
receiving benefits (including indirect beneficiaries of protectionist policies and tax subsidies) exceeds 50 percent. But, as noted above, some
important first steps have been taken in many of these economies.

There is one ironic advantage to Europe's much larger share of public spending and higher tax rates. An expansionary tax cut, to the extent
it succeeded in expanding employment, would produce a much *smaller*
deficit increase per unit of increase in employment. Expanded employment would increase revenues (because of high tax rates) and would
decrease transfer payments, which are much more generous than in the
United States or Japan. The net effect of the tax cut on the deficit is thus
likely to be a much smaller increase in the deficit compared to the size
of the cuts themselves than in the United States, above and beyond any
supply-side and income-reporting effects. The latter are also likely to be
larger than those documented in Chapter 8 for the United States because
marginal rates are so much higher.

Paradoxically, the temporary demand stimulus depends upon increasing disposable income to those persons who spend, rather than save, their
tax reductions (for example, because they are liquidity-constrained). Thus,
while the supply-side and income-reporting effects are likely to be greatest

at upper income levels where marginal tax rates are extremely high, the demand stimulus is likely to be greatest in middle- and lower-income groups. So there is a case for general across-the-board tax rate cuts in Europe, as well as reductions in the top marginal rates.[3]

Fortunately, there is some hope. Europeans are now willing to re-examine the nature of their welfare state, and in some cases, have actually made progress in slowing the growth of government outlays and reducing budget deficits and even cutting taxes. The German government, for example, has cut taxes and is committed to another tax cut in 1988. Great Britain, Italy, and Germany have been privatizing industry. Sweden has curtailed business subsidies. Several countries, including France, Holland, and Germany, have reduced unemployment benefits, and the United Kingdom has begun to tax them.

The only way for these economies to reduce permanently their share of taxes in GNP is to reduce their share of spending in GNP. To do that, they must reduce transfer payments to persons, such as social insurance benefits, which account for the majority of government's spending. Keep in mind that high benefits create a dependency on the safety net. The Reagan program sensibly tried to reduce the total amount of welfare-type spending, but to focus a larger fraction of the remainder on those who were below the poverty line. It has partially succeeded in doing so. That might be the first place to start for these economies. The next would be to render unemployment insurance more of a temporary safety net than a permanent substitute, and to increase the incentives to work by raising the disparity between their unemployment benefits and after-tax earnings for working. This will not be easy because it will be stoutly resisted by trade unions and current recipients. But these policies will have to be reformed or competition from abroad will inexorably erode the economies of Western Europe.

In reducing government expenditures, the other advanced democracies have one major advantage that the United States does not have: they rely upon us heavily for defense. The need for a rapid U.S. defense buildup would have been much less pressing had our allies kept up their own defense spending. On the other hand, one likely effect of the halt in the U.S. defense buildup will be increased pressure on them to share more equitably the burdens of our common defense.

Western Europe is now at a critical policy crossroad. Getting some control of government transfer payments *soon* is a necessity, for demographic pressures are sure to worsen matters in the years ahead. The demographics of Western Europe and Japan have shifted rapidly. As revealed

TABLE 12-4   Pensioners as % of Labor Force, Current and Projected

Year	US	Canada	Japan	France	W. Germany	Italy	U.K.
1985	24.0	16.0	18.3	31.0	29.0	27.1	30.3
2010	25.6	22.6	40.1	39.5	40.8	33.6	28.1
2030	41.5	39.4	42.7	54.6	63.6	46.5	37.6

Source: Projections based on OECD data.

in Table 4, over the next few decades the ratio of pensioners to the labor force will accelerate greatly in all advanced economies. The fraction of the population receiving old-age pensions as a percent of the labor force will double in Japan in the next twenty-five years and increase by one-third in West Germany. By the peak of the baby-boom generation's retirement, the ratio of old-age benefit recipients to the labor force in many of these economies will be only two or two and one-half workers per retiree, compared to the current three or four workers per retiree. This poses two tremendous challenges to these economies: first, to control the cost of public pensions in such a way that the funds are well targeted and cost effective; second, to achieve rapid economic growth so that the larger dependency ratio is less burdensome. A re-examination of the levels, rate of growth, eligibility standards, taxation, and multiplicity of retirement benefits is long overdue in all of these economies. It is a problem to be faced now because any sensible solution will require a broad base of agreement and legislation that can be phased in gradually to eliminate disruption caused by the rapid aging of the population. All of this takes time. The United Kingdom recently considered fundamental social security reform, but has since backed off. Those who will retire in several decades deserve some better notion of what their public support will be, so that they can plan accordingly in their private saving and insurance.

While detailed examination of each of the social insurance programs of these countries is beyond the scope of this volume, the general point is clear. An adequate social security system is necessary and desirable; social security cannot and should not be totally privatized, for reasons discussed in more detail elsewhere.[4] But the potential fiscal implications of the tremendous aging of the population are immense: tax rates for social security, already high in most of these countries, could double, choking off resources for continued economic growth. One interesting way to esti-

FIGURE 12-2   **Projected Public Debt/GNP Ratio, Current and Projected**

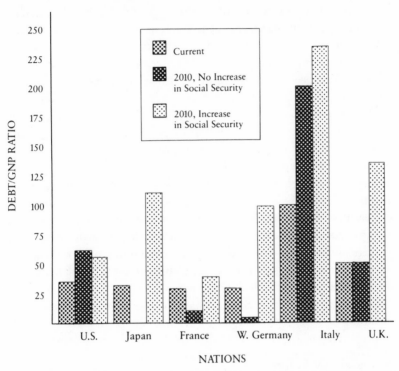

Source: Author's projections based on OECD data

mate the potential impact of the aging population on public finances is to examine what would happen to the ratio of the national debt to GNP over the next several decades if the noninterest part of the budget remained constant as a proportion of GNP. To figure this, the cost of the pensions automatically moving in line with demographic changes is calculated, with all other expenditures and taxes remaining constant as a proportion of GNP.

The results are presented in Figure 2. In Britain, the debt ratio would rise from 48 percent to 135 percent by 2010; in Japan, it would also exceed 100 percent, and in West Germany, it would rise to about 85 percent. Thus, looking down the road, these economies face great pressure to reduce other components of government spending and spur growth so that the greater

fraction of elderly retirees can be subsidized out of taxes on a larger future
real income. This necessitates lower tax rates. But countries like Japan
and Germany are reluctant to relax their fiscal policies. To reduce the
explosion of debt creates a painful choice between reducing pension
entitlements and cutting other expenditures, or increasing taxes substantially. A big tax cut now would worsen the situation and make it more
difficult in the future, unless it was heavily self-financing via revenue
reflows and reduced social spending on the newly employed.

Could these debt ratios rise dramatically without corresponding disruptions elsewhere in these economies? Who is willing to hold huge
amounts of Japanese, German, and British public debt? It is unlikely that
these countries can generate the same massive inflow of foreign capital
to offset the debt explosion as did the United States in the early 1980s.
I argued in Chapter 9 that the United States is unlikely to be able to continue to do so for the indefinite future, despite its special situation as a
safe haven, with the world's largest economy and the dollar as the major
trading currency. Thus, the gains from more efficient government spending, deregulation, and denationalization are not only likely to be important for the next few years in these economies, but will set the stage for
some sensible attempt to deal with what may prove to be an enormous
public finance crisis and a political battle between the generations.

Structural Tax Reform

As noted above, most other countries in the world have much higher marginal tax rates than the United States in both personal and corporate taxes.
Many of them also have substantial value-added or indirect taxes. For
the major industrialized countries in the world except Japan, the ratio
of taxes to GNP is higher than in the United States. In Sweden, marginal
tax rates for the *average* white collar worker have grown to over 80 percent. What can be done to reform the tax system in these countries?

First, it should be noted that firms and households as well as the political process in these economies have partially adjusted to these high tax
rates. Numerous special exemptions and deductions exist in order to overcome the most pernicious effects of high tax rates. For example, despite
very high tax rates, Japanese households can set aside large amounts in
tax-free saving accounts, thereby escaping or at least deferring taxes. Japanese corporations, while subject to an apparently high corporate tax,
finance almost 70 percent of their investment by debt, a ratio approxi-

mately twice that of U.S. corporations. Since interest payments on debt are tax deductible and the interest receipts are not taxable when provided by these tax-free saving vehicles, there really is no tax wedge going from a debt-financed investment back to the investor: the after-tax and before-tax rate of return on the marginal investment are the same. Analogous stories exist elsewhere. In Germany, there is partial integration of the corporate and personal tax. In the Scandinavian economies, which have extremely progressive tax rates with very high top marginal tax rates, the underground cash economy is the subject of so many anecdotal stories that one no longer considers them anecdotal. The value-added tax in most countries is riddled with so many exemptions that it does little to redress the potential regressivity and help the poor for whom these special exemptions (such as eliminating taxes on food and rent) were included in the first place.

Regardless of how much revenue these economies choose to raise, they would be much better off raising it with much broader-based taxes and lower marginal tax rates. This is true in both the corporate and personal tax, and in the value-added tax. A much more direct way to deal with potential regressivity or income redistribution problems in the value-added tax is simply to provide a refund for the value-added tax paid by poor persons, rather than by exempting the food purchased by rich and poor alike. The latter is a very inefficient, blunt instrument for trying to redress the burden of the tax on the poor.

European, Canadian, and Japanese saving and investment rates are much higher than in the United States. Hence, small increases in deficits cause less of a problem relative to the supply of domestically generated private saving. Since substantial tax cuts in order to achieve reduction in tax rates are unlikely to attract a corresponding amount of foreign capital and prevent the deleterious consequences of large budget deficits, structural tax revisions ought to be focused in those parts of the tax system which are most likely to generate a substantial revenue reflow. Both the American experience and logic show that the best areas for reduction are marginal tax rates that are extremely high and activities which are extremely sensitive to tax changes. In the Scandinavian countries, one could expect a reduction in the top marginal tax rate from, say, 80 percent to 70 percent not to lose very much revenue, as substantially more income would be reported.

To reduce the progressivity of their tax systems, these countries must overcome a much stronger resistance in the popular literature and press than in the United States. The tax rates in these countries are only nominally progressive and riddled with exemptions and deductions. Tax avoidance, the underground economy, special exemptions and features, and the fact that most of the revenue is used for redistributive outlays suggest that using the tax system as a primary vehicle for promoting equality in these societies is counterproductive. It is not uncommon in these countries, for example, for highly paid persons to report much of their personal consumption as business expenses, and therefore pay for it out of before-tax rather than after-tax dollars. Examples include the elaborate expense accounts and business dinners of the typical Japanese businessman, and the corporate amenities that go with highly paid positions in countries like Great Britain. While more obstacles must be overcome, the benefits from reducing very high marginal tax rates would be even greater in these countries than in the United States. Such reductions are probably necessary to sustain incentives to work, invest, and innovate—all preconditions for the growth necessary to ensure the future health of these economies.

The Reagan tax reforms—especially the 1986 Tax Reform Act, which shifts large tax burdens from the personal to the corporate income tax—may be appealing for the Europeans, but the dangers of increased corporate taxes in Europe are even greater than in the United States, as European investments have gone partly to replace high-wage European labor rather than to finance new technology or make existing labor more productive.

The Third World

I have focused throughout this volume on the United States, and occasionally discussed its interaction with major U.S. trading partners such as Germany, Japan, and Canada. But this discussion has great importance for the less-developed countries as well. Growth-oriented policies in the advanced world lead immediately to the most important and general kind of assistance that can be given to the lesser developed world: an increased demand for their exports. These beneficial effects far overshadow any indirect aid or direct foreign assistance. While the poverty and population problems in less-developed countries often cry out for direct assistance from the advanced economies, growth-oriented policies would do the most to improve the lot of the mass of mankind, tottering on the brink of subsistence. Not surprisingly, the Third World has become an ideological (and unfortunately, military) battleground between the democracies and relatively free markets of the West and the totalitarian economies of the

East, each group vying to be the role model for less-developed countries.[5]

Many components of Reaganomics are exportable, and nowhere is the message of Reaganomics — despite its flaws and unfinished agenda — more important than in the Third World. Limiting the role of government in the economy, lowering marginal tax rates on a broader base, deregulation, more careful targeting of transfer payments to the poor, a commitment to controling inflation, and attempting to raise economic growth to the top domestic priority are useful principles for all nations. History provides numerous examples of the benefits of doing so. To be sure, government is also a necessary and important component in the provision of preconditions for such long-term growth, from the public infrastructure and defense to a safety net for the indigent.

Conclusion

This brief tour of the problems, policies, and opportunities for improved performance in other countries indicates that acceptance of interventionist government economic policies ironically seems to be correlated with deteriorating economic performance. This manifests itself in various ways: erosion of incentives, diversion of resources, and at times, even simple mismanagement and waste. Governments play significant roles in societies, and the size of this role may understandably vary among types of economies and through time. For various reasons, the pendulum has swung too far, especially in the last two decades; in many countries continuing growth of government has brought with it at best diminishing benefits and at worst net losses to society. Space prohibits a detailed examination of specific programs for any other economy, but it is interesting to note that even Mexico, where a few years ago the subject of privatizing nationalized industries was not discussed in polite company, is now contemplating selling some government enterprises to the private sector. It is useful, however, to quote several tenets developed by the noted economist Arnold Harberger. In an important series of case studies of world economic growth in developed and developing nations, Harberger concludes by setting forth "some widely shared conclusions of policy professionals about the principal 'lessons' associated with successful growth policy":[6]

1. Keep budgets under adequate control. Budgets need not be balanced, but there are severe limits to budget deficits that can be incurred with relative impunity.

2. Keep inflationary pressures under reasonable control.

3. Make tax systems simple, easy to administer, and as much as possible, neutral and non-distorting with respect to resource allocation. (Harberger also concludes that the best tax for accomplishing all three purposes is the value-added tax.)

4. Avoid excessive income tax rates. There is little economic justification for rates exceeding 50 percent on any kind of income. Such rates distort behavior and create large disincentives to economic activity, while yielding little revenue.

5. Avoid excessive use of tax incentives to achieve a particular objective.

6. Make the borderline between public-sector and private-sector activity clear and well-defined. When the two compete in a given area, the same rules should govern their operation.

The core of these general rules is embodied in the Reagan economic program. The major exception is the large budget deficit, the most severe effects of which were not of immediate concern and have been ameliorated, at least temporarily, by a surprising volume of foreign capital flowing into the United States. Many foreign governments complained, while conveniently ignoring the beneficial effects of the U.S. trade deficit on the growth of their own economies. Of course, as severe pressure was placed on the dollar, the balance of trade deteriorated, imposing strains on various parts of the U.S. economy.

It is now a trite truism to say that the world is becoming increasingly interdependent. Clearly, assets denominated in U.S. dollars are much closer substitutes than ever before for assets denominated in leading currencies (especially the deutschmark or the yen). At the margin, at least over the short and medium run, we live much more in a world capital market than in a series of poorly linked domestic capital markets. It is dubious whether this free flow of capital at the margin could continue indefinitely into any one country, even one as large as the United States. But the substantial international flows of capital, as well as trade in goods and services, indicates that the results of any domestic economic policy, whether fiscal or monetary, are deeply influenced by corresponding policies pursued elsewhere.

In many economies, the role of government has grown to the point where it seriously impedes the performance of the economy. When substantially more than half the population is either employed by the gov-

TABLE 12-5   Public Sector Employment as Share of Total, 1981

Country	Percentage
Sweden	29.8
U.K.	21.5
Denmark	24.5
Germany	14.7
U.S.	12.0
Japan	6.5

Source: Author's calculations from various sources.

ernment (see the comparative data in Table 5) or receives transfer payments from the government, the prospect of shrinking the government diminishes rapidly. Many Western European countries are near or above this critical point. Many less-developed countries have important segments of the population dependent on public employment, and state-run enterprises. Worse yet, the aging of the population in these countries suggests that the pressures on public finances, as well as the share of persons receiving benefits from the government, will worsen drastically. The time has come for these countries to intensify their efforts to reduce excesses in government spending, taxation, regulation, and monetary policy. This is not a recipe for a return to a world where governments play no role in providing a safety net or public infrastructure; it is a recipe to restore some semblance of balance in preconditions necessary for economic growth. Some governments have recognized this, and have taken cautious initial steps on matters of spending, employment, transfer payments, and taxes. The enormous changes in the United States — e.g., the lowering of the top marginal tax rates from 70 percent to 28 percent in the course of eight years between 1980 and 1988 — must seem remarkable to foreign observers.

Reaganomics' most important contribution may well be speeding and accentuating the change in what is perceived to be the sensible role of government in the economy. If this legacy endures, it will undoubtedly affect public dialogue on economic policy in other countries as well. These will be driven primarily by the relationship between economic performance and expectations. One can only hope that the lessons of the Reagan economic program, both its successes *and* failures, will provide an added impetus and partial road map for other countries as they too seek to improve their economic performance.

Chapter 13

The Unfinished Agenda

In judging the successes and failures of the Reagan economic program, one must focus on the present, looking at what has been accomplished, what has failed, and how what has been done affects the policy agenda in the immediate future. Then, of course, there is the longer-term future, especially the question of whether the Reagan program will be viewed twenty years from now as a turning point, with many enduring accomplishments influencing economic policy and performance over the long haul, or whether it will be viewed only as an aberration—a temporary suspension of the long-run trend from Franklin Roosevelt's New Deal toward a European-style welfare state.

While Reaganomics has many accomplishments to its credit, it is important to make clear that it has *not* institutionalized either the basic principles upon which it stands or the continuation of its programs, through enduring structural changes in the budget process, monetary policy, or trade relations. If economic events and the political climate change, many of the Reagan initiatives may eventually be reversed. There are no guarantees that when the memory of double-digit inflation of the 1970s fades, future administrations or Federal Reserve Boards will not resort to inflationary monetary growth. Nor is there a guarantee that the spending programs curbed during President Reagan's term in office will not expand again in the future, although the large accumulation of public debt inherited by the next administration will temporarily exert downward pressure on spending growth.

The only thing that is certain is that if we do eventually return to the trend toward a European-style welfare state—where the share of taxes and government outlays often exceeds half the national income, marginal tax rates are exorbitant, and there is very little difference between after-tax earnings and public subsidies—the economy will lose much of its flexibility, vitality, and dynamism. The prospects for noninflationary long-term growth and international competitiveness would suffer substantially. Fortunately, many factors are working to thwart this potential slide. First, Reaganomics called a halt to this trend at a much lower level of government involvement in the economy than is the case in Western Europe. Second, the sorry performance of the inflexible economies of Western Europe, with their sluggish growth and enormous unemployment, serves as a cautionary example. We now see them retreating from their worst excesses. Third, labor unions represent a much smaller fraction of the labor force and are less powerful in dictating U.S. economic policy than in Europe, where they prevent the reallocation of the labor force in response to dynamic changes in technology, demand, and international competition.

The Administration's inability to institutionalize its philosophy and goals through structural reforms in monetary and fiscal policy (except for tax reform, which will eventually be affected by the budget deficit; Gramm-Rudman-Hollings, which is being honored through creative accounting as well as through observance; and indexed tax brackets, which lessen the revenue windfall due to inflation) means that economic policy is operating under a set of explicit rules similar to those of before. For this reason, the prospect of sustaining the Reagan program beyond the President's personal popularity remains in doubt. Nevertheless, much has been accomplished. The Reagan economic program, while far from perfect, has created an *opportunity* for a much-improved economy for the balance of the century, by eliminating rising and fluctuating double-digit inflation, explosive growth of nondefense government spending, high and rising marginal tax rates, ever-growing government regulation, and outright government control through incomes policies or wage and price controls. It is worth recalling that these were serious problems as recently as 1980.

In my view, however, the most important accomplishment of Reaganomics is intangible: Reaganomics changed the general understanding of what constitutes a reasonable economic policy. Only a few years ago, fine-tuning demand management, wage and price controls, incomes policies, retaliatory protectionism, expanding government regulation, public sector employment, industrial policy, public works programs, and national development banks were considered sensible economic policies. Some of them had been tried and found wanting, but were recycled once again. Today, one hears much less talk of such policies than even a few years ago. Perhaps this is because inflation has been substantially reduced. Bad ideas tend not to die out; they wait to be recycled. But the once-popular notion that the government, especially the federal government, is the proper answer to *all* of society's economic problems has been dealt a serious blow. Following the terrible economic performance of the 1970s, the Reagan economic program seems to have accomplished the important but intangible objective of discrediting this idea, making it more difficult for ill-advised policies to appear at the expense of the taxpayer and the economy. New spending programs will have to pass tougher tests for years to come, and that means less automatic budget growth in the future.[1] Even if nothing else is done, the repudiation of bad policies will stand as a major accomplishment.

Besides this intangible change, other, more concrete accomplishments can be outlined. The most important is the reduction of inflation at a much lower cost than had been predicted. The recession was severe, but it was not nearly as bad as critics predicted. Of course, the Administration did not forecast the recession as a result of the disinflation process, perhaps missing an important opportunity to educate the public to the idea that short-term sacrifices were necessary to reduce inflation. The Administration acted no differently than any other in this, and perhaps it would have been naive to expect more. Another major achievement was the focus of attention on the disincentives of high tax rates *at the margin.* The bad news is that we could not afford all the good news the Administration and Congress heaped on us. Since the original tax cuts, various tax increases have attempted to close some of the deficit, but it still remains large. Nor did we get the tax reforms quite right. Thus, much remains to be done in this area. However, compared to previous discussions of tax policy, the Administration has changed the focus to questions of efficiency and incentives, away from redistributing minor amounts of the tax burden by gerry-rigging the tax code.

The Administration was successful for several years in shifting priorities away from domestic spending toward defense. However, only limited success has been achieved in limiting the growth of nondefense spending. Grants-in-aid to state and local governments and means-tested welfare programs were both slowed substantially. The former certainly needed to be reduced and consolidated; the latter were burgeoning, and a tightening of eligibility standards was desirable. Both are major discre-

tionary spending categories, but the "uncontrollable" part of the budget
—items whose growth continues unless laws are changed—has been
much less affected. While the 1983 Social Security amendments moved
in the right direction, huge income transfers still occur in Social Security
and Medicare to well-off individuals at the expense of the average taxpayer. The Administration has not succeeded in decoupling these well-
off recipients from those who are needy. Indeed, since the 1981 political
setback on Social Security, the Administration has been reluctant to support even *targeted* reductions in Social Security benefits. A similar problem exists in agricultural subsidies, whose explosive growth is a major
disappointment.

Spending can be controlled only by a major attack on middle-class
entitlements. These programs, however, are hard to curtail precisely
because they reach a large number of beneficiaries and are administered
under a large number of complex rules. Nevertheless, the case for reduced
spending remains strong in a program such as Social Security, which pays
well-off elderly people many billions of dollars more than what they and
their employers paid in, plus interest.

The Administration has been only partially successful in instituting
a regime of rules to replace discretion in monetary and fiscal policies. The
three-year tax program certainly had this flavor, as did the Administration's support for the Fed's targets of monetary growth reduction. But there
have been several changes of tax policy since then, and the Fed has also
altered its monetary policy. The most enduring change is the indexing
of income tax brackets. The Administration has not been successful in
institutionalizing major budget reforms despite Gramm-Rudman-
Hollings, which is not surprising since it is having a difficult time controlling spending in general. Let's face it: it is awkward for an administration that is presiding over a doubling of the national debt to demand
a balanced budget amendment. However, the attempt to achieve institutional reform, structural reform, or constitutional amendment will
undoubtedly occupy a substantial part of the Administration's remaining time in office.

Similarly, reducing regulation has only been partially successful.
Interpretation and enforcement of existing laws has changed, but the basic
laws setting up the administrative apparatus to implement social regulations remains unchanged. Efforts made under the General Agreement on
Tariffs and Trade (GATT) have also made little headway in reducing
agriculture and non-tariff barriers, although the new round of negotiations provides some hope.

An Agenda for Economic Policy

While we have altered our monetary policy several times, dramatically changed budget priorities, sharply reduced and substantially reformed taxation, and reformed regulatory policy, we have not fundamentally modified the processes by which these policies are generated. There is a great need for a steady, coherent, coordinated, long-run set of goals, and for a general policy framework to achieve them. This will require either substantial structural reform of economic policy processes or continued efforts to alter the policies themselves. The unfinished agenda includes reforms of federal spending patterns and levels, further reform of the tax system, more regulatory reform, further trade liberalization, and reform of monetary policy.

Government spending has gone up, not down, under President Reagan. The discretionary part of nondefense spending has been controlled. But three major programmatic issues remain in budget policy. The first task is to decouple well-off recipients in government transfer programs such as Social Security, agricultural subsidies, and government loans in favor of those who are needy. The tightening of the eligibility standards in traditional welfare programs was an intelligent move in this direction. Sensible reforms for Social Security, Medicare, and other middle-class entitlement programs, which involve much larger expenditures, could make them less expensive and more effective. Welfare for the wealthy simply can no longer be afforded. It is not an ideological issue. More cost-conscious and target-effective spending on these programs will *preserve* benefits for the needy.

Second, the long-overdue defense buildup needs to be made as cost-effective as possible. Experts may differ in evaluating the need for specific items in the buildup, but that does not mean that the aggregate dollars are being spent as wisely as they should or could be. A very rapid defense buildup occurred in the first four years of the Reagan Administration, but, Congress has since made substantial cuts in the President's spending requests. Is a continued large defense buildup needed? If so, why? What needs to be built up? Attention in the press has focused on one or two large weapon systems and the Strategic Defense Initiative ("Star Wars"). The Soviets appear to have a Star Wars program of their own, and there is much disagreement among persons more knowledgeable than I on the desirability of pursuing SDI as currently proposed. There seems to be much less disagreement about the need to conduct the basic research than about issues of subsequent production and deployment. Careful and prudent observers from both parties support the development of the basic research, from Senator Sam Nunn (D-GA) to Senator Bob Dole (R-KA). But what other defense items are necessary and desirable? As programs approved in the first half of this decade go into production, is it realistic to think we could shut them down if we decided they were no longer desirable, given the employment built up around them?

Finally, a systematic re-evaluation of the desirability of federal participation in a wide range of programs is needed, examining opportunities for increased efficiency as well as the issue of whether the government should play any role at all. These programs range from the massive set of government loans, loan subsidies, and loan guarantees, to federal government ownership of assets that could be privatized. While we are better off in this regard than the European countries, there are many areas, such as transportation, energy, and utilities, where reforms and reductions in the federal role—or even privatization—would be highly desirable. Some of these opportunities for reform are discussed in detail in Chapter 7. Selling assets may help to reach a Gramm-Rudman-Hollings budget target temporarily but will not permanently reduce the deficit. In fact, selling assets will reduce the deficit for a given year, because of the cash-basis budget we employ, but not permanently.

Congress and the President are stalemated on these budget priorities. Congress does not want to reduce domestic spending any further, and is especially protective of middle-class entitlement programs (not surprisingly, since that is where the majority of votes are). Congress is also much less supportive of a continued defense buildup than it was a couple of years ago. In any event, the budget deficit not withstanding, we are spending too much, and not always wisely.

Large improvements have been made in the tax structure. The substantial lowering of tax rates in 1981–83, accelerated in the 1986 tax reform, is an enormous achievement. But problems will also undoubtedly result from the 1986 reforms, as discussed in Chapter 8. The reduction in tax rates will not fully offset the decline in saving and investment incentives. And our society already has the lowest saving and investment rate in the advanced world. Thus, developing effective saving and investment incentives remains a major goal. There are several ways this could be accomplished. A model favored by many economists is the gradual phase-in of a consumed-income tax, which unifies the corporate and personal tax. Such a tax system, which was proposed in a January 1977 plan by then Treasury Secretary William Simon, would redress the disincentives for saving and the double taxation of dividends that now exists,[2] but it would not, by itself, solve the problem of saving and investment.

Future changes in depreciation schedules, investment credits, preferential treatment of capital gains, and saving incentives must be thought out much more carefully than they were in the past. The combination of accelerated depreciation and investment tax credits, interest deductibility for leveraged investments, and the differential capital gains tax rates became the archetypical structure of a tax shelter: an asset was purchased, the investment incentives were front-loaded, often multiplied because the investment was leveraged with debt, and the asset, whose value would decline more slowly than the tax depreciation, was then sold, with the difference being taxed as a capital gain at preferential rates. Thus, investments have been made purely for tax benefits, rather than for economic productivity. This situation, in turn, has undermined confidence in the tax system. From the standpoint of saving and investment, it would be better to move to a system of consumed-income taxes, in which all net saving would be deductible from a much more comprehensive definition of income. Similar to the treatment of Individual Retirement Accounts in 1986, this would leave a very broad base of consumption as taxable income. Consumed income would become the tax base. The 1986 Tax Reform Act has major deficiencies in its treatment of investment and saving. These will have to be redressed or we run the risk of shutting down productive investment as well as tax shelters.

An alternative is to make changes at the margin: if additional revenues are sought, it is important that they come from a tax device that has desirable properties. A consumption-type value-added tax could be implemented at a modest rate that would both reduce the deficit and raise enough revenue to allow restoration of desirable features in corporate and personal income taxes. The base for such a tax should be quite broad, and it should avoid exemptions for specific items. Otherwise, the benefits of raising a lot of revenue on a broad base with low rates will be lost, and there will be little gain in redressing the regressivity of the tax since items such as food are exempted for rich and poor alike. A vastly superior method would be a refundable credit for low-income persons such as exists for Social Security taxes paid.

If these reforms prove too difficult to implement, we should retain the benefits of the 1986 tax reform — the substantially lower marginal tax rates — and seek additional revenue, as necessary, through a further broadening of the base. As discussed in Chapter 8, the base of the personal income tax was not broadened very much, and much of the broadening was done in saving and investment incentives. Taxation of fringe benefits could achieve this end. At present, a substantial fraction of income goes untaxed as fringe benefits (which have grown rapidly, partly because of their tax preference status).

Given the continuing fight over whether corporations pay their fair share of taxes, it is quite desirable to integrate corporate and personal taxes through a system to trace corporate-source income through the tax system and measure the tax paid on it, replacing the current system that ignores the corporate-source income taxed at the personal level. I believe this is part of the reason why there was such a dramatic shift of burdens from personal taxes to corporate taxes in the 1986 tax reform. Some part of this corporate tax is undesirable and will create future economic problems, such as lower investment rates.

None of these improvements in the tax system provides an incentive for improved spending decisions. It is very difficult to reduce spending in programs once they are implemented. The mid-1970s Budget Reform Act has simply not produced the results it was intended to achieve, which was to tie spending and tax decisions together. The spending goes on in separate appropriations bills, and honors the Budget Committee's dictates in the breach as well as in the observance. In recent years, appropriations bills have often reached figures much larger than the budget resolution would have allowed. Periodically, there was simply no budget resolution because Congress could not agree on the parameters for spending and taxes in time to pass a resolution.

Major institutional reform of the budget process is a key item in the agenda. The Administration has made several important suggestions. One is to bring federal credit programs back into the budget. Another is to extend a line-item veto to the president. While this is unlikely to pass because Congress does not want to surrender control to the president, some improved mechanism for reducing outlandish expenditures short of impoundment is imperative. Congress is overwhelmed every year simply in passing the bills necessary to run the government, let alone in evaluating the various programs. Thus, while zero-based budgeting and sunset legislation are appealing in principle, Congress does not have the time, expertise, and political will to implement them seriously. One step in the right direction would be to introduce multi-year budgeting, both to discourage fudging the figures for programs in order to slip them under a spending ceiling, and to allow for more rational debate and greater time to discuss specific items.[3] Another potential improvement would be a separate capital budget. With capital budgeting, there would be two budgets: a capital and an operating budget, with capital spending placed in the capital budget and a charge for depreciation and obsolescence of the capital stock made on the operating budget.

It is more appropriate (but not necessary) to finance long-lived investment (such as military buildups during — or to prevent — wars) by government borrowing, since the benefits will accrue for many years and future taxpayers may equitably bear part of the burden. There also may be small efficiency gains in smoothing tax rates over time. There is a fear that a separate capital account would lead to unnecessary spending, since proponents of specific capital projects delight in the exclusion of capital spending from the current services budget and deficit. I believe the opposite to be the case. First, anyone can add two numbers. The borrowing to finance investment spending would not be hidden. A capital budget properly implemented can bring capital investment spending under control and help us plan for future maintenance and repair costs, development, and financing. Second, how can the budget be made more comprehensive without a capital budget? To control off-budget spending, one must first realize that most of the spending is on capital items — explicit, implicit, or potential assets and liabilities, such as loans, guarantees, and unfunded pension plans.

Two additional reforms I favor — separately or in combination — are a super-majority requirement, say 60 percent, for approval of spending, and a marginal balanced budget requirement in which spending increases must be tied to sufficient finance — tax revenues or cuts in other spending programs — to prevent an increase in the budget deficit. Either or both of these proposals could be implemented by Congress itself and would greatly improve the budget outcomes, as spending would have to pass stiffer tests. Such reforms must be enacted during the next Congress, or pressure for a constitutional amendment to require much stricter spending limits or balanced budgets will obtain still greater momentum. Because such restrictions should only be used as a last resort, and because they will undoubtedly cause many distortions, a comprehensive budget reform is worth one more try. It should be viewed as precisely that: a last attempt at bringing a semblance of order to decision-making on public spending.

The large budget deficits and closely related trade deficits must be reduced, or the economy runs the risk of crowding out investment. The longer that large budget deficits require us to import vast amounts of foreign capital, the greater future payment of interest and dividends to foreigners will be. This in turn will require a still-greater excess of future exports over imports. We will not only have to balance our trade, but run a large surplus. This will cause tremendous reallocation of the economy's resources, as well as accompanying transition costs. We badly need to raise our national saving rate to that of our domestic investment, and the only way to do that rapidly is to reduce the federal deficit rapidly.

Throughout this volume, it is clear that I believe the budget deficits were the major flaw in the Reagan program. It is not obvious how to partition the blame for the budget deficits. In Chapters 4 and 9, we noted that *relative to the level of government spending and tax revenue projected prior to the Reagan program*, tax cuts were the major source of the deficit. But the level and composition of that spending, as analyzed in Chapter 7, were inappropriate. We needed some defense buildup and were spending large amounts on ineffective or poorly targeted programs. Despite the rhetoric that President Reagan has totally refused to increase taxes, the fact is that taxes were raised in 1982, 1983, and 1984 (see Chapter 8). Thus, blame for the deficits can be spread over both the legislative and executive branches, and ultimately rests with the public, which despite moralizing on deficits has refused to support either major spending reductions or a large tax increase. While some who place a great value on a smaller government believe any cost to the economy that starves Congress into cutting spending is worthwhile, the costs *are* substantial. Indeed, a cynic might argue that ultra-conservatives wanted large deficits to tie the hands of the next administration. While I share the goal of smaller government, I do not believe the current level of government spending to be so detrimental to the economy's health and personal freedom that it is worth any cost to reduce it.

But I do believe it can and should be reduced, and I have offered above my program for doing so. Stopping the evolution toward a European-style welfare state was more important than reducing spending below current levels, and was worth larger risks and greater short-run costs. Since I believe this has been partially, but perhaps only temporarily, accomplished, I favor a tax increase as a last resort, *if* spending cannot be reduced. It is also important that the increase be on consumption, not on investment. The President's fiscal legacy will depend heavily on the compromises reached in the next two years on the budget—how much and what spending will be cut and how much and how revenue will be raised.

Since I have stressed the complex nature of the effects of budget deficits and concluded large structural budget deficits are potentially quite harmful, it is important to note that budget deficits are not the sole cause of remaining economic problems, and that much-smaller deficits are not a guarantee of successful economic performance. It appears that the worst possibility—igniting a hyperinflation with runaway interest costs—has been forestalled. Several issues — the crowding out of investment, the possibility that the United States will have to become a large net exporter to cover interest payments to foreigners on a growing external debt, and the question of intergenerational equity — remain to be addressed. But a good idea — approximate budget balance over a time span longer than the typical business cycle, with all the measurement caveats discussed in Chapter 9 — will get a bad name if the public is misled into believing budget balance by itself will prevent a recession or inflation, or guarantee rapid growth.

As with tax reform and budget policy, so with regulatory policy. Americans clearly want safety on the job and reduced environmental pollution. The basic legislation needed to set up the agencies for enforcement of occupational safety and environmental preservation and safety have not really been amended under Reagan. Changes in interpretation and some selective deregulation have occurred, especially in traditionally regulated industries (where a pro-market, as opposed to pro-business policy emerged), but much less so in the new social regulation. Many of the agencies have had their budgets reduced and hence enforcement has been decreased, though in some cases enforcement was probably uneconomic. But another public scare and a change of administration will bring about a substantial increase in enforcement and a stricter interpretation of regulations. Taken to their extremes, the new social legislation could substantially reduce the ability of our economy to generate new technology and to grow. Clearly, balance is needed between economic and social priorities in the regulatory process. I believe that the Reagan Administration has moved in the right direction, but the failure to institutionalize the reforms leaves a great deal of uncertainty over the future of regulatory policy. It would be desirable to attempt to achieve a consensus on the appropriate balance and amend the enabling legislation accordingly, rather than leave interpretation up to political whim and court decisions.

U.S. trade relations have been strained because of our massive trade deficit. Pressure for protectionist legislation, while successfully resisted by the Administration in most instances, continues. Protectionist trade practices exist throughout the world, and much more forceful bargaining at the General Agreement on Tariffs and Trade is desperately needed if we are to prevent the continued threat of trade wars throwing the world into a recession. The GATT must deal sensibly with nontariff trade barriers and agriculture, *at the very least.* As this volume goes to press, tension in trade, from European Economic Community agriculture to Japanese semiconductors, is intense. Some retaliatory tariffs have been imposed both to respond to allegations of unfair trade practices and to head off still-greater protectionist legislation. The entire world economy runs the risk of a serious recession unless trade tensions can be quickly reduced. Some call for international monetary reform and a move back to fixed exchange rates. I believe this would be a mistake for both the United States and world economy. We ought not to interfere with the flow of resources by supporting various prices in the world economy above their natural levels, or placing ceilings to prevent them from rising to those levels. This is true in the domestic economy for everything from rent control to agricultural price supports, and equally true in foreign exchange markets.

If Reaganomics has stood for anything, it has stood for *rules rather than discretion* in both fiscal and monetary policies. Of course, the large budget deficits render much else uncertain. It is extremely important for the private sector to know in advance what taxes are likely to be in the future, what spending decisions are in the process of being made, and what the Fed is likely to do. This is why we should resist attempts to return to fine-tuning the economy, and why monetary growth targets need to be supplemented by additional indicators. Nominal GNP is one possibility,[4] more broad-based measures of money and credit another. This could lead to the implementation of rules rather than discretion, and yet allow some flexibility in the event of major, unforeseen changes in velocity. The rule should primarily focus on achieving a level of inflation low enough so that it does not seriously affect economic decisions, perhaps no more than 2 percent.

It is also clear that the Federal Reserve will have to pay much greater attention to the effect its monetary policy has on the monetary policy of the world's other major economies, represented especially by that of the Bundesbank and the Bank of Japan. As assets denominated in yen, deutschmarks, dollars, and other major currencies have become much closer substitutes for investment purposes in recent years, monetary growth in the rest of the world exercises increasing influence on how any given rate of domestic monetary expansion affects both the U.S. and the world economy. The Fed's ability to adopt sensible policy rules would also be improved by divesting it of its regulatory function. Currently, the majority of the Federal Reserve Board Governors' time is spent on regulatory matters, and relieving them of those responsibilities would increase the Fed's ability to focus on aggregate monetary policy.

In summary, the unfinished policy agenda includes improved spending controls, further tax reforms, and major structural or institutional changes in the budget process and monetary policy, encouraging more predictability and better outcomes. Although it is a challenging agenda for any administration, it encompasses those policies that will best encourage the goals of non-inflationary economic growth and efficient and target-effective government spending, while maintaining a humane social safety net. These policies are no guarantee against recession, sluggish growth, or other economic woes. They are only the framework which would maximize the opportunity to achieve a stable, growing, and efficient economy.

Our final assessment of the successes and failures of the Reagan economic program — as I noted at the beginning of the book — must be made in relation not to some idealized perfect economy but to the likely condition of the economy had the program not been implemented. As recently as 1980, high and fluctuating inflation, sluggish growth, high and rising taxes (especially marginal tax rates), and rapidly growing domestic entitlements (leading toward a European-style welfare state) were economic facts. In response, some presidential candidates proposed such solutions as a national industrial policy and a national reconstruction bank to regulate the flow of private capital. It is a tremendous accomplishment of the Reagan economic program that it was able to solve substantially many of the problems and that in the process, these ill-advised proposals have disappeared from our policy debate. In addition, the Reagan program helped to achieve rapid disinflation at much lower cost than was anticipated, a major change in budget priorities, and dramatic tax reform. Problems of course remain — especially the substantial budget deficit and related trade deficit. And there is uncertainty over the future course of monetary, fiscal, regulatory, and trade policies.

Despite the importance of the agenda proposed here, economic policy is less urgent than it was in 1980 because of the substantial improvements that have occurred since that time. While getting the fiscal deficit under control *is* an urgent priority, the reduction in inflation, reduced marginal tax rates, and partial control of domestic spending are major improvements since 1980. However, institutionalizing these improvements through changes in statutes and operating procedures remains a high priority. There are some hopeful signs in that direction: although the political process seems bogged down in dealing with these problems, many of these reforms are now espoused by economists from very different schools of thought and political orientations. The need for reform of the budget process is a concern of politicians both conservative and liberal (for example, the current and former directors of the Congressional Budget Office). Disagreements remain about the future course of tax policy — whether raising revenue will be necessary, and if so, how—and whether the 1986 tax reform will have to be amended to correct some of the problems it will create, notwithstanding its many desirable features.

This unfinished agenda is a challenge not only for Ronald Reagan in the last quarter of his term, but also for the United States and other nations for many years to come. We have the capability to improve economic policy and the policy process; whether we have the political will to do so remains to be seen. We can be sure of one thing: the failure to surmount the political obstacles to reform will extend well beyond our own economic well-being to that of our children and grandchildren. The ultimate impact of the Reagan economic program—its successes, failures, and the agenda it has set—will be judged by its impact many years beyond Ronald Reagan's term in office. A remarkable, if highly imperfect, start has been made, and an opportunity presented. Whether Reaganomics will be sustained and reinforced, or overturned, will greatly affect the future course of our economy and society.

One may hope that the experiences of the Reagan era, both good and bad, will lead our political institutions and processes toward policies that are more certain and more effective in creating an environment for improved long-run growth and short-run stability, while providing a humane safety net and preserving our personal freedoms.

◆ *Appendix* ◆

Tax Reform Proposals

Fundamental reform proposals can be grouped in several ways; perhaps the most useful and economically meaningful distinction would refer to whether they move us closer to a tax on consumption or to a tax on income (consumption plus saving). As Thomas Hobbes noted more than 300 years ago, it may be fairer and more sensible to tax people on what they withdraw from the common resource pool, roughly measured by their consumption, rather than on what they contribute to it, roughly measured by their income. I shall discuss some of the pros and cons of the two systems in more detail below.

As mentioned in Chapter 8, there were several major income tax reforms under consideration in the reform debate: the "FAIR" tax plan of Senator Bill Bradley and Representative Richard Gephardt; the Fair and Simple Tax plan (FAST) of Representative Jack Kemp and Senator Robert Kasten; a proposal put forward by the Treasury Department (Treasury I); and a plan partly based on Treasury I proposed by the President. Three basic expenditure tax reforms were also proposed. One was the personal cash flow tax, which I have elsewhere supported, and which was detailed in a landmark document prepared by the Teasury staff under the direction of David Bradford and released by Secretary William Simon as *Blueprints for Basic Tax Reform* in 1977. A close approximation was introduced by Representative Cecil Heftel as a substitute for current income taxes. One of the most important and intriguing tax reform proposals was the so-called flat-tax of Robert Hall and Alvin Rabushka, of the Hoover Institution at Stanford University. As a consumption tax it allows immediate write-off of all net (of borrowing) investment. A similar proposal was introduced as a bill by Senator Dennis DeConcini. The final consumption tax variant would be some form of a national retail sales tax or a value-added tax, which are used as major revenue devices in most Western European economies, have recently been adopted in New Zealand, and are under consideration in Japan.

A few words about fundamental tax reform are in order. To begin with, each of the plans was designed to be "revenue neutral"; that is, they were designed to raise the same amount of revenue as the taxes they propose to replace (generally individual and corporate income taxes). For most of the plans, however, revenue neutrality would probably have failed in the short run for two reasons. First, the method of estimating how much revenue would be generated generally underestimates the extent to which people will alter their behavior due to tax changes. Such an assumption is frequently unwarranted. Consider, for example, the proposal in Treasury I to eliminate the interest deduction on second homes. The Treasury assumed this would raise $10 billion in revenue. Unfortunately, anyone clever enough to hire a tax accountant would be advised to increase the mortgage on their first home and pay-off the mortgage on the second, thus rendering all of the interest deductible, and yielding the Treasury no revenue at all. Many other examples are available. It is unlikely that any of these proposals would fall drastically short of current revenue, but they would probably need tax rates a few percentage points higher to guard against this.

A second reason they would not be revenue neutral is that virtually all of the plans attempt to reduce tax rates by greatly broadening the tax base, i.e., by eliminating many exemptions and deductions. But, as noted above, these exemptions and deductions were originally designed to serve ostensibly noble social purposes. If so, one should expect that there would be enormous pressure to make up for any reductions in these tax breaks by alternative forms of government subsidies (loans or loan-guarantees) or direct outlays. For example, changing the accounting method which saves defense contractors billions of dollars may raise more revenue, but may require greater defense spending as these extra costs are passed on. Finally, working in the opposite direction, by lowering tax rates, and in some cases changing investment incentives, each of these programs has the potential for altering the future course of the economy, including income, the tax base, and future tax revenue. Thus, revenue neutrality must be understood as a very imprecise short-run static concept.

Virtually all of the proposals would have reduced the number of tax brackets in the individual income tax, raised the exemption levels so that more households at the bottom of the income scale would be free of any tax payment at all, greatly broadened the tax base by eliminating major deductions, and generally lowered tax rates. Were these features likely to lead to simplification of the tax system? I believe that the claims of how much these proposals would reduce the paperwork requirements of households and firms were hyperbolic. For example, it really is not very difficult to look one's tax up in the tax table once one has gotten down to what is called taxable income. The real difficulty is in working your way through the numerous special exclusions, averaging procedures, deductions, and so on; and, of course, arranging your economic affairs to reduce your tax burden. True simplification consists of reducing the number of special items and removing some people from paying tax at all, but has little to do with fewer tax brackets. *Lower* tax rates are desirable if the same amount of revenue can be raised through a broader base, but the reason is to reduce economic distortions, not to make the tax system simpler.

The major highlights of these various proposals are documented in Appendix Table 1. As indicated, there were substantial and important differences. For example, Bradley-Gephardt would have retained the deduction for state and local income taxes, while Kemp-Kasten and Treasury I would have abolished it. The latest version of Kemp-Kasten reinserted the capital gains differential, while Bradley-Gephardt eliminated it; and the Treasury proposal eliminated the distinction between capital gains and ordinary income but indexed the basis for calculating capital gains to adjust for inflation. The President's proposal contained a capital gains differential of 50 percent. Bradley-Gephardt and Kemp-Kasten retained the charitable contribution deduction, while Treasury I limited it to the amount contributed above 2 percent of income, besides changing several other features. There were also some differences in the number and range of tax rates among the proposals, although they all reduced tax rates and broadened the base.

It should be noted that proposals such as Kemp-Kasten and the Treasury plan, which would have eliminated the deduction for state income taxes, would have done less to reduce effective marginal tax rates than meets the eye. Consider a taxpayer in California or New York, states that have substantial and progressive income taxes. A large fraction of taxpayers in both states pay rates of 10 percent or more. Suppose someone is in the 50 percent bracket at the federal level and 10 percent at the state level. Their combined tax rate is 55 percent — 50 percent plus 5 percent (half the state rate because it is deductible from federal taxes). These people

Table A-1 Comparison of Former Law and Major Reform Plans

	Former Law	Reagan Plan
Individual tax rates	14 rates from 11% to 50%	3 rates: 15, 25, 35%
Personal exemptions	$1,080	$2,000
Mortgage Interest	Fully deductible for all mortgages	Principal residence deductible
Other Interest	$10,000 plus amount equal to investment income	$5,000 plus amount equal to investment income
Employer-provided health insurance	Not taxed	Taxed up to first $10/month for single; $25 for family
Retirement plans	IRAs deductible universally, up to $2,000 + $250 for nonworking spouse; 401(k) up to $30,000/yr	IRAs deductible; spousal IRA up to $2,000/yr 401(k) $8,000/yr limit with IRA offset
Charitable contributions	Fully deductible	Deductible, but only on itemized returns
State and local taxes	Fully deductible	No deduction
Capital gains	60% excluded for 20% top rate	50% excluded for 17.5% top rate but fewer items covered
Corporate tax rates	46% top, graduated rates up to $100,000	33% top rate, graduated rates up to $100,000
Depreciation	Accelerated	Somewhat accelerated, but less generous
Investment tax credit (ITC)	Generally 10%	Eliminated
R&D tax credit	25%, broad definition, due to expire	Extend; tighten
Alternative minimum tax	Modest	Strong

Ways & Means	Senate Finance	House & Senate Conference
4 rates: 15, 25, 35, 38%	2 rates: 15, 27%	2 rates: 15, 28%
$1,500 for itemizers $2,000 for non-itemizers	Increased to $2,000, phasing out as income increases	$2,000 (over three years) phasing out in higher incomes
Principal and second residence deductible	Deductible	Deductible; restricts nonhousing use
$20,000 plus amount equal to investment income, cap on tax shelters	Disallows consumer installment interest deduction	Disallows consumer interest deduction; investment interest deductible up to amount of investment income
Not taxed	Not taxed	Not taxed
IRAs deductible, but contributions offset against other deferred income, e.g., 400(k) $7,000/yr with IRA offset	IRAs non-deductible for person with pension, other types of deferred compensation limited e.g., 401(k) to $7,000/yr	IRAs deductible for low & middle income workers, phased out for higher incomes; 401(k) $7,000/yr limit
Fully deductible for itemizers, partly for non-itemizers	Deductible	Deductible for itemizers only
Fully deductible	Sales taxes not deductible	Sales taxes not deductible
42% excluded for 22% top rate in 1987	Taxed in full as ordinary income	Taxed in full as ordinary income
36% top, graduated rates up to $100,000	33%, graduated rates up to $100,000	34%, graduated rates up to $75,000
Slower depreciation; partly indexed for inflation	Faster for equipment, slower for structures; not indexed	Slower for both equipment & structures; not indexed
Eliminated	Eliminated	Eliminated
Extended	Extended	Extended 3 years at 20%, tightened eligibility
Very Strong	Very Strong	Very Strong

TABLE A-2 Major Features of Fundamental Tax Reform Proposals

	Basic Type	Major Changes in Base of Individual Tax
Bradley-Gephardt	Income	Eliminates: state & local tax deductions except income & real prop.; Capital Gains exclusion, medical & Life insur. prepaid by employer; two-earner deduc. dividend exclusion. modifies other fringe benefits, personal interest. Remaining deductions only at 14% rate.
Kemp-Kasten	Income	Eliminates: state & Local tax deduc. (except real prop.) Two-earner deduction; personal interest deduction; dividend exclusion; modifies medical deduction.
Treasury	Income	Eliminates: state & local tax deductions; interest deduction beyond principal residence, plus investment income, plus $5,500; dividend exclusion; capital gains exclusion. (indexes basis); many fringe benefit exclusions; modifies charitable contributions; increases IRA and Keoghs.
Heftel/Cashflow	Consumption	Eliminates: State & local taxes (except income), two-earner deduction; capital gains exclusion.
Hall-Rabushka	Consumption	Eliminates: interest deduc. (home mortgage & Personal); state & local tax deductions charitable contribution deductions; two-earner deduction and almost all other deductions except modification of retirement plan contribution.
Value-Added Tax[a]	Consumption	Individual tax eliminated, Replaced by VAT.

[a] No specific proposal in legislation. Refers to generic form in use in many other countries which contains exlusions for housing, education and religious activities. Author's calculations.

Major Changes in Base of Corporate Tax	Rates Indiv/Corporate	Special Features
Eliminates investment tax credit and ACRS. (Replace with slower modified ADR), R&D Credit, special mineral industry expensing. (These are depreciated)	14%–30%/30%	Removes indexing
Eliminates investment tax credit; mineral industry expensing. (these are depreciated)	25% (Soc. Sec. offset)/ 30% Corp.	Retains indexing
Eliminates investment tax credit, ACRS (replaces w/ slower RCRS, mineral industry expensing (depreciated)	15%, 25%, 35%/33%	Extends indexing
Tightens R&D Credit		
Allows 50% dividend deduction.		
All special provisions eliminated	10%–30%/30% (retained earnings only)	Retains indexing, gifts & bequests taxed unless reinvested
Eliminates ACRS, ITC (Expensing), R&D Credit, interest deduction, percentage depletion (retains expensing for mineral industry) allows carry forwards with interest indefinitely.	10%/19%	personal exemption indexed
All value added (revenues less cost other than labor costs) with exemptions. Investment expensed; corporate income tax eliminated.	20%/20%	Could include credits for low-income tax relief.

would have moved, under the Treasury plan, to 35 plus 10 percent, or 45 percent total, a reduction from 55 to 45 (not 50 to 35) percent—a far smaller reduction in percentage terms than meets the eye by simply examining the federal rates.

The most important differences among the early plans, besides those just mentioned for the individual tax—such as differences in the treatment of capital gains, charitable deductions, tax rates, and the deductibility provisions—concerned treatment of capital income, primarily in the business tax. Bradley-Gephardt and the Treasury proposal would have abolished the investment tax credit and the accelerated cost recovery system. Bradley-Gephardt and Kemp-Kasten would have eliminated the R&D tax credit. What these investment features would have been replaced with differs radically. In Hall-Rabushka, consistent with consumption tax principles, investment was expensed, i.e., written off in the year made. This is still more rapid than the accelerated cost recovery system currently allowed, but of course with the investment tax credit removed and the changes in interest taxation and deductibility, this change would have greatly harmonized and rendered much more neutral investment incentives both with respect to spending and among different types of investment. Bradley-Gephardt replaced the accelerated cost recovery system with slower depreciation, while Kemp-Kasten retained an accelerated cost recovery system (called the neutral cost recovery system). The Treasury proposal reversed this and replaced ACRS with RCRS, the real cost recovery system. This system increased the number of asset classes, stretched the depreciation for longer-lived assets, but allowed an inflation adjustment to the base that is being depreciated so there would not be an artificial reduction in the real value of depreciation allowances because of inflation. Most of the proposals, Table 2 shows, also reduced the corporate tax rate. The Treasury proposal allowed an exclusion for the corporate tax of 50 percent of dividends paid, a partial attempt to reduce the double taxation of dividends at the corporate and personal level.

Each of these proposals represented a serious attempt at comprehensive reform of the antiquated and problematic tax laws. Because the proposals were so sweeping and so complex, and because taxes are so important in citizens' lives, each had strong supporters and detractors. Indeed, it is somewhat remarkable that fundamental tax reform came out in the open as a major public policy issue. While each of the proponents of these proposals deserves credit for contributing to the debate, there still existed great differences among them. Many of them, for instance, were anti-investment relative to the current tax system and had the potential for substantially curtailing capital formation and future growth. This is particularly true of the Treasury proposal and of Bradley-Gephardt.

It was unfortunate that we invested large amounts of political capital, with substantial capital gains and losses incurred because of major changes in the tax treatment of different assets, and in the end raised no more revenue than under old laws while discouraging investment and saving. It would have been even more ironic if an anti-investment tax reform were used to generate additional revenue to reduce the deficit. The major potential problem caused by a long string of very large deficits relative to GNP and private saving is the possibility of substantial crowding out of private investment. Thus, an anti-investment structural tax reform used to raise more revenue to reduce the deficit in order to prevent crowding out of investment would be entirely counterproductive.

We needed a better tax system. The 1978 and 1981 tax reforms moved us, no matter how imperfectly, toward a tax system focused on consumption, but they inadvertently generated a decreased sense of fairness. The good and bad qualities of the recent fundamental tax reform are discussed in Chapter 8. New proposals should be considered from the perspective of whether they move us toward or away from a comprehensive consumption tax, preferably one that unifies the corporate and personal tax. Consumption-type tax plans are neutral with respect to the consumption/saving choice: they tax saving only once, when it is consumed. Income taxes distort the saving decision by taxing saving twice, first as part of income and again if it earns interest or dividends as a part of saving or investment. The cash-flow tax, the valued-added tax, and Hall-Rabushka all would have moved us close to that ideal. While each of these proposals contained some features I would have liked to have seen improved (for example, I think Hall-Rabushka would have been improved by including a deduction for contributions to charity), they were greatly preferable to Bradley-Gephardt or the Treasury proposals. Kemp-Kasten fell somewhere in between.

In summary, in evaluating these proposals, the phrase "modified flat-tax" did not apply to all of them. These proposals differed drastically in their likely economic impact on the economy, and the consumption-type variants are far preferable to those that would move us back toward income taxation and reverse the substantial improvements made in 1978 and 1981.

NOTES

Chapter 1

1. *Program for Economic Recovery,* 1981, p. 133.
2. *The Washington Post,* February 7, 1984.
3. "The Education of David Stockman," *The Atlantic,* December 1981.
4. "Reaganomics" in the most general sense still has more than a year of direct policy involvement, plus an undetermined policy legacy. The long-run growth effects—if an incentive-oriented policy survives—will take many years to evaluate. By analogy, FDR's New Deal looked different in 1938 than in 1958, or in 1978, following the growth of government, heavily influenced by the legacy of the New Deal.
5. Compare the United States to Western Europe, where until recently, governments nationalized a growing share of major industries.

Chapter 2

1. Many empirical studies documented the deleterious effects of this erosion of incentives on U.S. saving and investment. See, for example, M. Feldstein and L. Summers, "Inflation and the Taxation of Capital Income in the Corporate Sector," *National Tax Journal,* 1979, and M. Boskin, "Taxation, Saving, and the Rate of Interest," *Journal of Political Economy,* April, 1978. An alternative view, that incentives were not very important, was stressed by Brookings economists Barry Bosworth and Edward Denison.
2. This includes not only the direct effect of rising energy prices, but also the effect of higher prices of goods and services because of higher energy cost to produce them.
3. For example, see M. Feldstein, "The Fiscal Framework of Monetary Policy," *Economic Inquiry,* January, 1983, and S. Fischer and F. Modigliani, "Towards an Understanding of the Real Effects and Costs of Inflation," *Review of World Economics,* 1978.
4. See M. Weidenbaum, *The Future of Business Regulation,* New York, Amacorp.

Chapter 3

1. Many caveats have been raised to the Barro proposition. For example, only a small fraction of decedents leave direct bequests to their heirs. Many would like to leave negative bequests, but because these are not enforceable, they leave nothing. Most important, the theorem is true *only* if the taxes *do not* distort other decisions, a blatantly inaccurate assumption. An empirical test of the Barro hypothesis—which rejects it—is presented by M. Boskin and L. Kotlikoff, "Public Debt and United States Savings: A New Test of the Neutrality Hypothesis," in K. Brunner and A. Meltzner, eds., *The New Monetary Economics: Fiscal Issues and Unemployment*, Carnegie-Rochester Conference Series on Public Policy, Vol. 23, 1985.

2. Of course, numerous other studies could be cited, and these studies have been superseded by others with improved data, theory, or econometric technique, but these are cited because they were enormously influential among economists and in the policy community approaching the Reagan Presidency.

3. Indeed, at a Commerce Department-sponsored conference on supply-side economics, one of the country's leading econometric modelers, the late Otto Eckstein of DRI, credited supply-side economics for providing more accurate estimates of potential GNP for use in macroeconometric models.

4. The literature on optimal taxation is by now voluminous. While determining the most desirable tax and transfer structure depends upon a number of factors, such as the underlying inequality in the ability to generate income, the degree of social risk aversion to inequality, the rate at which the *marginal* value of income declines, and the response of labor supply and capital formation to taxation, the statement above is a summary of the primary results so long as there is some disincentive effect of higher tax rates. Contrast this with the situation where there are *no* disincentive effects of higher taxes. If "social welfare" is defined to be the sum of individual utilities and the marginal utility of income falls, it would be optimal to equalize incomes, as each dollar taxed away from a wealthier household and transferred to a poorer one would raise social welfare.

Chapter 4

1. Indeed, former OMB Director David Stockman makes much of this miscalculation of reduced revenues as if it comes as a total surprise. This implication of the overly optimistic forecast was mentioned by numerous commentators, the present author included.

2. See *Program For Economic Recovery*, 1981.

3. Of course, since the major spending was on Social Security and Medicare, tightening eligibility standards for other programs, while desirable, could not save very much. Much larger unintended benefits were being paid out in Social Security and Medicare to wealthy individuals far above and beyond anything they paid in plus interest. As we shall see below, it was inordinately difficult to make any progress on these much larger amounts.

4. Capital gains revenue rose subsequent to the reduction in the fraction of long-term capital gains included as taxable income with the 1978 tax reform. Sorting out the fraction of the increase due to the rate reduction versus other factors is tricky, but most economists now concede that at the very least, there is a substantial response of capital gains realizations to the rates, and that rate increases are unlikely to generate very much revenue, if any.

5. The magnitude of these deficits amounted to approximately $1.8 trillion in the OASDI part of Social Security, and two to three times this amount in HI, in inflation-adjusted discounted dollars. See M. Boskin, *Too Many Promises: The Uncertain Future of Social Security*, Dow Jones-Irwin, Homewood, Ill., 1986.

6. The TEFRA increase was overwhelmingly in business taxes; the individual tax rate cuts were kept largely intact. This is the beginning of a reversal which culminated in the 1986 Tax Reform Act to be discussed below.

7. This is explained in detail in M. Boskin, *Too Many Promises*, op. cit.

Chapter 6

1. See P. Cagan, "Containing Inflation," in P. Cagan, ed., *The Reagan Program*, American Enterprise Institute, 1986.

2. See W. Fellner, *The High Employment Deficit and the Potential Output*, American Enterprise Institute, 1981.

3. As discussed in detail in Chapters 2 and 3.

4. See Alan Blinder, "The 1971–74 Control Program and the Price Level: An Econometric Post-Mortem," *Journal of Monetary Economics*, 1981.

5. See my debate with Walter Heller in *Taxing and Spending*, 1978.

6. Thus, in Palmer and Sawhill, *The Reagan Record*, Urban Institute, 1984, they suggest that the decline in inflation has only been about two thirds of what the official statistics reveal. I believe this to be an understatement, but the basic point is correct: purged of the energy component, the CPI fell from 11.7 to 5 percent, rather than 12.2 to 4.1 percent from 1980–84.

7. The numerous and insidious costs of continued, and even anticipated, inflation were documented in Chapters 2 and 3.

8. See L. Summers, "Why Is the Unemployment Rate So Very High Near Full Employment," *Brookings Papers on Economic Activity*, 1986, for a discussion of these *long-term* costs of short-lived recessions.

9. This is a common view. See, for example, the discussion in Palmer and Sawhill, op. cit.

10. As noted in Chapters 2 and 3, supply-side economics was concerned with long-run growth, not short-run fluctuations. This distinction seems to have been lost by many, especially in the media.

11. See Thomas J. Sargent, "The Ends of Four Big Inflations," R. Hall. ed., *Inflation: Causes and Effects*, University of Chicago, 1981, for a discussion of these estimates, with which he strongly disagrees. Also Perry and Gordon for a basic study of these Phillips Curve phenomena. Also, the "Okun's law" plus the Phillips Curve estimate of 9 percent of a year's GNP in lost output per percentage point reduction in inflation is still often used, although as noted above, it is far too high after the Reagan disinflation.

12. Thus, Palmer and Sawhill estimate that the lost output relative to a stable 6 percent unemployment rate will amount to $900 billion by the time the economy returns to that rate of full employment in another two years.

13. See Herbert Stein, "Looking at the Record," *AEI Economist*, October 1984.

14. See Cagan, op. cit., for a further elaboration.

15. While no one can be sure whether the stop and go cycle of accelerating and decelerating inflation is over for the foreseeable future, it is quite remarkable how the issue of a modest, stable inflation rate has lost its grip on the media.

16. Because the investment tax credit and ACRS are only available on domestic investment.

17. See Alice Rivlin, ed., *Economic Choices*, Brookings Institution, 1984, and Palmer and Sawhill, op. cit.

18. Several important contributions to the discussion of institutionalizing procedures for fiscal and monetary policies to obtain the outcome of lower government spending, bal-

anced budgets, and more stable monetary growth, appear in J. Moore, ed., *To Promote Prosperity*, Hoover Institution Press, 1984. See especially the discussions by Martin Anderson, Milton Friedman, and Robert Hall.

19. Anyone who uses the federal government's budget documents or the Congressional Budget Office's annual analyses of the President's budgetary proposals, as well as the alternative proposals offered by others in Congress, is struck by such a change.

20. See J. Moore, op. cit.

21. See A. Schick, *Crisis in the Budget Process*, American Enterprise Institute, 1985.

Chapter 7

1. Much of what might be considered government spending shows up in the national income accounts as private spending, e.g., to comply with mandated private activity, which might instead have been financed by taxation accompanying direct government provision.

2. These issues are discussed in more detail in Chapter 10.

3. I do not pretend to any particular expertise in evaluating the benefits and costs of the defense buildup. At one extreme, it may have substantially furthered the likelihood of major arms control with the Russians; on the other, there are those who believe the opposite is the case.

4. See M. Boskin, *Too Many Promises: The Uncertain Future of Social Security*, Dow Jones-Irwin, 1986, for a detailed discussion of these issues.

5. ibid.

6. Indeed, administrations of both parties have attempted to reduce or eliminate some of these programs in the last decade. However, the extreme concentration of interested beneficiaries usually overwhelms the diffuse interests of the taxpayers.

Chapter 8

1. For example, as documented in M. Boskin, "Taxation, Saving, and the Rate of Interest," *Journal of Political Economy*, 1978; L. Summers, "Capital Taxation and Accumulation in a Life-cycle Model," *American Economic Review*, 1981; and Hall and Jorgenson, "Tax Policy and Investment Behavior," *AER*, 1967.

2. "Front-loading" of deductions, such as with ACRS and the ITC, unfortunately opens avenues for tax abuse via uneconomic shelters. The basic scheme of a shelter is to take the deductions more rapidly than the decline in value of an asset and then pay only the capital gains rate on the difference. This burgeoning industry was one reason the Treasury proposal (discussed in detail in the appendix) went to indexed economic income and eliminated the capital gains differential. I am in favor of shutting down abusive shelters, but the Treasury proposal was much more likely to shut down real investment and risk-taking. Tax shelters should be put out of business via comprehensive consumption taxes.

3. As estimated in Boskin, op. cit.

4. See S. Venti and D. Wise, "IRAs and Saving," in *The Effects of Taxation on Capital Accumulation*, M. Feldstein, ed., University of Chicago Press, 1987, for estimates of the effects of IRAs on saving.

5. See M. Boskin, "A Closer Look at Tax Neutrality Toward Investment," *Tax Notes*, November 1985; and J. Shoven, et al., "Gains from U.S. Income Tax with a Progressive Consumption Tax," *Journal of Public Economics*, 1983.

6. See M. Boskin, "Some Issues in Supply Side Economics," Carnegie Rochester Conference Series, 1981.

7. See Boskin, ibid.

8. This is a one-time effect. Once the new higher desired level of capital stock is reached, a continuation of this effect cannot be expected without further tax incentives. Therefore, this offset against the potential deleterious effects of large deficits is only temporary.

9. See L. Lindsay, "Taxpayer Behavior and the Distribution of the 1982 Tax Cut," NBER Working Paper No. 1960, October 1985.

10. As detailed in R. Hall and A. Rabushka, *Low Tax, Simple Tax, Flat Tax*, McGraw-Hill Book Company, 1983.

11. See Summers, op. cit.

12. An astoundingly large and rapid shift in demographics toward the elderly in Japan, for example, may cause their saving rate to plummet, leaving a smaller excess of saving over Japanese investment to export to the United States.

Chapter 9

1. 1. See M. Boskin, "Concepts and Measures of Budget Deficits and their Effects on Aggregate Demand and the Composition of Output," in K. Arrow and M. Boskin, eds., *The Economics of Public Debt*, Macmillan for the International Economics Association, forthcoming, 1988.

2. Barro and others have argued that the prospect of future taxes to pay higher future interest payments on the larger debt will lead to increased saving to pay those future taxes. This analysis is intriguing, and probably partially correct, but the conditions required for it to happen are quite restrictive; thus, there is little empirical support for it (witness the current low saving rate). Also, Keynesians argue that if GNP expands, saving should increase. But to offset the deficit this would require people to save a much larger fraction of their increased disposable income, and a corresponding expansion in GNP, much larger than historical experience suggests, would have to occur.

3. See M. Boskin, "Federal Government Deficits: Some Myths and Realities," *American Economic Review*, May 1982, and the forthcoming *The Real Federal Budget*, Harvard University Press, and Robert Eisner, *How Real is the Federal Deficit*, Basic Books, 1986.

4. See R. Penner, "Forecasting Budget Totals: Why Can't We Get It Right?," AEI Economist, 1981.

5. Robert E. Hall, "Federal Deficits in the Longer-Run," unpublished mimeo, 1984.

6. Robert Barro, "Are Government Bonds Net Wealth?" *Journal of Political Economy*, 1975.

7. Obviously, supply-side measures that lower tax rates might create a greater labor supply for example, and therefore, lead to an increase in GNP because people substitute work in the market place for leisure or work at home. This is in addition to any impacts that larger private incomes have on spending.

8. See J. Palmer and I. Sawhill, *The Reagan Record*, Urban Institute, 1984.

9. When I first presented such calculations in 1983, there was considerable alarm over the debt/GNP trend. For more details on such calculations, see M. Boskin, "Deficits, Public Debt, Interest Rates and Private Saving," in M. Boskin, J. Fleming, and S. Gorini, eds., *Private Saving and Public Debt*, Basil Blackwell, 1987.

10. See T. Sargent, "The Ends of Four Big Inflations," R. Hall, ed., *Inflation: Causes and Effects*, University of Chicago, 1981.

11. Most of the state and local surplus is in pension funds, which are simultaneously accruing future liabilities.

12. There are slight conceptual differences between the national income account's measure of the budget deficit used here and the numbers used by the CBO and OMB.

13. From the 1940s to 1982, the United States rarely was a net borrower.

14. See R. Eisner and P. Pieper, "A New View of Federal Deficit and Debt," *American Economic Review*, 1984; M. Feldstein, "Government Deficit and Aggregate Demand," *Journal of Monetary Economics*, 1982; and M. Boskin, "Alternative Concepts of Government Deficit and Debt, and Their Impact on Economic Activity," In K. Arrow and M. Boskin, eds. *The Economics of Public Debt*, Macmillan for the International Economics Association, forthcoming, 1988.

15. See L. Summers, "Issues in National Savings Policy," in G. Adams and S. Wachter, eds., *Saving and Capital Formation*, D. C. Heath, 1985.

16. See M. Boskin, in K. Arrow and M. Boskin, *The Economics of Public Debt*, op. cit.

17. ibid.

Chapter 10

1. There are no deductions or exemptions in the payroll tax, although the earned income credit in the income tax provides a rebate of Social Security taxes for low-income persons who file income tax returns.

2. Lawrence Summers concludes that labor market segmentation, in which persons losing high wage jobs take quite a long time to accept lower wage jobs, is a major reason for the rise in "normal" unemployment. See "Why is the Unemployment Rate So Very High Near Full Employment?" *Brookings Papers on Economic Activity*.

3. The Administration clearly favored the idea, but felt it could not take the lead on it for political reasons.

4. See J. Weicher, "Reaganomics and the Fairness Issue," *AEI Economist*, August 1984.

5. These figures are derived from the various technical reports of the US Department of Commerce, Bureau of the Census, *Current Population Reports*, Money Income and Poverty Status of Families and Persons in the United States, annually.

6. See Rebecca Blank and Alan Blinder, "Macroeconomics, Income Distribution and Poverty," unpublished paper, April 1985. Sheldon Danziger and Peter Gottschalk, however, conclude that it was about half program cuts and half the rise in unemployment. See their "Macroeconomic Conditions, Income Transfers and the Trend in Poverty," in D. Lee Bowden, ed., *The Social Contract Revisited*, Urban Institute, 1984.

7. J. Weicher, op. cit.

8. This has led to calls for protection from foreign competition. But recall the loss to American consumers if free trade is abandoned.

9. See M. Boskin, *Too Many Promises: The Uncertain Future of Social Security*, Dow-Jones Irwin, 1986.

10. John Palmer and Isabel Sawhill, eds., *The Reagan Experiment*, Urban Institute, 1982.

Chapter 11

1. Some of the failures in this regard are also documented in previous chapters.

2. There is a widely held view that such innovations must often be financed by venture capital which will only be forthcoming for such risky investments if there is the possibility of very large returns on investment. This conclusion was a major impetus toward the reduction in capital gains taxes in 1978.

3. See J. Kendrick, *The Formation and Stocks of Total Capital*, NBER, 1979.

4. See M. Feldstein and C. Horioka, "Domestic Savings and International Capital Flows," *Economic Journal*, 1980.

5. See E. Denison, *Accounting for U.S. Economic Growth, 1929–69*, Brookings, 1974 and "Effects of Selected Changes in the Institutional and Human Environment upon Output per Unit of Input," *Survey of Current Business*, 1979; R. Siegel, "Why Has Productivity Slowed Down?" *Data Resource (DRI) Review*, 1979; L. Thurow, "The U.S. Productivity Problem," *DRI Review*, 1978; and D. Jorgenson, "Productivity and Economic Growth," paper presented to the Annual Meeting of the American Economic Association, New Orleans, December 1986.

6. J. Kendrick, "Recent Productivity Trends," *AEI Economist*, August 1986.

7. M. Baily, "What Happened to Productivity Growth?" in *Science*, Oct., 1986.

8. See A. Blinder, "Reaganomics and Growth," in C. Hulten and I. Sawhill, eds., *The Legacy of Reaganomics*, Urban Institute Press, 1984.

Chapter 12

1. See the *AEI Economist*, June 1986.

2. See *AEI Economist*, October 1986.

3. While I am only willing to claim that the deficit increase is likely to be much smaller than the tax cuts, a recent study by O. Blanchard and L. Summers, "Fiscal Increasing Returns, Hysteresis, Real Wages and Unemployment," NBER Working Paper #2034, suggests that the deficit might actually fall.

4. See Chapter 7 and my *Too Many Promises: The Uncertain Future of Social Security*, Dow Jones-Irwin, 1986.

5. The performance of the Communist economies, as near as one can tell from the notoriously unreliable data, appears to have deteriorated markedly in the last decade relative to the United States, Japan, and Western Europe. Indeed, pressure for reform by giving a greater role to private enterprise is increasing. The most successful of such countries appears to be Hungary, which is the most market-oriented. China and others are also in the midst of liberalizing reforms.

6. I focus here on a subset of those tenets. See Arnold Harberger, ed., *World Economic Growth: Case Studies of Developed and Developing Nations*, ICS Press, San Francisco, 1985.

Chapter 13

1. Of course, credit must be shared for this accomplishment, as its antecedents predate the Reagan presidency.

2. See D. Bradford, *Untangling the Income Tax*, Harvard University Press, 1986, for a detailed, but readily accessible, discussion of the major issues.

3. See A. Rivlin, *Economic Choices*, Brookings Institution, 1987, and R. Penner and A. Schick, *Crisis in the Budget Process*, AEI, 1986, for discussions of some of these issues.

4. See R. Hall, "Monetary Policy for Noninflationary Growth," in J. Moore, ed., *To Promote Prosperity*, Hoover Institution Press, 1982, for a discussion of alternative monetary policy rules.

Suggested Reading

For additional reading on the Reagan economic program, recent economic performance, and evaluations of economic policy and policy alternatives, I recommend the volumes listed below. They provide a spectrum of analyses and perspectives, some similar, others quite divergent, from that offered in this volume. One word of caution: the data are often not directly comparable across the studies, as they may refer to dollars for different years unadjusted for inflation, forecasts from different time periods, and even different versions of the same data (for example, the national income accounts were recently revised comprehensively).

Philip Cagan, ed., *The Impact of the Reagan Program*, American Enterprise Institute, 1986 (and the other recent volumes of AEI's annual Issues in Contemporary Economics Series).

J. Palmer and I. Sawhill, eds., *The Reagan Record*, Urban Institute Press, 1984 (and other volumes in the Urban Institute Changing Domestic Priorities Series).

A. Rivlin, ed., *Economic Choices 1987*, Brookings Institution (and the other annual volumes in Brookings Economic Choices Series, and its predecessor, Setting National Priorities Series).

Of course, the numerous studies cited in the text and footnotes, and the many references therein, offer substantial opportunities for further elaboration of the issues raised in the text.

Index